International Organizational Anarchy

"As the place of international organizations in world politics seems to be changing, Zamudio and Arellano-Gault have written a sophisticated and engaging book that maps out what is changing as well as what is not. They range widely across themes, organizations, and region to show how organizational features interlace with internal and external politics. This is a book worth having for all scholars of world politics."
—Ian Hurd, *Northwestern University*. Author of *International Organization: Politics, Law, Practice*

"This is a must-read for anyone interested in understanding International Organizations' impact and their role in our current international system. Zamudio and Arellano-Gault combine two perspectives that interact exquisitely, providing an excellent document that broadens the knowledge of international relations and organization theory scholars."
—Esther Coronado, *Professor of International Law, UNAM, Mexico and International Relations Scholar*

"This timely book elegantly reviews endogenous and exogenous drivers of IOs agency, flexibility, and connectivity. It shows how they build a global normative order in a disorganized world, despite unequal levels of rationality in their respective decision-making processes. In the end, interdependence and networking overwhelm fragmentation and rivalry. Successfully combining organizational theory and international studies, the book brings a much-needed and remarkable clarity to a complex field."
—Yves Schemeil. Emeritus Professor, *Institut Universitaire de France, politique globale et comparée, Grenoble. Author of the book: The making of the World: how International Organizations shape our future*

Laura Zamudio-González
David Arellano-Gault

International Organizational Anarchy

International Organizations as Full Actors in the Global Arena

Laura Zamudio-González
International Relations
Universidad Iberoamericana
Mexico City, Mexico

David Arellano-Gault
Public Administration
Centro de Investigación y Docencia
Económicas, CIDE
Mexico City, Mexico

ISBN 978-3-031-82391-6   ISBN 978-3-031-82392-3   (eBook)
https://doi.org/10.1007/978-3-031-82392-3

© The Editor(s) (if applicable) and The Author(s), under exclusive license to Springer Nature
Switzerland AG 2025

This work is subject to copyright. All rights are solely and exclusively licensed by the
Publisher, whether the whole or part of the material is concerned, specifically the rights of
translation, reprinting, reuse of illustrations, recitation, broadcasting, reproduction on
microfilms or in any other physical way, and transmission or information storage and retrieval,
electronic adaptation, computer software, or by similar or dissimilar methodology now
known or hereafter developed.
The use of general descriptive names, registered names, trademarks, service marks, etc. in this
publication does not imply, even in the absence of a specific statement, that such names are
exempt from the relevant protective laws and regulations and therefore free for general use.
The publisher, the authors and the editors are safe to assume that the advice and information
in this book are believed to be true and accurate at the date of publication. Neither the
publisher nor the authors or the editors give a warranty, expressed or implied, with respect
to the material contained herein or for any errors or omissions that may have been made.
The publisher remains neutral with regard to jurisdictional claims in published maps and
institutional affiliations.

This Palgrave Macmillan imprint is published by the registered company Springer Nature
Switzerland AG.
The registered company address is: Gewerbestrasse 11, 6330 Cham, Switzerland

If disposing of this product, please recycle the paper.

ACKNOWLEDGMENTS

We would like to express our sincere gratitude to Zaira I. Chávez and Gabriel S. Rojas—both outstanding individuals and dedicated research assistants—whose support at various stages proved instrumental in the completion of this long-term project. Over the past decade, we have explored the intersection between international relations and organization theory as a framework for understanding International Organizations, and their contributions were invaluable throughout this endeavor.

We are also deeply thankful to several cohorts of undergraduate students from Universidad Iberoamericana and graduate students from CIDE (Centro de Investigación y Docencia Económicas, Center for Research and Teaching in Economics), both in Mexico City, who participated in our courses on International Organizations. Their intellectual engagement, insightful questions, and collaborative discussions significantly enriched our thinking and helped shape the ongoing theoretical dialogue between organizational theory and the study of International Organizations—those increasingly central, yet often crisis-ridden, actors in the evolving international order.

CONTENTS

1 **Introduction: International Relations, Organizational Theory, and the Role of IGOs. Connecting the dots**   1
References   9

2 **International Organizations from an International Relations Perspective: Agency, Autonomy, and Accountability Issues**   11
Introduction: The Surprising International Organizational Explosion   11
Navigating in a Minefield   14
The Story of a Crowded Neighborhood   16
Theory for Understanding Black Boxes   19
A Theory for Inhabited Instances   23
Discussions and Trends   28
Meta-organizations and Inter-organizational Relationships Between IGOs   31
Organizational Pathologies in IGOs   33
IGOs as Organized Anarchies   34
Concluding Remarks   35
References   38

vii

viii CONTENTS

3 Organizations as Systems: IGOS Coping with the Systemic Impact and the Inability of Full Control 45
Introduction 45
Systems Theory in International Relations: Just a Useful Metaphor? 49
    Early Systemic Theories in IR: The Modeling Tradition 51
    Complexity and Unexpected Effects 54
Other Applications of Systems Theory in IR 56
The Organizational Basis of Systems Theory 58
    General Theory of Systems: Web of Relationships, Interactions, and Interdependencies 59
    The Structural-functionalist Approach: How Do Organizations Become a Form of Structure? 64
    Contingency Studies: How Do Organizations Survive in Volatile Contexts? 66
The Paradox of Organizations as Systems: The Never-ending Process of Differentiation 68
    Complexity and Self-organizations 70
    Organizations as Complex Adaptive Systems 73
    Organizations as Decision Systems: The Luhmannian Proposal 74
Concluding Remarks 86
References 88

4 Organizations as Localized Domination Constructions: IGOs at the End of Bureaucratic Pathologies and the Beginning of Political-Strategic Constructs 95
Introduction 95
IGOs as International Bureaucracies 101
International Public Administrations 104
IGOs as Organizations: Spaces of Constructed Order 108
IGOs: Strategic Games and Organizational Battles 115
    The Bureaucratic Phenomenon (Or Why Bureaucracies are More Competent Than Assumed) 116,
Organizational Order: Between Chaos and Interdependence 128
Concluding Remarks 133
References 135

5 Organizations as Machines of Meaning: IGOs as a Result of Bounded Rationality and Meaning Producers   143

Introduction   143

Sensemaking in IGOs: From Constructivism to the Ambition of Global Governance   147

Bureaucratization: Between Pathologies and Technical Legitimization   150

Regimes or the Dream of General Legitimate Shared Rules   152

Network Governance: The Deep Web of IGOs, Actors, Governments, Regimes   154

Bounded Rationality IGOs: Heuristics and Tactics for Acting and Not Dying in the Attempt   159

IGOs: Constructs of Multiple Negotiated Rationalities   160

IGOs: People Acting, Deciding, and Behaving   162

    IGOs and Their Bounded Rationality Strategies   165

    IGOs and Sensemaking: The Important Question Is, What Situation Are We Facing?   167

Sensemaking: The Creation of Solid Organizational Commitments   171

Concluding Remarks   181

References   184

6 Organizations and Institutions: IGOs Decisions, Adjustments, and Transformation Within the Context of the Technical-Political Discourse in the International Arena   189

Introduction   189

Institutions and Regimes in IR: the Search for Order in Anarchy   194

    Institutions: The Long and Confusing Path of a Concept   195

    Neorealism and Neoliberalism   197

    Constructivism   199

    International Regimes   201

Organizations and Institutions: The Internal Organizational Logic of Institutions   203

Politics and Rational Organizational Technic: Necessary But Uncomfortable Bedfellows   206

The Institution of the Decision: Rationality and Irrationality   214

Concluding Remarks   220

References   223

x CONTENTS

7 Conclusions: The Power of Interdisciplinary
   Cross-Fertilization Between International
   Relations and Organization Studies   229
   References   235

Index   237

CHAPTER 1

Introduction: International Relations, Organizational Theory, and the Role of IGOs. Connecting the dots

International Governmental Organizations (IGOs) play a significant role in the global sphere and have become an integral part of the daily lives of individuals, for better or worse. For instance, in August 2017, hundreds of Guatemalans rallied before the Constitutional Court to express their unwavering support for a team of prosecutors and international experts, under the umbrella of the International Commission against Impunity in Guatemala (CICIG) working since 2006 to combat corruption. During this event, the protesters also called for the presence of Commissioner Iván Velásquez, a Colombian prosecutor whom the government had labeled persona non-grata after launching an investigation into the use of illicit funds in political campaigns, implicating the ruling party.

In March 2020, as the SARS-COVID-19 pandemic spread worldwide, various neighborhoods in Mexico City showcased banners expressing their commitment to adhering to the health protection guidelines provided by the World Health Organization (WHO), such as wearing masks, practicing social distancing, and utilizing tests. Conversely, at the federal level, the Mexican president asserted that the disease was less virulent than

© The Author(s), under exclusive license to Springer Nature Switzerland AG 2025
L. Zamudio-González, D. Arellano-Gault, *International Organizational Anarchy*,
https://doi.org/10.1007/978-3-031-82392-3_1

1

influenza. He urged the populace not to follow the recommendations of the WHO or those of its experts, whom he labeled as interventionists.

The Finnish Parliament's approval of the accession of the country to the North Atlantic Treaty Organization (NATO) in March 2022 is noteworthy. This decision followed a citizens' initiative that evidenced a significant level of acceptance among the population of abandoning the policy of strict neutrality that Finland had followed for nearly 80 years. Similarly, Kenya witnessed three days of violent demonstrations in June 2024. Protestors, numbering in the dozens, stormed Parliament in opposition to a controversial tax increase bill that was supported by the International Monetary Fund (IMF).

International governmental organizations (IGOs) are just one part of a diverse array of international organizations that include non-governmental organizations, trans-governmental organizations, hybrid international organizations (HIGOs), quasi-non-governmental organizations (QUANGOs), business non-governmental organizations (BINGOs), and governmental NGOs (GONGOs). All these organizations have an impact on governance in countries around the world. They negotiate and implement agreements, create regulations, and design instruments for humanitarian action, crisis management, and governance. They also network and link with other organizations, both within and outside of states, and they can even create new international organizations (Kilroy et al., 2013).

This book examines IGOs, which have been observed to possess a prolonged lifespan. Moreover, these IGOs are complex to eradicate, and their impact extends beyond their structural boundaries. Governments and individuals continue to be influenced by the numerous normative, regulatory, and legal frameworks established by these IGOs, even outside their organizational framework. Although IGOs are not always effective and may sometimes contribute to the problem rather than to the solution, their interactions have steadily grown, resulting in an institutionally intricate and diverse international environment.

The field of International Relations (IR) has devoted increasing attention to these organizations but with varying foci (Ruíz Cabañas et al., 2023). At times, they have been incorporated as components of the so-called "International Organization"—that is, the self-organizing propensity of the international system in a context of anarchy devoid of an international government. Alternatively, they have been perceived as power instruments manipulated by the interests of various states, sometimes as facilitators of cooperation among them, or as bureaucratic entities that are often ineffective. Most of these investigations have concentrated on a single research question: why do states establish them? Although this is an important question, it overlooks the fact that IGOs articulate the interests that arise from within their own governing bodies and the interests of states from outside. Thus, IGOs operate at multiple levels, addressing external state interests and endogenously generated concerns.

To expand upon the comprehension of IGOs beyond the realm of state interaction and to grasp their functioning, it has been emphasized in various forums that it is essential to pose novel queries. What precisely are they, what duties do they perform, and what objectives do they attain? How do they formulate, legitimize, and implement decisions? How did they broaden or modify their mandates? How do they interpret, simplify, or skew reality? How do they exercise agency? How diverse are they within themselves, and how do their members pursue differing interests and adopt various strategies? Furthermore, why do IGOs strive to legitimize themselves because they possess specialized technical neutrality?

To enrich the study of IGOs within the IR field, debates from midrange disciplines such as organization theory, sociology of organizations, and organization studies, should be an integrated whole. For the sake of simplicity herein, we refer to these disciplines as *organizational theory*. Organizational Theory posits that all organizations, whether governmental, private, non-governmental, social, or judicial are not mere machines that blindly follow orders, nor are they unified rational actors that respond solely to efficiency-based logic. Instead, organizations—of any kind—possess a certain level of rationality—although never complete—and can make decisions but facing numerous unavoidable uncertainties. Moreover, organizations are persons, and they have unique interests, including professional, political, and group-based, which can lead to complex internal and external interdependencies. By incorporating these perspectives from Organizational Theory, the study of IGOs can be enhanced and further developed within the IR field.

Thus, organizations are collective actors, they are formed, recreated, and set in motion by individuals with an agency who face uncertainty, lack resources and incomplete information, and confront a changing reality. They also compete for power, form relationships, and commitments, and seek to imbue meaning to their actions. At the same time, they strive to gain political space and participate in decision-making. Organizational theories provide helpful frameworks for understanding why, at times, IGOs effectively fulfill their mandates and values while being seen as "the missionaries of our time" (Barnett & Finnemore, 1999). However, at other times, they exhibit hypocrisy and biases and end up causing fiascos.

This book is the result of a collaboration between two students of IGOs: one with an internationalist perspective and the other grounded in organizational theory. This interdisciplinary effort aims to foster a comprehensive and rigorous analysis of IGOs by incorporating the strengths of both disciplines. Each chapter strives to merge these two fields of study, aiming to advance the organizational analysis of IGOs in a nuanced and sophisticated manner.

The book analyzes IGOs as an organizational phenomenon, broadening the typically centered on studying companies or public administration organizations. By doing so, the book contributes to the study of IR by identifying the organizational gears, dynamics, and challenges that occur daily in all IGOs and presents potential lines of research that can be derived from different explanations of their challenges and dynamics.

The discipline of IR has engaged in extensive and profound discussions which regard the international system as anarchy (Havercrofft & Prichard, 2017; Lechner, 2022). Both realism and neo-realism, as well as neoliberals, have established anarchy as a fundamental pillar of the discipline, together with the English School or the School of International Society, and even since Kant's well-known text of perpetual peace (Buzan & Little, 2001; Powell, 1994; Waltz, 1979). Anarchy, as understood in this context, refers not to chaos but to a form of order that emerges from multiple interactions among entities without the need for a centralized authority or hierarchy (Buzan & Little, 2001; Herz, 1942; Powell, 1994; Waltz, 1962, 1979).

One of the classic texts in this field, Bull's (1984) work and subsequent discussions, emphasize the self-constructed nature of order based on struggles, balances, conflicts, and interdependencies that, whereas they may not culminate in a stable and universal peace, they can generate a certain logic of stability and contribute to the improvement and expansion of order (Alderson & Hurrell, 2000; Bull & Watson, 1984; Wendt, 2003; Williams, 2005). Consequently, it is typical for the IR discipline to discuss anarchy and the paradoxical order constructed and reconstructed through it.

The central idea of this book is the notion of an ***organized anarchy***. This refers to the idea that IGOs are spaces where individuals work together to achieve coordination in a disorganized or chaotic environment. These individuals engage in organizational games over which they may not have complete control, and the contexts in which they operate are complex and constantly changing. It is also important to note that IGOs extend beyond individuals, encompassing relationships, interactions, patterns, and interdependencies that can lead to unpredictable outcomes. In essence, IGOs are organized anarchies that exist within the anarchy of the international system, yet they can maintain a certain level of rationality and achievement.

Organizations classified as organized anarchies are characterized by three dynamics (Cohen et al., 1972; Cohen & March, 1974; March & Olsen, 1979; Musselin, 1997): first, the objectives and preferences of individuals affecting the organization are diverse, heterogeneous, and even conflicting. Second, the complexity of the objectives sought is such that there is no single precise technique or path to achieve them. Third, multiple agents and groups participate in decision-making, making it intricate and dynamic. Organizations cannot establish a linear path or a single process to harmonize means and ends when these dynamics crystallize. The key to organized anarchy is negotiation in spaces of intricate interdependence, interaction with multiple stakeholders, and the constant search for legitimacy to survive in a chaotic environment. This implies a widely changing, dynamic, and uncertain decision-making and action process. Uncertainty is an endogenous element, not an accident neither something to be discarded nor eliminated. In this type of organization, an individual must proactively learn to live with uncertainty and play with it. The anarchy of these dynamics does not imply that IGOs cannot achieve their objectives and results. This implies that knowing how to administer and manage anarchy is essential to achieving these outcomes.

IGOs function as organized anarchies characterized by many agents with diverse objectives, mandates, and varying levels of power. IGOs often have ambitious goals such as reducing poverty, preventing war, controlling the proliferation of weapons of mass destruction, and managing pandemics. To achieve these objectives, IGOs rely on negotiated, agreed-upon, and legitimized instruments that are sometimes tested in practical applications. It is important to note that IGOs operate within a complex environment of negotiations and conflicts between states and the increasing participation of corporate interests, non-governmental organizations (NGOs), and other international actors.

The management, direction, and control of IGOs are complex and multifaceted. No single recipe or instrument can effectively guide an organized anarchy such as an IGO in the pursuit of its objectives. This book aims to organize and systematize various theories of organization and critically examine lessons from the field of IR to identify viable strategies and approaches for leading and managing IGOs.

This book comprises seven chapters and explores into organizational behavior by examining the phenomena and debates that have shaped it, as well as studies from IR and organization theories that have significantly contributed to our understanding of these phenomena.

The second chapter examines the concepts of agency, autonomy, and accountability within IR. These concepts are often viewed as organizational anomalies or dysfunctions, and this chapter explores how organizations are required to act with discretion while also grappling with the problem of accountability for their decisions, the power they wield over states through regulatory mechanisms and the establishment of new governance spaces. This creates concerns for governments, who view these issues as anomalies or dysfunctions within organizations, but this is not the case. In this section, the focus is on understanding why it has been difficult to recognize the agency of IGOs and why it is challenging to address actors such as IGOs, which are supposed to be subordinated to the power and decisions of the states that establish them, yet require a certain level of autonomy to be effective in practical applications.

The third chapter delves into the concept of complexity, which originates from the systemic impact of social interactions and the inability to regulate context. According to the systemic perspective, every organization relies heavily on its context and must adapt or differentiate from the context of survival. No organization exists in isolation, and there is no way to foresee or control the events that unfold in the environment. How can the outcomes of an IGO's operations be evaluated if they ultimately result from interactions out of their control? Additionally, how do IGOs acquire influence and power in an environment where states are in anarchy and have no centralized or supranational authority?

The fourth chapter reviews organizations as structures of localized dominance. The primary proposition is that organizations comprise individuals engaging in actions, yet they have attained a status and existence that extends beyond the individuals who form them. Legally and symbolically, organizations have developed their own life and an autonomous presence in the realm of modernity. The impersonal nature of domination has been the driving force behind the transformation of organizations into entities with a life of their own due to the process of rationalization. How is this metamorphosis conducted in practical terms? In other words, organizations are venues for people to interact with each other. The specific manner in which these interactions and relationships generate interdependencies is critical to the empirical comprehension of the actions and decisions of an organization. IGOs, as organized anarchies, are political constructs originating from states that are, in turn, involved in diverse relationships regarding resources, influence, and power. These dynamics are essential to understand the decisions and actions of IGOs. Consequently, Chap. 4 also examines the components of the dynamics of authority and domination within IGOs and examines their hierarchical spaces, governance, and decision-making processes. Thus, what might be perceived as a bureaucratic malady from a normative standpoint might, from another perspective, be observed as a concrete decision-making process that resolves a power, uncertainty, and risk dilemma in action.

The fifth chapter explores the concept of organizations as machines for creating meaning and limited rationality. It has been argued that individuals within IGOs grapple with perpetual uncertainty, possess limited information, and recognize that their actions will yield unforeseeable consequences. To cope with this reality, these individuals practice bounded rationality by attempting to restrict their environment through habits, norms, institutions, relationships, and commitments. Bounded rationality, for both individuals and organizations, entails adopting strategies that enable decision-making and action in an inherently unpredictable reality. Although such strategies carry inherent risks and limitations, they allow for some semblance of control over reality by imparting meaning, direction, and bias. However, these strategies are not foolproof as the environment may change, rendering prior logical and practical approaches ineffective and insufficient. Organizational change is always necessary but never comes with a guarantee. IGOs, as entities within an organizational reality characterized by anarchy, continuously create meaning, adopt strategies of limited rationality, introduce biases, and simplify reality.

The sixth chapter examines the relationship between organizations and institutions, focusing on how organizations legitimize decisions, changes, and transformations under a technical-political discourse. By reducing uncertainty, organizations develop strategies of limited rationality that can be highly stable and serve as widely accepted guides in various arenas. As a result, organizations create potent institutions, such as the institutions of rational decision-making and planned and strategic change. Organizations justify their existence based on expert knowledge, sophisticated techniques, and robust decision-making and action instruments. These positions are powerful because organizations legitimize themselves by making decisions, implementing changes, and claiming to be technical and highly proficient. They are still institutional realities, meaning they are political arguments and rhetoric that usually work and are necessary. Although there may be no control over the complex reality, it is assumed that rational instruments can provide a means of managing it. Although these processes of rational change may fail today, organizations can initiate a rational change and reform tomorrow that can alter everything. Such processes of rational change are still constructions of limited rationality and political discourses that allow organizational stability and legitimacy. IGOs must legitimize themselves, and in doing so, they create institutions. However, how do they direct changes and present themselves as rational, technical, and neutral IGOs? How do they reconcile the contradiction between the illusion of neutrality and technical capacity and the political and operational reality of any organization facing uncertainty? How do they understand the expectations of neutral and obedient IGOs, with the necessity to legitimize themselves politically and the capacity to create institutions? Institutions play a critical role in an anarchic international order that achieves order through intelligent and flexible strategies typical of organizational anarchy.

The ultimate aim of this book is not to replace the approach of International Relations (IR) with organization theory (OT). Instead, the goal is to complement it and gain deeper insights into the operations, actions, and processes that organizations deploy to survive. In other words, the objective is to promote the 'organizational turn' in the study of IGOs by incorporating diverse and robust organizational theory perspectives that go beyond those currently dominating IR, such as principal-agent theories or institutionalist views. This interaction between the two disciplines is undoubtedly a productive path to revitalizing the study of IGOs, enabling society and governments to better understand, manage, and improve them. IGOs, as organized anarchies, are dynamic, vibrant, and fluid; they cannot be controlled or directed in a linear fashion, as if they were mere instruments or robots. However, with analytical humbleness and respect for the people and social logics that drive them, it is possible to understand them as powerful social entities that, with intelligence and flexibility, can be guided, shaped, empowered, and monitored.

REFERENCES

Alderson, K., & Hurrell, A. (2000). *Hedley Bull on International Society*. Palgrave Macmillan.

Barnett, M. N., & Finnemore, M. (1999). The politics, power, and pathologies of international organizations. *International Organization, 53*(4), 699–732.

Bull, H. (1984). The emergence of a Universal International Society. In H. Bull & A. Watson (Eds.), *The expansion of International Society*. Clarendon Press.

Bull, H., & Watson, A. (Eds.). (1984). *The expansion of International Society*. Clarendon Press.

Buzan, B., & Little, R. (2001). Why international relations has failed as an intellectual project and what to do about it. *Millennium: Journal of International Studies, 30*, 19–39.

Cohen, M., & March, J. (1974). *Leadership and ambiguity*. Harvard Business School Press.

Cohen, M., March, J., & Olsen, J. (1972). A garbage can model of organizational choice. *Administrative Science Quarterly., 17*(1), 1–25.

Havercrofft, J., & Prichard, A. (2017). Anarchy and international relations theory: A reconsideration. *Journal of International Political Theory, 13*(3), 1–15. https://doi.org/10.1177/17550882177199

Herz, J. (1942). Power politics and world organization. *American Political Science Review, 36*(6), 1039–1052.

Kilroy, R., Rodríguez, A., & Hataley, T. (2013). *North American regional security: A trilateral framework?* Lynne Rienner.

Lechner, S. (2022). Anarchy in international relations. In *Oxford research encyclopedia of international studies*. Oxford University Press. https://doi.org/10.1093/acrefore/9780190846626.013.79

March, J., & Olsen, J. (1979). *Ambiguity and choice in organizations*. Universitetsforlaget.

Musselin, C. (1997). *Les universités sont-elles des anarchies organisées?* Presses Universitaires de France, pp. 291–308. Hal-03567656.

Powell, R. (1994). Anarchy in international relations theory: The neorealist-neoliberal debate. *International Organization, 48*, 313–344.

Ruíz Cabañas, M., Schiavon, J., & Velázquez, R. (2023). *Introducción al estudio de los organismos internacionales. Perspectivas históricas, conceptuales y teóricas*. TEC de Monterrey, CIDE, CESPEM, Universidad Autónoma de Baja California.

Waltz, K. (1962). Kant, liberalism, and war. *American Political Science Review, 56*(2), 331–340.

Waltz, K. (1979). *Theory of international politics*. Addison-Wesley.

Wendt, A. (2003). Why a world state is inevitable. *European Journal of International Relations, 9*(1), 19–38.

Williams, P. D. (2005). International peacekeeping: The challenges of state-building and regionalization. *International Affairs, 81*(1), 163–174.

CHAPTER 2

International Organizations from an International Relations Perspective: Agency, Autonomy, and Accountability Issues

INTRODUCTION: THE SURPRISING INTERNATIONAL ORGANIZATIONAL EXPLOSION

International Governmental Organizations (IGOs) are one of the most striking phenomena in the contemporary world. Over the last century, these creatures grew rapidly and steadily, acquired relevance, became institutionalized, and they really affect the lives of millions of persons all over the world.

The Russian invasion of Ukraine in February 2022, which led to violence and war in Europe and displaced approximately 6.4 million Ukrainians, cannot be fully understood without considering the expansion of the North Atlantic Treaty Organization (NATO), whether such expansion was deliberate or not. The World Health Organization (WHO), its regional organizations, and a series of public-private partnerships, including Global Alliance for Vaccines and Immunization (GAVI), Global Outbreak Alert and Response Network (GOARN), and Emergency Medical Teams (EMT), coordinated and essentially led the global response to the unprecedented SARS pandemic Covid-19 (2020–2022), which weakened economies and impacted individuals worldwide. The potential rebuilding of the Gaza Strip in the aftermath of the Israeli-Hamas conflict that began in October 2023 is being discussed in the context of a

---

© The Author(s), under exclusive license to Springer Nature Switzerland AG 2025
L. Zamudio-González, D. Arellano-Gault, *International Organizational Anarchy*,
https://doi.org/10.1007/978-3-031-82392-3_2

11

proposed United Nations Transitional Administration, similar to the one established in East Timor in 1999 (UNTAET), when the region was devastated by war.

Despite their numerous differences and unique characteristics, IGOs have become a significant aspect of contemporary global reality. These organizations, which include organizations like NATO, the Office of the United Nations High Commissioner for Refugees (UNHCR), the International Organization for Migration (IOM), United Nations Transitional Administration in East Timor (UNTAET), the Organization of American States (OAS), the European Union (EU), the African Union (AU), and many others, operate either independently or as part of a network and address a variety of transnational problems, crises, wars, emergencies, and disasters (Culebro & Romo, 2023; Muñoz, 2021; Urbano, 2008). However, their effectiveness remains a topic of debate. While some argue that they are inefficient and costly, and contribute to the problems they aim to solve, others recognize their innovative mechanisms of cooperation and governance. Some even view them as the only potential solution for survival and refer to them as "true missionaries of our time" (Barnett & Finnemore, 2004).

Given the current state of knowledge about them, it is challenging to settle this controversy. There have been instances where its usefulness has been demonstrated. For instance, the International Commission against Impunity in Guatemala (CICIG) serves as a prime example. This small organization, comprised of prosecutors and international criminalistics experts, successfully dismantled over 60 criminal and corruption networks in Guatemala in a five-year period. Additionally, the CICIG was responsible for removing a sitting president and vice president involved in a customs corruption network. Another notable example is the World Health Organization (WHO), the specialized agency of the United Nations focused on health issues. The WHO has made significant strides in eradicating smallpox globally, has made considerable progress in the fight against measles, and has accelerated the development and distribution of vaccines to combat Covid-19.

Regrettably, these entities have also often failed. The instances of Somalia, Rwanda, and Bosnia in the nineties exemplify genuine humanitarian disasters, during which the intervention of the United Nations with peacekeeping forces or "blue helmets" demonstrated unjustifiable organizational failures that failed to halt the genocide or mitigate the escalation of violence, irrespective of the decisions and policies adopted by the great powers (Dallaire, 2004; Gourevitch, 1998). In other situations where the consequences have not been as dire, concerns regarding bias have emerged, such as in the case of the International Criminal Court, an unprecedented organization of perpetual justice that has made it possible to prosecute and penalize perpetrators of serious crimes against humanity but has primarily focused on African officials and cases.

Human rights organizations are often criticized for their inability to enforce compliance with their recommendations, which is sometimes referred to as their "lack of teeth". Some organizations, such as the United Nations General Assembly, issue non-binding resolutions, while others, like the European Union, have the authority to impose sanctions on individuals or companies in different countries. In rare cases, organizations have been granted temporary executive, legislative, and judicial powers to administer and reconstruct governments, as in the case of the United Nations Transitional Administration in East Timor (UNTAET) or the UN Interim Administration Mission for Kosovo (UNMIK). Specialized organizations, such as the Permanent Court of Arbitration, or the Internationalized or hybrid courts, like the Special Court for Sierra Leone or The Extraordinary Chambers in the Court of Cambodia, can also enforce compliance by applying international laws or hybrid schemes that combine national legislation.

The above can be applied when examining their decision-making processes and governance structures. It is generally believed that all IGOs automatically respond to and reflect the interests of powerful actors, as they were *de facto* created as their instruments. Nevertheless, it is easy to find IGOs with complex networks of stakeholders beyond the states. Like the African Union (AU), which seeks to reveal its own ancestral cultures by nominating a Panel of the Wise (POW) composed of five individuals recognized for their contributions to peace and security in various African countries. Additionally, the International Labor Organization (ILO) includes states as members but also integrates employers, trade unions, and workers' organizations into its decision-making structures, although their objectives and purposes are not always aligned. Furthermore, organizations with dual decision-making structures, such as NATO, which have both civilian and military components or organizations composed of "parts of states", such as the International Criminal Police Organization (INTERPOL), which is organized through police offices in multiple countries, are also included. Additionally, some organizations resemble the Russian matryoshkas, which are composed of varying degrees of autonomy and specificity, as is the case with the World Health Organization, which is composed of regional organizations, such as the PanAmerican Health Organization (PAHO), which was established before the WHO itself. (Blavoukos & Bourantonis, 2017: 305)

In summary, we possess limited knowledge about the vast and diverse array of IGOs that involve themselves in armed conflicts and civil wars, as well as in the formulation of agendas for democracy or development, that establish norms to standardize critical activities such as aviation, navigation, or the management of nuclear issues, and define response mechanisms for emergencies such as earthquakes and hurricanes. These organizations operate independently and coordinate multiple public and private actors in horizontal relationship structures; they experience success and failure; they respect sovereignty, support, and bolster responses commanded by governments and challenge, intervene, or reconstruct them. The message is clear, and we must further study these entities which have gained enormous influence and even power in the present world (Schemeil, 2023: 20). Determining whether they possess autonomy and agency and whether we can effectively create, direct, and control them seem to be crucial questions to be answered.

Navigating in a Minefield

The IGOs discussed in this book are typically established by states cooperating and collaborating to address a diverse range of issues, including delegating authority and providing resources to a specialized body expected to direct and manage these challenges effectively. These IGOs are officially created through formal agreements or treaties between two or more states with a shared interest and a secretariat (Bauer & Ege, 2016). They are also governed by specific representation and decision-making mechanisms that lead their operations. These organizations typically have an official headquarters and a distinct logo, and as former US Secretary of State Henry Kissinger once joked, they often have at least one telephone line for communication purposes.

IGOs are expected to act in the best interests of their multiple creators. However, if these organizations fail to meet their objectives or experience clear disagreements about their functioning, states can disband them as it was the case with the League of Nations in 1946, the Warsaw Pact in 1991, or the CICIG in 2019. States can also choose not to finance these organizations, as was the case with United Nations Educational, Scientific and Cultural Organization (UNESCO) in 2011 when the United States and Israel stopped providing resources due to the membership of Palestine, or the WHO in 2020 when the United States withheld funding under President Donald Trump due to disagreements with China's handling of the pandemic.

While not all IGOs are created by states, the latter do not always have the means to control them. Many IGOs create other organizations that emerge through normal processes of internal decisions without state intervention or the signing of treaties. In 1992, it was reported that 70% of international organizations in operation were emanations; of these, 25% were second, third, and even fourth generation organizations (Shanks et al., 1996: 594). For example, the European Commission for Agriculture has created approximately other 20 organizations, and the United Nations Security Council has the authority to establish subsidiary bodies to implement sanctions.

In addition, it is important to recognize that organizations are not homogeneous. As Allison (1971) stated, they are more like an arena where various agents interact and within which other organizations are situated rather than a unified rational monolith. The Asian Infrastructure Investment Bank is often seen as a simple appendix of Chinese government ambition, even though it comprises 57 countries from different continents. On the other hand, the Shanghai Cooperation Organization, also known as the NATO of the East, which enshrines emerging powers and core powers that compete for the creation of a new multipolar order, such as Russia, China, and India, presents a complex situation whereby respecting the sovereignty of governments and meeting the mandates of its multiple principals becomes challenging for the endogenous functioning of the organization (Hawkins & Jacoby, 2008). Similarly, organizations such as the UN, with 193 member countries, and the World Trade Organization (WTO), with 153 member countries, also have diverse structures and administrative sections which made them something much more complex than a monolithic-vertical-simple structure.

To endure, IGOs endeavor to balance diverse interests, acquire resources, engage in negotiations and bargaining with multiple stakeholders, establish specialized bureaucratic structures, monopolize technical knowledge, align with other organizations or groups, and more. One noteworthy example of this is the institutionalization of cooperative relations between the North Atlantic Treaty Organization (NATO) and the United Nations (UN), as evidenced by the presence of a NATO office within the UN building in New York (Kille & Hendrickson, 2012). Thus, the dynamics of inter-organizational relations are characterized by a multitude of issues and fragmentation, alongside interaction, cooperation, and institutionalization, which embody novel forms of international governance (Hale & Held, 2011; Toro, 2023).

While acknowledging that IGOs operate within a complex environment characterized by diverse and potentially competing national interests, this book offers a nuanced understanding of IGOs that goes beyond the conventional viewpoint that these organizations are solely created, directed, and controlled by governments. We aim to develop a specialized and in-depth analysis that transcends the state-centric perspective and the logic of anarchy that often underpins existing scholarship on IGOs.

The Story of a Crowded Neighborhood

In his book After Victory (2001), John Ikenberry posits that periods of international order-building emerge following significant conflicts and are distinguished by dominant states making decisions looking to apply their newly acquired power. According to Ikenberry, the nature and stability of the order depend on the capacity of the states to establish institutional mechanisms for restraining power and committing to long-term obligations or "bindings" (Ikenberry, 2001: 10). These are critical historical periods marked by remarkable activity, innovation, and experimentation, which, as in the case of the 1945 order, involve exceptional processes facilitated by the action and creation of a diverse set of international institutions and organizations (Ikenberry, 2001: 8).

In truth, the formation of IGOs does not progress linearly, but rather, as Peter Katzenstein points out when discussing the transformation of the international system, it involves a series of "irregular sequences of big bangs" (Ikenberry, 2001: 7). Throughout history, the processes associated with the establishment of international institutions often commenced in Europe during the Nineteenth Century, with the initial organizations emerging from the Congress of Vienna (1814–1815) following the Napoleonic Wars (Reinalda & Verbeek, 2011). However, the development of different international institutions was not restricted to these significant events. Numerous organizations also emerged due to the intensifying, sustained, economic, political, and commercial interactions between states stimulated by industrialization and globalization (Claude,

1964). Furthermore, others were established based on learning processes that embraced existing organizational models to adapt to new realities.

The system of periodic conferences that serves as the foundation of contemporary international politics was established in 1815 during the Congress of Vienna. At this time, the five victorious powers agreed to establish mechanisms for permanent consultation and joint decision-making. They aimed to create a system of balanced and contained power. This system has since defined platforms and mechanisms for collective agreements, such as treaties or conventions, which are essential components of international politics.

Although the conferences did not officially qualify as IGOs, owing to their lack of permanent headquarters and a secretariat, they nevertheless enabled consultation processes and the formulation of agreements to such an extent that, by the close of the century, the European powers had successfully managed to divide and colonize the entire African continent. The system of consultation between the great powers referred to as the pentarchy, was later revived by the United Nations Security Council.

During the latter half of the Nineteenth Century, following the Crimean War (1853–1856) and the national unification conflicts in Italy (1861) and Germany (1871), which resulted in shifts in territorial balances and spurred industrial and arms races, international organizations and formal bodies emerged to regulate and restrict the use of force in conflicts, as well as to develop mechanisms for mediation, conciliation, and arbitration to prevent and de-escalate disputes (Reinalda & Verbeek, 2011). Examples of such organizations include the Permanent Court of Arbitration, the Hague Conferences, and humanitarian organizations such as the International Committee of the Red Cross (ICRC). Although the ICRC is not classified as an IGO, its work played a significant role in defining the Geneva Protocols, which regulate the military relationships and practices of the states towards civilians. The Hague Conferences were particularly noteworthy regarding organizational learning, as they laid the groundwork for convening nations in large assemblies, which are the bodies within IGOs where decisions are democratically made.

The secretariats, an emblematic component of IGOs, originated from creating specialized entities to strengthen commercial standardization, facilitate communications, and promote economic exchanges. Many of these early international organizations have endured and served as models for subsequent organizations, such as the Central Commission for the Navigation of the Rhine (CCNR), which was established in 1815 during the Congress of Vienna and paved the way for the formation of other European River Commissions, including the Danube River Commission, as well as the Trifinio Plan, a regional organization created in 1988 as part of the Central American Integration System (SICA) to manage and safeguard water resources in El Salvador, Guatemala, and Honduras.

The emergence of technical unions in the mid-Nineteenth Century, such as the Universal Postal Union (UPU) and the International Telegraph Union (ITU), led to their integration as specialized agencies within the United Nations. Today, this family of technical and, in theory, apolitical organizations has expanded significantly. Examples include the International Civil Aviation Organization, International Meteorological Organization, World Health Organization, and International Atomic Energy Agency.

The two world wars of the Twentieth Century resulted in the establishment of the first collective security organizations, the League of Nations and the United Nations, which have universal membership and sophisticated organizational mechanisms associated with specialized agencies addressing various economic, social, cultural, and other issues. Additionally, there are regional organizations, funds, and diverse programs. After World War II, there was a significant increase in the number of IGOs, which expanded to cover almost all areas of international life. Some examples of IGOs include the International Monetary Fund (IMF) for monetary and financial stability, NATO and Sout Asian Treaty Organization (SEATO) for peace and collective security, the World Bank and Organisation of Economic Co-operation and Development (OECD) for poverty reduction and technical assistance for development, the International Atomic Energy Agency (IAEA) for nuclear arms control, the International Criminal Court (ICC) for human rights protection and defense, the Office of the United Nations High Commissioner for Refugees (UNHCR) and the International Organization for Migration (IOM) for migration and refugee assistance, the World Trade Organization (WTO) for trade promotion, the European Union (EU) and the Organization of American States (OAS) for democratization, and INTERPOL for the control and detection of criminal networks (Legler, 2015; Cooper & Legler, 2006). There are also organizations focused on environmental care, such as the United Nations Environment Programme (UNEP) and the Artic Council.

Consequently, the creation and learning process of an international order has resulted in the IGOs significantly impacting the global stage (Biermann & Koops, 2017). According to the Union of International

Associations (UIA, 2015), the number of IGOs has increased firmly from 1039 in 1981 to 1690 in 1992. Additionally, the number of non-governmental international organizations increased from 200 in 1900 to 4000 in 1980 and 7600 in 1993. Furthermore, the number of what some call "intergovernmental organizations" has increased from three in 1909 to 380 in 1980. Moreover, approximately 1200 new international organizations of various types are estimated to be added annually.

Studying and classifying the complex and diverse IGOs that currently inhabit our world is a noteworthy achievement. This task is akin to the challenge described, satirically, in Jorge Luis Borges' short story "The Analytical Language of John Wilkins" (1964), where in the imaginary Chinese encyclopedia "Celestial Emporium of Benevolent Knowledge" animals are classified into various categories such as Emperor's relatives, embalmed, trained, piglets, mermaids, and those that from afar, look like flies. Despite numerous studies and classifications of IGOs, Brechin and Ness (2013) highlight the difficulty in finding a comprehensive theory to encompass the wide range of social creatures that international organizations represent. These include international governmental and no-governmental, intergovernmental, transnationals, technical unions, courts and tribunals, and even public-private partnerships, among others. The sheer heterogeneity of international organizations makes finding a theory that can effectively encapsulate their various forms and functions a daunting task.

Theory for Understanding Black Boxes

Despite the considerable achievements of IGOs, there has not been a corresponding focus on their systematic study. The examination of IGOs within the International Relations (IR) field has been sporadic and disjointed, with periods of frank abandonment (Rochester, 1986). In the words of Verbeek (1998), this research agenda has been relegated to the status of an "ugly duckling" in IR. As a result, influential works such as Cox and Jacobson (1973), which delved into decision-making processes within organizations as an essential aspect of their study, and Graham Allison's (1971) seminal work on decision-making in the political realm, applied to the Cuban Missile Crisis, have not had the impact that they should have had. The lack of attention given to IGOs within the academic community is perplexing, given the significance of these organizations in shaping global politics.

An essential reason is that the IR field primarily focuses on large analytical frameworks that concentrate on the International Organization or the International System. This focus often leaves IGOs, and other actors subsumed within these broad categories. It is worth noting that the term "International Organization" in the singular refers to a distinct category from "international organizations" in the plural. The former implies a system of interrelationships that generates a particular effect or order, while the latter refers to a group of entities and persons interacting for a specific purpose. Unfortunately, the relationship and difference between these topics are not widely discussed within the IR discipline, as they are often assumed to be part of the same field. However, the International Organization, a leading journal in the IR field, has been instrumental in the study of both international organization and organizations since its inception in 1947. More recently, the Journal of International Organizations Studies (JIOS), established in 2010, has sought to specialize in investigating IGOs in their specificity.

In contrast, distinguishing the boundaries between institutions and organizations within the discipline is highly intricate. The discourse surrounding international institutions and organizations is often contentious. In essence, IGOs frequently assume subservient or ancillary positions within the extensive network that studies rules, institutions, powers, and regimes.

This bias is comprehensible due to the absence of a superior organizing entity in the international arena, resulting in anarchy-based order. Such an order lacks a central or supranational authority. Given this self-organization logic, characterized by a lack of hierarchy or central authority, the question of how stable, peaceful, and orderly systems can be fostered under these conditions arises. This issue has been at focus since the classical reflections of Kant (1957). A significant concern is to create and maintain order in the face of an unequal distribution of power, conflicting interests, and unequal shares of power. The aim has been to establish a decentralized system of political authorities centered on states as constitutive authorities, capable of developing mechanisms to govern relations between them without relying on a centralized government. This concept has been explored by scholars such as Nicolaidis and Shaffer (2004), Reinicke and Copeland (1998), and Rosenau and Czempiel (2009).

IGOs have been integrated into a broader study of international institutions. These institutions are viewed as specific types of rules, norms, and regimes that function as tools or instruments of an anarchic international system capable of self-organization. A central debate revolves around the efficacy of these institutional tools in generating cooperation and achieving predetermined or intended outcomes. This is a highly ambitious objective, as it entails molding a semi-anarchic system of IR to achieve specific results through certain instruments. Institutions aim to enhance cooperation among states, and among their instruments, they employ organizations equipped with rational mechanisms such as hierarchy, staff, resources, and management technologies (Bauer & Ege, 2016).

However, the assumption that organizations are merely instruments is one of the Achilles' heels of this perspective. Organizations can undoubtedly be seen as instruments, but they are also social entities composed of real people. Assuming that these social entities (and the individuals who inhabit them) behave purely as instruments would indeed simplify matters. In this way, they could be managed by higher rationalities, such as those of states. However, this book presents a reality that is quite different. When discussing organizations, it is imperative to acknowledge that persons play a crucial role (Simon, 1947). As is widely recognized in organizational theory, actions and decision-making are impossible without a certain level of discretion and autonomy. Organizations confront their unique environment and dilemmas of action, coordination, and capability. It is not unexpected that IGOs manage resources and employ various forms of power and influence within their organization and globally. Consequently, IGOs have evolved to an extent that their founders may never have envisioned or perhaps intended.

Assuming, as a realist in IR thinking does, that IGOs are merely instruments in the hands of states, serving their interests, aims, and objectives without analyzing these organizations as entities in their own right is of limited utility for empirically studying the dynamics of IR. Presuming that only states are actors and the consequences or implications of IGO can only be comprehended in terms of the constraints and political logics of power relations and asymmetries is not adequately supported by empirical evidence. It is increasingly challenging to view IGOs as opaque entities, assuming that whatever transpires within these entities will be determined by the power dynamics between states (Reinalda & Verbeek, 2011). These assumptions provide scant room for understanding IGOs as social entities composed of individuals, groups, and coalitions (Claude, 1964; Le Roy, 1995; Mearsheimer, 1995).

Other theories, such as neoliberal IR theory, emphasize the role of IGOs relative to the state-centric realist paradigm. This theory contends that IGOs are essential for facilitating cooperation, as with regimes (Krasner, 1983). There are numerous instances in which IGOs play a critical role in the international political system by permitting member states to assess the intentions of other states and monitor their compliance with agreed-upon international norms and rules (Reinalda & Verbeek, 2011). However, as this book will show, the challenge lies in understanding how various organizations, which have been established or designed to achieve specific objectives, require the creation of certain conditions, such as rules, structures, hierarchies, and capacities, to act on the intentions, interests, and identities of their creators.

The theoretical approach of constructivism carries significant importance in the field of IR. According to this school of thought, IGOs establish rules, norms, and arguments that dictate the parameters in which they negotiate, make decisions, and determine what is deemed legitimate, rational, and necessary (or not). Despite being viewed as a cohesive entity, IGOs are comprised of diverse actors both inside and outside the organization, each with unique goals and challenges. This perspective is further explored in Chap. 5. When taken as a whole, both constructivism and liberalism serve to ground the discipline in an endogenous and specialized understanding of IGOs.

It is currently possible to observe a growing interest among IR in extending the analysis of IGOs beyond the limitations of viewing them solely as instruments. Slowly, the debate has broadened to include discussions on whether IGOs possess legitimacy for the execution of their duties, how they establish their objectives, and how they achieve them. Certain studies have demonstrated that these organizations possess technical and political capabilities, essential for fulfilling their mandates in practical application. It is increasingly understood that, as organizations, they require agency and discretion to build the ideological legitimacy of their actions. Researchers are now paying greater attention to how IGOs, like any organization, seek to shape their environment rather than simply being shaped by it. The relationships between IGOs, experts, public, and private actors, and how these interactions add resources and capabilities by transferring knowledge are increasingly studied. Researchers are also examining how instruments and capabilities impact sovereignty, how they are shaped, and how they impact performance. It is now widely acknowledged that IGOs comprise people who negotiate, bargain, cooperate, and act like any other organization (Oestreich, 2012; Ahrne & Brunsson, 2008; Zamudio-Gonzalez et al., 2015; Trondal et al., 2010; Verbeek,

1998; Reinalda & Verbeek, 1998, 2004). Organizations have been studied as such intensively by disciplines like Organizations Studies for decades now. The rapprochement between the disciplines of IR and Organization Studies has been slow, as Ness and Brechin (1988) noted in 1988 and reiterated twenty-five years later in 2013 (Brechin & Ness, 2013). However, progress has been made in bringing these two disciplines closer together.

A Theory for Inhabited Instances

IGOS are organizations and as such they are inhabited entities (Hodson et al., 2012). IGOs operate within specific contexts where decisions are made, negotiated, and bargained for. Within these contexts, various actors compete for resources and interact with one another, while policies are discussed and legitimized through the exchange of information and technical knowledge. These dynamics have significant implications for a field of study that typically employs large analytical frameworks to view IGOs as black boxes and defines its research agenda around a singular question: why do states establish them?

Understanding IGOs entails examining their internal agency and how it is constructed rather than just responding to external factors. It is crucial to assess whether these organizations can define their interests and how they are held accountable. As a result, various "black box" elements are emerging as significant factors in understanding the international arena (Abbott et al., 2015; Avant et al., 2010; Archer, 2001; Barnett & Finnemore, 1999, 2004; Diehl, 2005; Ege et al., 2023; Ege et al., 2021; Reinalda & Verbeek, 2011; Shanks et al., 1996).

Therefore, it is necessary to enhance the study of IGOs by strengthening the theoretical and analytical tools. The field of Organizational Theory (or Organizational Studies) has generated a wealth of approaches, concepts, and perspectives that can enrich the analysis of IGOs. In recent years, discussions in IR on principal-agent relationships, pathologies, and dysfunctions could be enriched by understanding and applying the many other perspectives and tools that the study of organizations has advanced. This book aims to progress in the use of a sophisticated body of organizational theories and perspectives in the study of IGOs, which is on par with what already exists in the study of governmental and private organizations. There is a vast body of literature on case studies, theoretical analyses, and prescriptions for studying these types of organizations, and it should be applied to the study of IGOs.

The study of IGOs, such as international bureaucracies, has not received as much attention as necessary from an IR perspective. IGOs are considered an epiphenomenon of the distribution of power, and thus, the need to examine their dynamics, decision-making processes, and mechanisms of action has not been a priority. The lack of knowledge regarding the decision-making processes of IGOs, their effect on other actors, their relationship with and competition against other organizations, and their impact on international governance is significant. Additionally, little is known about the unique management and organizational *techniques* that IGOs have developed in practice and their organizational dilemmas. While governmental organizations have mandates given from the outside and must deal with multiple external agents, such as businesses, citizens, and non-governmental organizations (NGOs), IGOs also have to manage relationships with all states and governments, networks of companies, and NGOs in an interconnected system without a common hierarchical or legal center. Although the organizational, political, and management techniques of IGOs may resemble those of governmental organizations, they are highly specialized and different indeed. Furthermore, there is a lack of knowledge about this technique and its associated capabilities. One good example is the lack of understanding of the management challenges that the specificities of budgeting the IGOs face. Budgets often are not annual but bi or tri-annual and they are quite scarce for the high expectations their missions endorse. Their assets might be regular, but they also have occasional contributions, donations, and other sources which generally are strictly earmarked, leaving a null or very low maneuverability. And finally, depending on the source and the size of contributions, there might be an important difference of influence among the principals of an IGO (Schemeil, 2023: 137).

Despite these quite interesting and even strange specificities of IGOs, organizational theorists have had very little interest and curiosity to study them. They primarily focus on studying governmental, private, and non-governmental organizations, and there are just a handful of organizational theories that have offered solid studies regarding international organizations. As Schmeil (2023: 37) summarizes: "Psychological and cognitive approaches are little solicited [by IR discipline], while Organization Theory remains ignored. What is lost in translation here (meaning translation from national to an international idiom) is essential to an analysis of

IOs: creativity versus routine; transformative leadership of powerful states versus weak leadership of powerless institutions; and politics versus administration".

Although the complementary nature of these disciplines is evident, they start from different ontological, epistemological, and methodological assumptions, which can make conversations and conceptual rapprochement between the two not entirely natural. The first question that must be addressed in analyzing these disciplines is whether IGOs are mere instruments to serve the power and interests of the states that created them. Alternatively, are they mechanical and automated black boxes where well-defined inputs are aggregated to produce predictable and controllable outputs? Or do they possess the capacity to act like any other organization, with a certain degree of autonomy and self-management? Achieving goals in such organizations involves aligning the behaviors of specific individuals dealing with uncertain environments and limited resources and technologies. In other words, understanding the black box of organizational decision-making and actions is critical to comprehending the effects and outcomes that any organization can achieve. The black box comprises concrete individuals facing uncertain environments with limited resources and rationality. Organized action consists of discretion, cooperation, meaning creation, conflict, group interaction, and coalition-building within the organization. With this, there is the possibility of pursuing the objectives.

The normative question of how the creators of an organization manage to maintain control of the creature they have created is relevant. However, it is only one of several important questions, and it is crucial to examine the positive ways in which individuals organize and collaborate to attain desired outcomes. For many years, organizational research has established how organizations and the individuals within them function, although the cooperation and coordination are diverse, heterogeneous, and subject to change. There is no single blueprint or universal set of tools for individuals confronting the uncertainties of their environment to organize themselves and collaborate without friction or risk. As Fukuyama (2004) has informed economists, international experts, and political scientists, there is not a single organization and management theory, but rather many. It is impossible to have one theory, let alone an infallible one: organizations are social constructs that necessitate the expertise, discretion, and political and relational capabilities of specific individuals confronting particular circumstances.

Pursuing an advanced integration of organizational studies knowledge into understanding IGOs is a lengthy and optimistic endeavor. The discourse that occurred in the 1990s between neo-realism and liberal neo-institutionalism is a significant event. This debate has bolstered and contextualized the conversation on international institutions and their importance in state cooperation (Reinalda & Verbeek, 2011). However, this view is not accepted by neorealists, as they assert that cooperation is rare since states are primarily driven by a desire to ensure their survival in an environment of highly disproportionate power distributions (Reinalda & Verbeek, 2011). From this perspective, which is highly influential within the IR field, IGOs cannot escape the constraints imposed upon them. Their autonomy and agency are ultimately diminished and insignificant, as they possess minimal instruments and capabilities that influence the behavior or overriding interests of states.

Despite their shared assumptions about the state, utility-maximizing behavior, and the rationality of actors, neorealism and neoliberalism have divergent views on cooperation. While neoliberalism posits that cooperation is frequent, feasible, beneficial, and facilitated by international organizations and institutions, neorealism asserts that cooperation is not prevalent, enduring, nor advantageous.

In this manner, both theories espouse an anarchic system characterized by the absence of a supranational authority. This structure of the anarchic system is deemed substantive in defining the behavior and interests of states (Reinalda & Verbeek, 2011). Contrarily, traditional realist theories posit that the behavior of states is rooted in a question about selfish and, to some degree, malevolent human nature. In contrast, neorealism and neoliberalism emphasize the structure of the international system. It is this anarchic structure of the international system that shapes the interests and behavior of states.

The international system is often portrayed as a collection of self-interested states that strive to maximize their benefits. Without a governing body, these states are left in perpetual insecurity, as they have no central authority to turn to in times of crisis. As Keohane (2005) notes, this environment defines the lack of a central authority. Consequently, states define their interests in terms of their survival and autonomy within the competitive system. To attain these goals, they must possess power, and any cooperation is determined solely by absolute gains: will cooperation yield more benefits for me than for others? The potential benefits to be obtained in the future are considerable.

The allocation of power is contingent; therefore, the absolute gain is a pivotal element for states to collaborate. On the other hand, neoliberalism, which shares the same assumptions, is more amenable to cooperation due to intricate interdependence. Axelrod and Keohane (1985) posited that although states interact in an anarchic system, shared interests necessitate coordination and cooperation, which can be attained through international institutions based on transaction cost theory. Consequently, institutions facilitate state cooperation by aligning with the principles of relative gains and mutual interests.

The dynamics of complex interdependence indicate that cooperation is a recurring process that yields reputational consequences. If a state fails to cooperate at a particular moment, it will likely encounter reputational issues, which may deter other actors from cooperating. In this regard, the international order can be perceived as emerging from below, stemming from the diverse and multiple actors, namely states, each with distinct agendas, logics, resources, and capabilities.

Although states strive to shape a global order that aligns with their interests, they cannot guarantee complete control. This order often emerges from unpredictable forces that are not hierarchically structured, but it establishes a collective order that may not necessarily involve cooperation. Sometimes, the order arises from conflicts, wars, or legal processes that may be part of the problem. It is crucial to note that this order is not intentionally designed by any actor but rather emerges from the interactions among them. Despite this, some actors, such as the United States in the past century, have wielded significant influence over the international system, allowing them to pursue more effective dominance strategies than other states. However, this influence does not equate to absolute control over the system. Another critical issue in cooperation is compliance, ensuring that agreements are followed. The challenge of compliance arises when actors attempt to manage the dynamics while simultaneously being the first to violate the agreements they have established. (Chayes & Chayes, 1993, 1998).

The ensuing debate led to the presentation of various viewpoints, disregarding the cautionary tales of neo-realism. Instead of questioning their relevance, the focus shifted toward understanding their actions, decision-making processes, and organizational structures. Although these entities may seem insignificant and powerless, they have permeated everywhere and proliferated. Consequently, the field of IR has incorporated certain theoretical frameworks and perspectives to study these seemingly irrelevant yet rapidly growing entities.

Institutionalism, which encompasses both economic and sociological theories, is widely acknowledged in academic circles as a powerful perspective. Institutionalism then has been significantly influenced by the principal-agent theory in economic institutionalism and is considered an essential pillar of organizational studies, as recognized by March and Olsen (1984, 1998). In this logic, the actions of individuals or agents with varying degrees of autonomy and discretion must be a focal point when studying IGOs as spaces for coordination and cooperation. According to this view, agency can shape the interests and behaviors of states through the power of organized action (March & Olsen, 1984, 1998).

DISCUSSIONS AND TRENDS

The examination of IGOs finds itself grappling with three distinct inclinations: the assertion of their insignificance from the perspective of neorealism, the pursuit of overarching theories that would enable IGOs to be permanently integrated into the framework of the international system, and the assimilation of organizational theories that could potentially elucidate their part in the study of the global order by delving into the "black box" of organized action. While progress has been more substantial in the second inclination than in the third, it is evident that considerable advancement has been made in this area.

One theory that arises from the second trend posits the concept of international regimes (Keohane, 1986; Krasner, 1983). This approach is premised on understanding regimes as specific types of institutions, as defined by Krasner (1983), who posited that regimes are a set of explicit and implicit principles, norms, rules, and decision-making processes around which the expectations of states on an issue converge. Thus, regimes are attempts to regulate specific issues such as trade, the use of certain weapons, the protection of whales, and the protection of refugees. In this manner, the expectations and interests of stakeholders are expected to converge around an issue with a robust regulatory emphasis. The primary function of regimes is to reduce information costs, as they are predicated on providing information and monitoring compliance. Consequently, this theory aligns with Keohane (1986). Keohane (1982) also focuses on the issue of the reputation of regimes by providing appropriate standards of behavior upon which the conduct of states is established.

Subsequently, this led to a discussion between rationalists and constructivists, resulting in two distinct regime perspectives. Rationalists emphasized the finalistic (pursuing certain ends) nature of regimes, while constructivists focused on shared and intersubjective meanings, more than on specific results (Barkin, 2006). The discourse on international institutions within regimes also involved to drive away the study of international organizations from the field of IR, while the concept of an organization is absent from the definition of regimes. Although decision-making processes are incorporated, it is implied that organizations exist, but there is no explicit organizational vision.

The notion of international regimes can be perplexing for those outside the field of IR. Comprehending this abstract idea can be likened to grasping the concept of tools and levels of formality. While institutions can be viewed as existing or constructed phenomena, regimes seem more connected to design, with components such as laws, rules, principles, and customs that are mainly agreed upon and explicit. This structure appears to suggest a greater degree of design than in the case of institutions. However, the debate about the distinctions between regimes and institutions persists, as does the role of international organizations in these contexts. Questions about regimes pertain to what role the organizations play within the regimes and, in turn, how the regimes can influence the behavior of states.

Constructivism is a significant theory that begins with a distinct ontology that refuses to recognize the state as the primary actor, thereby rejecting the assumptions of neo-realism and neoliberalism. Proponents of constructivism contend that institutions play a critical role in shaping the interests and practices of states, as well as their identities in the global arena (Finnemore, 1993).

Constructivism posits an intersubjective domain that possesses meaning for those who occupy it. Generally, intersubjectivity encompasses the shared comprehension, experiences, and social knowledge that stem from institutions. In this regard, organizations are enduring configurations of identities and interests that cannot be separated from the perceptions of actors. In contrast to neorealism, Wendt (2005) contends that anarchy is not an inherent feature but a product of the interactions between states and that states reciprocally define each other, thus lending meaning to anarchy. On the other hand, Finnemore (1996) posits that the preferences of the states are not immutable, and they may not always be aware of what they desire; instead, they are receptive to acquiring knowledge about what is suitable and practical. Therefore, organizations can facilitate the resolution of issues by inculcating their norms, values, and principles, and constructivism asserts that organizations are significant constituents in shaping the identities of states.

Furthermore, other theories fall within the mid-range of significance in the field and are starting to question the role of IGOs. To organize these theories, one can delineate three distinct levels: the first level seeks to clarify the origins or reasons for the existence of these organizations, the second level aims to elucidate their structural design, and the third level examines how they function.

The mid-range theories that center around the creation or demand of international organizations are the functionalist or neo-functionalist theory, which is a project that initially opposed integration processes but later shifted towards them through technical cooperation schemes (Mitrany, 1966, 1975; Haas, 1964; Gehring, 1996; Pollack, 2001). For these theories IGOs are created to minimize the territorial nationalism attachment or achieve integration processes. The hegemonic stability theory, rooted in realism, posits that cooperation is necessary for states to create IGOs, which facilitate the hegemony of dominant states. In this sense, establishing the International Monetary Fund (IMF) maintains the hegemony and dominance of countries such as the United States.

Concerning the explanation of the design, there are theoretical frameworks that are not strictly IR theories but they are adapted, such as Rational Choice or the agent-principal model, and even the sociological neo-institutionalism. These frameworks are utilized to explain the diversity of international organizations based on the nature of the problem at hand.

The perspective of Rational Choice theorizes that design is a response to the challenges faced by an organization, and factors such as the number of members, scope, subject matter, centralization, control, and flexibility play a significant role in shaping this response. However, this perspective does not delve into the delegated functions, or the controls exercised. Principal agent theory investigates the issues of control of an agent once the conditional delegation of authority has taken place. Constructivism views design as a non-material element intimately connected to adopting legitimate and acceptable norms and practices that shape preferences and identities. Sociological Neo-Institutionalism shifts the focus from the agency of states to the influence of organizations, highlighting their role in shaping preferences and identities.

In the realm of operation and functioning, the theories under consideration are not restricted to a particular discipline. Instead, they draw upon ideas from Bureaucratic Theory and the pathologies identified by Weber (1922/2019). Barnett and Finnemore (1999) thoroughly examined the operation of IGOs, beginning with an analysis of bureaucratic pathologies.

META-ORGANIZATIONS AND INTER-ORGANIZATIONAL RELATIONSHIPS BETWEEN IGOS

From the perspective of organizational theory, the paradox of IGOs stems from the fact that they are both created and bound by states through their laws, rules, and mandates, yet they are also independent organizations that must operate within their context and generate their own logics of action and survival. This endogenous life of organizations is a fundamental problem in the field of IR, but organizational studies have provided ample empirical evidence to support this concept. Organizations exist and function daily through the process of organizing, which involves coordinating individual actions and resources to achieve collective goals. This process is critical to understanding how organizations operate and evolve, and it encompasses not only the creation of structures and systems but also the fostering of a culture that supports ongoing adaptation, innovation, and coordination. IGOs cannot avoid the dynamics of organizing, as they are involved in global projects and must participate in these activities to survive and succeed (Scott & Davis, 2007; Scott et al., 2011).

Thus, the inherent logic of IGOs is neither a disease nor a malfunction but rather a natural state for any organization. Therefore, connecting this specificity with the general logic of the international order and governance is crucial. A manifestation of this paradox can be seen in the intricate inter-organizational relations that have been growing among IGOs themselves (or with International Non.-Governmental Organizations (INGOs). In this regard, the idea of a meta-organization is highly beneficial for analyzing these interactions.

Meta-organizations, as defined by Ahrne and Brunsson (2008), are composed of organizations whose members are other organizations, rather than individuals. This concept addresses the paradox of autonomy, where meta-organizations possess autonomy while simultaneously requiring cooperation and coordination among various actors. According to this theory, the complexity of international problems necessitates the involvement of meta-organizations, which seek greater autonomy from the states to which they belong. However, this creates a paradox without a clear solution, as these organizations strive for autonomy while simultaneously relying on cooperation and coordination with other actors and organizations, leading to a certain level of dependency or interdependence.

To comprehend the intricacies of any IGO, one must first grasp its' inter-organizational logics. Unlike the conventional theory of governance, the theory of meta-organizations posits a varied distribution of powers and an unbalanced correlation of forces between different international organizations and states. This imbalance, however, does not preclude cooperation and coordination, as these can be achieved through political action, agreements, and negotiations that establish objectives. While cooperation and coordination can be generated, they are not necessarily achieved through a hierarchical or procedural process. Instead, IGOs must establish control through negotiation processes rather than directing their members. Nonetheless, it is essential to note that not all IGOs are without coercive mechanisms. For instance, the International Monetary Fund employs loan mechanisms and conditionality to exert its influence. Therefore, the idea that IGOs lack coercive instruments is not universally applicable.

Organizations must develop political strategies to expand their autonomy. Autonomy is a central concept in the discussions, but it is important to distinguish between different types of autonomy. A meta-organization possesses two main characteristics: the first is the capacity to collaborate when the parts do not follow a hierarchical and repetitive structure, and the second is that meta-organizations typically have fewer resources than the organizations that make them up. Thus, how does a meta-organization with limited resources establish mechanisms that provide it with legitimacy, normative authority, or soft governance?

The issue of the influence of IGOs secretaries has sparked a debate. Bauer and Ege (2016) investigated the autonomy of IGOs relative to states, while Reinalda and Verbeek (2011) examined the influence of IGOs at different stages of subnational public policy formulation. IGOs are evident in shaping public agendas, as demonstrated by the Sustainable Development Goals and conferences. Haas (2002), Barnett and Coleman (2005), and Reinalda and Verbeek (2011) indicate that IGOs are increasingly involved in the design and implementation of public policies. IGOs can induce state behavior without relying on direct authority or coercive mechanisms, relying instead on legitimacy and neutrality. IGOs benefit from this arrangement, as they can use symbolic language and call their guidelines recommendations. IGOs base their political logic on mechanisms such as discussion, negotiation of agreements, creation of language, and establishment of shared norms and principles that can become more powerful and mandatory regulations over time. Additionally, there are instances where IGOs can temporarily govern, as seen in Timor Leste, Sierra Leone, and Kosovo, where they assume legislative and judicial executive power.

Organizational Pathologies in IGOs

Organizational pathologies or dysfunctions have been considered part of the analysis of the functioning of IGOs as actors. The main idea of Barnett and Finnemore (1999, 2004), based on DiMaggio and Powell's (1983, 1991) work, is that the same sources of bureaucratic power can lead to pathological behaviors in IGOs. They proposed a typology that distinguishes between internal and external dysfunctions and between material and cultural causes of such dysfunctions (Barnett & Finnemore, 1999). In this context, they present theories such as Allison's (1971) bureaucratic theory, which suggests that competition between subunits of an organization can result in inefficient or undesirable behavior. Additionally, theories like institutional realism and neoliberalism argue that states, rather than the organizations themselves, are responsible for the dysfunctional behavior due to their preferences, interests, and resources.

From a deeper perspective, specific theories examine dysfunction from a cultural standpoint and outside the organization itself; that is, they consider the environment rather than the organization. These theories assert that organizations prioritize legitimacy over efficiency and that the cultural environment significantly influences this legitimacy. The cultural factor is essential in comprehending the occasionally dysfunctional behavior of organizations, as the cultural environment may present contradictory norms and principles that affect the actions of organizations. One category identified in the literature is the "world policy model" (Barnett & Finnemore, 1999).

Internal cultural dimensions are essential in the field of international organizations. Barnett and Finnemore (1999) assert that pathologies arise from categorizing these organizations as bureaucracies, viewed as social forms. Bureaucracies are considered rational means of achieving collective goals and instilling specific values. They acquire social knowledge and expertise to achieve this, thereby exercising their power. However, this organizational structure can lead to dysfunctions and pathological behaviors (Hodson et al., 2012). These structures are governed by rules, routines, and standardized procedures that produce predictable responses. While this makes them effective for complex tasks, it can also compromise the rationality of the means.

Likewise, regulations and customs can result in habitual actions and forming subgroups detached from the broader social context. Furthermore, specialization and fragmentation can impede decision-making and restrict officials' perspectives, ultimately causing maladaptive behaviors. In brief, Barnett and Finnemore (1999) postulate that the characteristics of bureaucracy, such as legal rationality and expertise, grant the ability to act independently but can also lead to dysfunctional outcomes. Adhering to Barnett and Finnemore's (1999) framework, they identify five mechanisms through which bureaucracies can give rise to pathologies: the paradox of rationality, the principle of universality, the normalization of deviant behavior, institutional isolation, and cultural conflict. However, from an organizational standpoint, pathology is a controversial perspective subject to significant scrutiny and debate. This book will discuss this interesting debate in Chap. 4.

IGOs as Organized Anarchies

IGOs are quite complex and amazing organizations. They are organizations, persons acting and making decisions in a context of multiple state actors, populations, firms, NGOs, and facing wicked problems like poverty, education, telecommunication, armed conflict, or the need to make peace between states and within states. The organizational point of departure in this book, as explained in the introduction, is that rather than being instruments under the control of their creators, IGOs are organized anarchies.

An organization faces a peculiar way of organizing when: firstly, the objectives and preferences of those influencing the organization are varied, heterogeneous, and sometimes conflicting. Secondly, the scope of the objectives sought is such that there is no one clear, definitive technology or method to achieve them. Thirdly, decision-making processes involve numerous agents and groups, resulting in complex and dynamic procedures. When these dynamics are set, it becomes challenging for organizations to follow a straightforward path or a singular process to align means with ends. Negotiation, interaction, and legitimacy-seeking are critical to managing. And this is why some propose that complex organizations are generally organized anarchies, with an acute capacity to process multiple feedbacks and offering flexible responses. The anarchic nature of these dynamics does not mean that objectives will not be met, and results will not be achieved. Rather, it suggests that effective management and administration of this anarchy are essential for success (Cohen et al., 1972; Cohen & March, 1974; March & Olsen, 1979; Musselin, 1997).

An organized anarchy, in essence, exists in a perpetual state of ambiguity: there is no clear understanding of precisely what needs to be achieved, nor is there a consensus on the best methods to accomplish these vague objectives. Additionally, it remains unclear which agents, in what capacities, are responsible for making decisions and being accountable for the outcomes.

How, then, do IGOs function as organizations? This book aims to progress the task of integrating various organizational theories into the study of IGOs, thereby laying a foundation for understanding these entities as both remarkable and anarchic collectivities. Despite their anarchic nature, IGOs can accomplish critical tasks, adapting to, and helping to resolve complex global challenges.

Concluding Remarks

Considering IGOs as organized anarchies is an interesting and challenging endeavor. Numerous debates arise in the nascent literature that attempts to relate IGOs from IR to Organizational Theory, and fresh avenues for analysis and contemplation come to the fore. The development of robust bureaucracies, characterized by civil services built on technical criteria, a certain degree of autonomy, and a defined ethos that fosters a sense of belonging and identity among members, as described by Bauer and Ege (2016), raises important research questions. These bureaucracies, which interact formally and even institutionally with other organizations in dyads, triads, and networks, and sometimes intervene intrusively in the domestic affairs of governments, demonstrate both agency and distinct interests. This situation prompts new inquiries: What challenges emerge from these bureaucratic dynamics at the international level? How do these bureaucracies acquire an authoritative character, and what variables do they use to evaluate their performance?

Without question, incorporating bureaucratic logic into the examination of functioning has elevated its status as a significant factor for comprehending their performance and objectives (Bauer et al., 2024; Ege et al., 2021; Schomaker et al., 2022). Nevertheless, substantial difficulties persist in the theoretical construction of IGOs and their preliminary investigation, primarily concerning their autonomy, agency, and accountability.

The primary issue at hand is examining the role of IGOs in global governance, considering the institutional density and intricate nature of transnational problems. Considering this, states require adaptable and comprehensive solutions that involve numerous actors with multi-centered and networked organizational models and coordination structures rather than traditional centralizing models. Present-day global challenges necessitate the resources and abilities of multiple public and private actors, as well as multilevel governance systems characterized by decentralized coordination and compliance mechanisms, inter- and intra-organizational cooperation mechanisms, and active civil society participation. The emergence of regimes, global agreements, public-private partnerships, and multi-stakeholder alliances underscores the need for the diversity and density of current institutional arrangements. It is crucial to investigate the participation of IGOs in these processes, including their functions and responsibilities, as well as the impact of their participation in regional and global governance networks (Biermann & Koops, 2017; Karns et al., 2015; Avant et al., 2010).

The second challenge is part of an ongoing debate among IGOs: States are key actors in global governance, but they are not the only ones with the capacity for independent action. IGOs act independently and in ways not dictated or intended by the states that created, maintained, and supported them (Oestreich, 2012; Collins & White, 2011; Reinalda & Verbeek, 1998). The state-centric paradigm that dominates the field of IR limits theoretical tools to explain the agency of IGOs. Furthermore, it raises questions about the accountability of IGOs, how it occurs, and to whom they are accountable.

Applying theories from economics (principal-agent) or sociology (bureaucratic theory) to IGOs has been instrumental in challenging the prevailing theoretical paradigm. It is crucial to demonstrate that IGOs are not merely instruments but also arenas where power asymmetries, divergent objectives, informal interactions, and bureaucratic logic, previously referred to as the logics of decision-action which are endogenous to organizations, exist. This poses several substantive challenges for the field of

IR: recognizing IGOs as political actors that are neither wholly neutral nor objective and that they compete, negotiate, and pursue their interests, even if it means going against states. While there have been analyses of this perspective, the conceptualization of power remains superficial and imprecise, providing ample room for further discussion on this critical element.

The third challenge problematizes the status of IGOs as agents and sites of authority, shifting the study of IGOs toward bureaucratic perspectives (Barnett & Finnemore, 1999, 2004; Bauer et al., 2016). By treating IGOs as bureaucracies, this approach not only offers new insights into their behavior but also demystifies them by recognizing that they possess inherent discretionary spaces, which can foster informal structures, patrimonialism, deviations, and other natural characteristics of bureaucracies that are not necessarily pathological or dysfunctional.

IGOs are subject to certain limitations, including finite resources, uncertain contexts, and the inherent complexity of their instruments, which often fall short of the complexity of reality. However, it is crucial to investigate the impact of the bureaucratic culture, including its rules, procedures, and routines, on organizational outcomes. This approach enables a more holistic understanding of organizations that acknowledges their capacity to succeed and fall short of achieving the common good. By engaging in such discussions, IGOs are incorporated into broader Public Administration and Organizational Theory debates.

The study of collaboration and interactions with IGOs has a long history. However, there has been a growing interest in understanding the partnerships and potential synergies between IGOs and intergovernmental, non-governmental, and private organizations in recent years. Examples of joint work between organizations such as the United Nations (UN) and North Atlantic Treaty Organization (NATO) in peacekeeping operations, the increasing involvement of NGOs in civil-military state reconstruction operations, and networks involving various public-private actors such as the Gavi Alliance have shifted the field of IR towards the theoretical and empirical examination of inter-organizational relationships. The significance of analyzing these relationships lies not only in their relevance in the international arena but also at the organizational level; they pertain to coordination, cooperation, negotiation, and adaptation abilities that are unique, as they occur in highly specific contexts both within organizations and in the spaces where they operate (Biermann & Koops, 2017).

In summary, there is a pressing need to examine International Governmental Organizations (IGOs) within an interdisciplinary framework. As these organizations increasingly wield significant power and influence, understanding them as entities comprised of individuals engaged in the 'organizational game' becomes crucial. The forthcoming chapters of this book introduce several organizational theories that shed light on the internal dynamics within IGOs—often considered a 'black box.' These chapters will elucidate the decision-making processes, the pursuit of ambiguous objectives, and the complex interactions involving various agents, governments, and organizations within these entities.

Moreover, the text will explore how these organizational elements are essential for understanding not only the performance of IGOs but also their ability to remain viable, legitimate, and operational in a world marked by uncertainty. The narrative acknowledges that these organizations sometimes fail and sometimes succeed, as they are inhabited by individuals navigating a complex environment. In essence, this book aims to advance the critically needed 'organizational turn' in the study of international organizations (Schemeil, 2023: 47).

References

Abbott, K., Genschel, P., Snidal, D., & Zangl, D. (2015). *International Organizations as Orchestrators*. Cambridge University Press.

Ahrne, G., & Brunsson, N. (2008). *Metaorganizations*. Edward Elgar.

Allison, G. (1971). *Essence of Decision*. Little, Brown and Company.

Archer, C. (2001). *International Organizations*. Routledge.

Avant, D., Finnemore, M., & Sell, S. (2010). *Who Governs the Globe?* Cambridge University Press.

Axelrod, R., & Keohane, R. O. (1985). Achieving Cooperation Under Anarchy: Strategies and Institutions. *World Politics, 38*(1), 226–254.

Barkin, S. (2006). *International Organization. Theories and Institutions*. Palgrave Macmillan.

Barnett, M., & Coleman, L. (2005). Designing Police: Interpol and the Study of Change in International Organizations. *International Studies Quarterly, 49*(4), 593–619.

Barnett, M., & Finnemore, M. (1999). The Politics, Power and Pathologies of International Organizations. *International Organization, 54*(4), 699–732.

Barnett, M., & Finnemore, M. (2004). *Rules for the World. International Organizations in Global Politics*. Cornell University Press.

Bauer, M., Eckhard, S., Ege, J., & Knill, C. (2024). Means of Bureaucratic Influence: The Interplay Between Formal Autonomy and Informal Styles in International Bureaucracies. In H. Jörgens, N. Kolleck, & M. Well (Eds.),

International Public Administrations in Environmental Governance: The Role of Autonomy, Agency and the Quest for Attention. Cambridge University Press. https://doi.org/10.1017/9781009383486.002

Bauer, M., Knill, C., & Eckhard, S. (2016). International Public Administration: A New Type of Bureaucracy? Lessons and Challenges for Public Administration Research. In M. Michael Bauer, C. Knill, & S. Eckhard (Eds.), *International Bureaucracy: Challenges and Lessons for Public Administration Research* (pp. 179–198). Palgrave Macmillan.

Bauer, M. W., & Ege, J. (2016). Bureaucratic Autonomy of International Organizations' Secretariats. *Journal of European Public Policy.* https://doi.org/10.1080/13501763.2016.1162833

Biermann, R., & Koops, J. (Eds.). (2017). *Palgrave Handbook of Inter-Organizational Relations in World Politics.* Palgrave Macmillan.

Blavoukos, S., & Bourantonis, D. (Eds.). (2017). *The EU in UN politics.* Palgrave Macmillan.

Borges, J. L. (1964). *Other Inquisitions (1937–1952).* University of Texas Press.

Brechin, S. R., & Ness, G. D. (2013). Looking Back at the Gap: International Organizations as Organizations Twenty-five Years Later. *Journal of International Organizations Studies, 4*(1), 14–39.

Chayes, A., & Chayes, A. (1993). On Compliance. *International Organization, 47*(2), 175–205.

Chayes, A., & Chayes, A. (1998). *The New Sobereignty: Compliance with International Regulatory Agreements.* Harvard University Press.

Claude, I. (1964). *Swords into Plowshares. The Problems and Prospects of International Organization.* Random Hause.

Cohen, M.D., March, J.G. (1974). *Leadership and Ambiguity: The American College President* McGraw Hill.

Cohen, M. D., March, J. G., & Olsen, J. P. (1972). A Garbage Can Model of Organizational Choice. *Administrative Science Quarterly,* 1–25.

Collins, R., & White, N. (2011). *International Organizations and the Idea of Autonomy. Institutional Independence in the International Legal Order.* Routledge; Taylor and Francis Group.

Cooper, A., & Legler, T. (2006). *Intervention Without Intervening? The OAS Defense and Promotion of Democracy in the Americas.* Palgrave Macmillan.

Cox, R., & Jacobson, H. (Eds.). (1973). *The Anatomy of the Influence. Decision Making in International Organization.* Yale University Press.

Culebro, J., & Romo, G. (2023). Nuevas aproximaciones organizacionales a la crisis y la gestion de crisis. *Revista Digital de Estudios Organizacionales, 3,* 7–11.

Dallaire, R. (2004). *Shake Hands with the Devil. The Failure of Humanity in Rwanda.* Carroll & Graf Publishers.

Diehl, P. (Ed.). (2005). *The Politics of Global Governance. International Organizations in an Interdependent World*. Lynne Rienner Publishers.

DiMaggio, P., & Powell, W. W. (1983). The Iron Cage Revisited: Institutional Isomorphism and Collective Rationality in Organizational Fields. *American Sociological Review, 48*, 147–160.

DiMaggio, P. J., & Powell, W. W. (Eds.). (1991). *The New Institutionalism in Organizational Analysis*. University of Chicago Press.

Ege, J., Bauer, M. W., & Wagner, N. (2021). How Do International Bureaucrats Affect Policy Outputs? Studying Administrative Influence Strategies in International Organizations. *International Review of Administrative Sciences, 87*(4), 737–754. https://doi.org/10.1177/00208523211000109

Ege, J., Bauer, M. W., Wagner, N., & Thomann, E. (2023). Under What Conditions Does Bureaucracy Matter in the Making of Global Public Policies? *Governance, 36*(4), 1313–1333.

Finnemore, M. (1993). International Organizations as Teachers of Norms: The United Nations Educational, Scientific, and Cultural Organization and Science Policy. *International Organization, 47*, 565–597.

Finnemore, M. (1996). *National Interests in International Society*. Cornell University Press.

Fukuyama, F. (2004). *State-building: Governance and World Order in the 21st Century*. Cornell University Press.

Gehring, T. (1996). Integrating Integration Theory: Neo-functionalism and International Regimes. *Global Society. Journal of Interdisciplinary International Relations, 10*(3), 225–253.

Gourevitch, P. (1998). *We Wish to Inform You that Tomorrow We Will Be Killed with Our Families. Stories from Rwanda*. Picador.

Haas, E. B. (1964). *Beyond the Nation State: Functionalism and International Organization*. Standford University Press.

Haas, P. M. (2002). UN Conferences and Constructivist Governance of the Environment. *Global Governance, 8*(1), 73–92.

Hawkins, D., & Jacoby, W. (2008). Agent Permeability, Principal Delegation and the European Court of Human Rights. *Review of International Organizations, 3*, 1–28.

Hale, T., & Held, D. (Eds). (2011). *Handbook of Transnational Governance: Institutions and Innovations*. Polity Press.

Hodson, R., Martin, A. W., & Roscigno, V. (2012). Rules Don't Apply: Kafka's Insights on Bureaucracy. *Organization, 20*(2).

Ikenberry, G. (2001). *After Victory. Institutions, Strategic Restrain and the Rebuilding of Order After Major Wars*. Princeton University Press.

Kant, I. (1957). *Perpetual Peace*. Macmillan.

Karns, M., Mingst, K., & Siles, K. (2015). *International Organizations. The Politics and Processes of Global Governance*. Lynne Rienner Publishers.

Keohane, R. O. (1982). The Demand for International Regimes. *International Organization, 36*(2), 325–355.

Keohane, R. O. (1986). Reciprocity in International Relations. *International Organization, 40*(1), 1–27.

Keohane, R. O. (2005). *After Hegemony: Cooperation and Discord in the World Political Economy*. Princeton University Press.

Kille, K., & Hendrickson, R. (2012). NATO and the United Nations: Debates and Trends in Institutional Coordination. *Journal of International Organizations Studies, 2*(1), 28–48.

Krasner, S. (1983). *International Regimes*. Cornell University Press.

Le Roy, A. (1995). *International Organizations. Principles and Issues*. Prentice-Hall.

Legler, T. (2015). Beyond Reach? The Organization of American States and Effective Multilateralism. In J. Dominguez & A. Covarrubias (Eds.), *Routledge Handbook of Latin America and the World* (pp. 311–328). Routledge.

March, J., & Olsen, J. (1979). *Ambiguity and Choice in Organizations*. Universitetsforlaget.

March, J., & Olsen, J. (1984). The New Institutionalism: Organizational Factors in Political Life. *American Political Science Review, 78*(3), 734–749.

March, J., & Olsen, J. (1998). The Institutional Dynamics of International Political Orders. *International Organization, 52*(4), 943–969.

Mearsheimer, J. (1995). The False Promise of International Institutions. *International Security, 19*(3), 5–49.

Mitrany, D. (1966). *A Working Peace System*. Quadrangle Books.

Mitrany, D. (1975). *The Functional Theory of Politics*. Martin Robertson.

Muñoz, T. (2021). Los retos de la ONU para alcanzar la gobernanza en materia de protección a desplazados forzados a 75 años de su fundación. In N. Pérez & G. Pérez (Eds.), *A 75 años de la Organización de las Naciones Unidas. Riesgos Globales* (pp. 141–162). UAM.

Musselin, C. (1997). Les universités sont-elles des anarchies organisées? In *Désordre(s)* (pp. 291–308). Presses Universitaires de France.

Ness, G., & Brechin, S. (1988). Bridging the Gap: International Organizations as Organizations. *International Organization, 42*(2), 245–283.

Nicolaidis, K., & Shaffer, G. (2004). Transnational Mutual Recognition Regimes: Governance Without Global Government. *Law and Contemporary Problems, 68*, 263.

Oestreich, J. (Ed.). (2012). *International Organizations as Self-Directed Actors*. Routledge.

Pollack, M. A. (2001). International Relations Theory and European Integration. *Journal of Common Market Studies, 39*(2), 221–244.

Reinalda, B., & Verbeek, B. (Eds.). (1998). *Autonomous Policy Making by International Organizations*. Routledge.

Reinalda, B., & Verbeek, B. (2004). *Decision Making Within International Organizations*. Routledge.

Reinalda, B., & Verbeek, B. (2011). Policy Autonomy of Intergovernmental Organizations: A Challenge to International Relations Theory. In R. Collins & N. White (Eds.), *International Organisations and the Idea of Autonomy. Institutional Independence in the International Legal Order* (pp. 87–103). Routledge.

Reinicke, W. H., & Copeland, D. (1998). Global Public Policy: Governing Without Government? *International Journal, 53*(3), 597.

Rochester, M. (1986). The Rise and Fall of International Organization as a Field of Study. *International Organization, 40*(4), 777–813.

Rosenau, J., & Czempiel, O. (2009). *Governance Without Government: Order and Change in World Politics*. Cambridge University Press.

Schemeil, Y. (2023). *The Making of the World. How International Organizations Shape Our Future*. Verlag Barbara Budrich.

Schomaker, R. M., Bauer, M. W., & Ege, J. (2022). Bureaucracy and Internationalization. In A. Farazmand (Ed.), *Global Encyclopedia of Public Administration, Public Policy, and Governance*. Springer. https://doi.org/10.1007/978-3-030-66252-3_3748

Scott, R., & Davis, G. (2007). *Organizations and Organizing*. Routledge.

Scott, R., Levitt, R., & Orr, R. (2011). *Global Projects. Institutional and Political Challenges*. Cambridge University Press.

Shanks, C., Jacobson, H., & Kaplan, J. (1996). Inertia and Change in the Constelation of International Governmental Organizations 1981–1992. *International Organization, 50*(4), 593–627.

Simon, H. (1947). *Administrative Behavior*. Macmillan.

Toro, C. (2023). The Two US-Mexico Borders and the Limits of the North American Project. In E. Hershberg & T. Long (Eds.), *North American Regionalism: Stagnation, Decline, or Renewal?* (pp. 46–67). The University of New Mexico Press.

Trondal, J., Marcussen, M., Larsson, T., & Veggeland, F. (2010). *Unpacking International Organizations. The Dynamics of Compound Bureaucracies*. Manchester University Press.

Union of International Associations (UIA). (2015). *Yearbook of International Organization 2015–2016*. Walter de Gruyter.

Urbano, J. (2008). La migración de terceros países a la Unión Europea: la fortaleza se cierra. In R. Peña (Ed.), *México-Unión Europea. Asociación estratégica para la gobernabilidad y la inclusión social*. UNAM-Plaza y Valdéz.

Verbeek, B. (1998). International Organizations. The Ugly Duckling of International Relations Theory. In B. Reinalda & B. Verbeek (Eds.), *Autonomous Policy Making by International Organizations*. Routledge.

Weber, M. (1922/2019). *Economy and Society. A New Translation by K. Tribe.* Harvard University Press.

Wendt, A. (2005). La anarquía es lo que los Estados hacen de ella: la construcción social de la política de poder. *Relaciones Internacionales, 1*, 1–47.

Zamudio-Gonzalez, L., Arellano-Gault, D., & Culebro, J. (Eds.). (2015). *Puentes, Fronteras y Murallas Disciplinarias en torno a las Organizaciones Internacionales.* CIDE.

CHAPTER 3

Organizations as Systems: IGOS Coping with the Systemic Impact and the Inability of Full Control

INTRODUCTION

The United Nations (UN) is a well-known international organization that can be viewed as a system comprising numerous elements, such as other organizations, agencies, programs, mandates, missions, conventions, and conferences. In terms of its organizational structure, the UN is a decentralized system of specialized bodies, each with its own constitution, mandate, governance, and budget. It consists of six fundamental organs, 15 specialized agencies, and several funds or programs. Examples of these organizations within the UN system include the Food and Agriculture Organization (FAO), the International Monetary Fund (IMF), and the United Nations Development Program (UNDP). The UN has offices worldwide, employs 125,436 officials, and has a budget of 65.8 billion dollars (UN System Chief Executives Board for Coordination [CEB-UN], n.d.-a, n.d.-b). It serves as a vast administrative structure organized as a system for developing policies through the legitimacy of its quasi-universal membership (Weiss et al., 2004).

The UN was initially established as a decentralized entity comprising interconnected components (Ruggie, 2003: 302). Some of its specialized agencies, such as the International Telecommunication Union (ITU) and the FAO, were established before the UN's formal creation or

© The Author(s), under exclusive license to Springer Nature Switzerland AG 2025
L. Zamudio-González, D. Arellano-Gault, *International Organizational Anarchy*,
https://doi.org/10.1007/978-3-031-82392-3_3

45

concurrently with it (Childers, 1995). Each agency has its unique charter, membership, assembly, and secretariat, with an executive head elected by the member governments (Art. 57 Chap. IX charter). The Economic and Social Council (ECOSOC) incorporated these agencies into the UN through collaborative agreements (Childers, 1995). Hierarchically, organizations within the UN create and coordinate with other organizations: ECOSOC consults and provides recommendations and, in turn, delegates implementation to other organizations that require a certain level of autonomy to manage and take action effectively (Karns & Mingst, 2004: 116).

Systemic logic extends beyond the mere nesting of subsystems such as organizations. It includes other related subsystems or instruments, such as funds and programs. These are often considered emanations of the UN, as they are subsidiaries of the General Assembly and answer to the Secretary-General (Childers, 1995: 18). However, they also possess a certain degree of operational autonomy. This is because they frequently have their own governing bodies, staff, and resources (McLaren, 2001: 321). In essence, some funds and programs are proper organizations in their own rights.

From an administrative perspective, each instance serves a specific purpose or function. In other words, they do not exist independently; their existence depends on their ability to contribute to the overall system. Each component must fulfill a specific function in light of the broader goals of the system. For instance, in the case of international organizations, the general functions are quite broad, encompassing issues such as health, education, disarmament, trade, peace, and development. If all system components can be connected and related to one another, it may be possible to achieve peace incrementally, as suggested by Mitrany (1966). The interaction of these elements can produce positive outcomes, although the complexity of the interactions and interdependencies within the system makes it difficult to predict precise results.

The UN serves as a good example of systemic high expectations, demonstrating the capacity of diverse elements to generate positive outcomes in the face of intricate problems, such as global crises. Although it is impossible to anticipate or predict the entirety of the consequences produced by a complex IGO such as the UN, the inherent dynamics of systems, including the search for equilibrium, constant adaptation, interaction, interdependence, and order, enhance the likelihood of achieving favorable and enduring results in dynamic and uncertain environments.

The term *system* has been an essential component of the language of International Relations (IR) at least since Wallerstein's seminal works on the *world system* (Wallerstein, 1979, 2005; Osorio, 2015). Wallerstein (1979) defines a system as a complex network of interrelationships and interactions between diverse entities, such as states and their governments. Although the system is not entirely designed, it is characterized by a lack of formal higher authority, resulting in each actor, such as states, playing in the system according to their interests, histories, resources, and geography. Despite this lack of centralized authority, the interactions between actors generate interdependencies that ultimately give rise to ordered and agreed-upon patterns of behavior, rules, and relatively stable norms. This systemic order does not require a central authority to direct everything. Instead, it emerges from the complex relationships between actors.

The systemic perspective has gained considerable appeal in several social sciences and has the potential to serve as a robust epistemological framework. This is because systems provide a comprehensive understanding of order through the continuous interactions between their constituent parts and the environment in the context of inherent uncertainty and the possibility of chaos always present.

A significant proportion of systemic currents hold universal aspirations. If systems are present, their fundamental principles are consistent: interaction and adaptation to the environment, interdependence among the various elements and subsystems. The processes of change, adaptation, differentiation, and dynamic stability, adhere to the primary principle of any system: survival. The systemic perspective is often deployed in a more adaptable manner, serving as a practical metaphor that connotes an elaborate process, resulting in a relatively organized whole. It has also been criticized for oversimplifying and reducing everything to the relationships between the parts and the whole without addressing the underlying axioms.

Returning to the UN, which can be viewed at both a systemic level composed of subsystems and a systemic level nested within a more extensive system, the complexity of the analysis becomes evident. The UN is not only a system in its own right, with its constituent subsystems, but also forms part of a supra-system that comprises states, other International Governmental Organizations (IGOs), International Non-governmental Organizations (INGOs), and companies, which collectively contribute to the creation of the global order. For instance, states are part of the UN's environment and are also constitute elements of some of its subsystems, such as the General Assembly, the Security Council, or as members of its various agencies. From a functionalist perspective, IGOs are gears of the international system created and driven by states. In this view, IGOs perform a specific role or function within the system, which is crucial for order maintenance and survival. In this sense, the functionality of IGOs can be evaluated based on their ability to fulfill their roles, act rationally, and align themselves with the interests and strategies of states. Within this context, IGOs can be considered second-level elements of the international system, subordinate to the primary elements, namely states, and their functionality can be measured or assessed accordingly.

However, from a systemic perspective, IGOs can be viewed as systems in and of themselves. If the international system has the highest level of aggregation from a systemic viewpoint, then the states are subsystem. In turn, IGOs are disaggregated subsystems of the supra-system, the international system. As subsystems, IGOs face states as part of their environment and must devise strategies to adapt and survive in a mobile and threatening context or navigate a minefield. A system fulfills its function if it adapts and differentiates itself. Consequently, IGOs must differentiate themselves from their creators, the states, as their survival depends on this differentiation. This suggests that systemic vision is more complex and dynamic than simple functionalism. IGOs, as systems in and of themselves, cannot be merely obedient functional parts of state-centric systems.

Systemic logic is not necessarily a rigid theory, as the relationship between systems, subsystems, and supra-systems can overlap, be somewhat disordered, and prone to change. For instance, Sitter (2005) examined the history of the European Union (EU) and found that over the past few decades, the EU has created and organized a series of IGOs within itself, often under incrementalist rather than rational logic. Other European international organizations have overlapped, sometimes closer and sometimes further away from EU structures.

Several analytical elements require further investigation in this initial and brief interpretation of IGOs as systems. The application of systems theory to IGOs as organizations is a potent way to understand the organizational nature of such entities. Systems theory, at its core, is a theory of organization in the most extensive sense of the word, not solely as a theory for comprehending formal organizations but as a means of understanding how reality organizes and even self-organizes.

This chapter summarizes the key elements of systems theory and its application to IGOs. The chapter begins with a brief overview of studies that have utilized systems theory within the realm of International

Relations (IR), intending to assess its usefulness and the types of research conducted. Subsequently, the chapter focuses on the principles of systems theory when viewed through the lens of organizational theory to gauge its applicability to the study of IGOs as organizations. As the chapter progresses, several of the concepts presented in the introduction are further elucidated.

SYSTEMS THEORY IN INTERNATIONAL RELATIONS: JUST A USEFUL METAPHOR?

The field of IR has traditionally employed systemic analysis to understand the international dynamics. However, it is basic to note that the idea of systems is frequently used as a metaphor rather than concise theoretical concept stemming from a particular theory or approach (Albert et al., 2010: 47).

Systemic vision, widely employed in understanding contemporary international realities, has been crucial because it recognizes an interconnected world in which no state or organization can effectively tackle global problems without engaging other actors (Bousquet & Curtis, 2011). As evidenced by the recent COVID-19 pandemic, the Westphalian model of state interaction has become outdated. The emergence of private and social actors has necessitated the development of flexible, more horizontal, and decentralized structures of influence and authority. Intergovernmental and non-governmental international organizations have become key players in shaping the global system with their unique capacities and tools (Hardt & Negri, 2000; Alba, 2020; Avant et al., 2010). Moreover, the capabilities of private and social actors have significantly increased on various global issues. For example, individuals can now promote human rights actions before institutions specifically designed for that purpose, such as the International Criminal Court, which prosecutes individuals responsible for genocide or crimes against humanity (Barnett & Sikkink, 2009). Additionally, the World Bank's Inspection Panel is an independent complaint mechanism available to individuals and communities who have been or believe they have been affected by a World Bank-financed project.

Indeed, the emphasis on relational analysis in systems thinking provides an avenue for contemplating concepts such as globalization, global governance, global society, and world society (Barnett & Sikkink, 2009;

Biermann et al., 2009; Schmidt, 2021: 98), extending beyond conventional levels of analysis (Waltz, 1959).

Systems thinking argues that actors are neither completely free agents capable of transforming the social systems in which they operate, nor are they entirely trapped or determined by social structures -organizations, rules, norms-. Actors, although, have scarce control over them (Buzan, 1993). Agency and structure are interdependent, with each shaping the other: the actions of agents influence structural configurations, which in turn guide the actions of these agents. In more radical frameworks, such as Luhmann's concept of *global society*, agency and structure are indistinguishable. This is because, in the global society model, viewed as a singular system, all elements are equally significant without any one element generally outweighing another (Albert, 2010).

While systems thinking is arguably essential for understanding global issues, the field of International Relations (IR) appears to lack a well-established and cohesive tradition for, under the umbrella of system theory, analyzing international politics (Albert et al., 2010; Braumoeller, 2012; Stephens, 1972; Tierney, 1972). Early efforts at systemic theorizing in the 1950s and 1960s were based on von Bertalanffy's general systems theory (1956), which emphasized scientific rigor and isomorphism. These ideas later influenced cybernetic and functionalist developments. However, the momentum of these advancements diminished in the 1970s with the rise of structural neorealism. The concept of *system* has historically been applied in various ways, including: (1) as a theoretical lens for interpreting political phenomena, (2) as an integrated set of relationships based on a hypothetical set of political variables, such as an international system with a world government, (3) as a set of relationships between political variables in an actual international system, and (4) as any set of interacting variables (Dougherty & Pfaltzgraff, 1993: 134). To reinvigorate and strengthen systems thinking in IR, it is crucial to take these contexts into account and begin with broader reflections on how systems thinking might contribute to the study of international politics, rather than narrowly focusing on defining an operational concept.

In the following sections, some trajectories and efforts within the discipline of International Relations (IR) will be outlined (in an illustrative but not exhaustive manner) that have been directed toward studying large-scale social forms. From a holistic perspective, these efforts seek to uncover the structural dynamics and logics of systems, specifically their processes of stability, change, and evolution (Albert et al., 2010: 9–10). It will be seen, through this exploration, that despite the logical assumption that systemic theories would analyze IGOs (as valid subsystems alongside states), this has not occurred, at least not in a structured manner.

Early Systemic Theories in IR: The Modeling Tradition

The inception of systemic theorizing in the field of IR is intimately tied to general systems theory and adaptive functional systems (Stephens, 1972: 322). Systems theory emerged as a result of the work of Ludwig von Bertalanffy, a biologist who proposed the unification of science through isomorphism, which entails the formulation of principles that apply universally to all systems irrespective of the nature of their constituent parts and relationships (González-Uresti, 2021: 392–393). With the concept of isomorphism, regularities or *laws* in political life were identified. It was posited that the structures that explain behavior in one organization could also be used to describe it in others (Brodbeck, 1968; Del Arenal, 2007: 213; Kaplan, 1964; Stephens, 1972: 323).

Isomorphism reveals the structural nature of all physical and biological systems (Stephens, 1972: 323). For instance, this concept has been applied to identify similarities between communist countries (Robinson, 1969). However, its universal claims and positivist assumptions were met with skepticism, and it did not gain traction in IR (Blauberg et al., 1977; Stephens, 1972; Tierney, 1972: 6). Nonetheless, researchers with mathematical and computer science backgrounds made significant advancements in other areas, such as von Neumann and Morgenstern (1947), who established the foundation for game theory.

Subsequent research abandoned isomorphism and aimed to elucidate the behavior of the international system as a distinct system in its individuality (Braumoeller, 2012: 159). Such efforts resulted in two distinct traditions: agent-based mathematical modeling (ABM) and equation-based mathematical modeling (EBM), as well as a tradition among internationalists who endeavored to apply system theory to international politics to detect recurring patterns and stable behavior.

The modeling tradition has contributed significantly to Axelrod and Hamilton's (1981) work on cooperation, and Cederman's (1997) to study emergent actors in world politics. These studies introduced macromodels that utilized multiple variables and databases. However, systemic theorists in the IR field have not yet fully exploited this agenda, as noted by Braumoeller (2012: 160).

A second tradition of studies has been widely acknowledged. It commenced with Morton Kaplan's work in 1957 and continued with Kenneth Waltz's contributions in 1979, both of whom advocated for advancing the discipline of IR scientifically. Morton Kaplan believed strongly in the necessity of transforming the IR discipline into a scientific field where regularities and patterns could be systematically studied. He utilized von Bertalanffy's isomorphism as a foundational concept and defined systems as a series of interrelated elements distinct from their surroundings due to specific patterns and regularities.

Kaplan (1957) proposed a typology that included six hypothetical international systems of world reality: the balance of power, flexible bipolar, rigid bipolar, universal international, hierarchical or unipolar international, and veto international systems. The balance of the power system was characterized by states with similar capabilities and strengths. These states exhibited behavioral patterns aimed at negotiation and avoided direct conflict. They also demonstrated a greater willingness to negotiate and reach agreements periodically through consensual changes between parties. In models of bipolarity, which could be either rigid or flexible, the basic organizational structure is composed of opposing blocs headed by a national actor. These blocs were characterized by the presence or absence of non-aligned national actors, and behavioral patterns were more competitive. States were willing to draw and defend zones of influence but took care not to escalate local conflicts. In this system, international organizations formed a subsystem. They supported states as long as their interests were contrary to those of another bloc or when the possibilities of change were riskier.

After World War II, the international system resembled Kant's concept of a confederation of states united by cooperation and stability, with international organizations facilitating coordination. Unlike the international veto system, this system leaned towards isolationism and sought to maintain stability through a decentralized deterrence scheme involving several nuclear-armed states (Boulding, 1958: 330).

Kaplan argued that systems possess rules or essential requirements which define the behaviors necessary for systems to remain in equilibrium (Stephens, 1972: 331). He did not rule out the possibility of instability and transformation from one system to another (Del Arenal, 2007: 218). Still, his major concern was to explain stability.

The revival of the custom of constructing models, either actual or hypothetical, of the international system was initiated by Rosecrance and

Modelski in 1964. Rosecrance (1963), like Kaplan, aimed to explain stability conditions through a historical analysis of nine European international systems between 1740 and 1960. He identified the capabilities, attitudes, and resources of the ruling elites, as well as the capacity of the systems to maintain equilibrium, as fundamental determinants. Rosecrance (1963) subsequently applied systemic theory to the study of war and peace, using the same historical systems, and identified the variables and determinants of crises (Del Arenal, 2007: 221). George Modelski (1964) distinguished two types of international systems: the industrial and the agrarian. These were considered the extreme ends of a continuum of analysis suitable for analyzing change in social systems (Del Arenal, 2007: 224).

Kenneth Waltz (1979) structural realism profoundly impacted theorizing about the international system for the following two decades. Waltz posited that the global system comprises autonomous, self-sufficient entities functioning in a self-reliant environment. This anarchic environment, devoid of rules, regulations, and supranational authority, shaped the behavior of these entities and prompted them to adopt strategies of survival, self-preservation, alliances, and balance of power (Bousquet & Curtis, 2011: 50). While Buzan and Little (2000) contend that Waltz's work focuses more on structure than the system, they argue that he neglects to explain international politics by disregarding the state and its foreign policies.

Snyder (2013) also notes that Watlz's argument aligns with Durkheim's concept of mechanical society, where the units are separate, and their main characteristics are autonomy and self-sufficiency. Conversely, in an organic society, the parts are united by their differences, with mutual dependence as a fundamental element. In this regard, Snyder pointed out that the transition from a mechanical society to an organic society occurs through an increase in interactions between the units, a concept he referred to as dynamic density. Thus, the greater the dynamic density, the greater the specialization and integration among the units. In the context of globalization, states tend toward integration, in contrast to anarchy.

The general theory of systems has primarily influenced the field of IR by concentrating on stated-centered international systems that pertain to politics (Calduch, 1991; Del Arenal, 2007: 208). This is because the dominance of structural realism has led to a preference for micro-level approaches, in which the state and its foreign policy are the primary units of analysis.

Complexity and Unexpected Effects

The 1980s and the 1990s were marked by the integration of complexity research into the social sciences and the revitalization of systems thinking, which created opportunities for a creative shift in the IR paradigm (Bousquet & Curtis, 2011: 43). For some analysts, this development may have sparked a fifth disciplinary debate: the idea that rather than order and hierarchy as basis of the international order, diversity and *panarchy* (the intricate coupling of human and nature systems) are the real key elements of the international (Kavalski, 2007).

Complexity theory employs various methods that challenge Enlightenment principles by analyzing linear causality, predictability, and order (Capra, 1996; Kavalski, 2007: 437). Complexity theorists argue that social reality encompasses a spectrum of events, some of them ordered, some disordered, and some basically probabilistic (Geyer, 2003). This perspective suggests that linear causality and the idea that systems are merely the sum of their parts are inadequate.

One of the most interesting categories of complex systems is what is referred to as emergent properties, that is, unexpected effects that are impossible to predict, derived from the interaction of actors with each other and with their environment (Kavalski, 2007: 439). The interaction of multiple components simultaneously prevents any possibility of control or linear causality (Waldrop, 1992: 86). Emergent effects give rise to uncertainty and change at the systemic level (Cederman, 1997).

These contexts demonstrate the potential for autonomous interactions among individual units to give rise to self-organization or emergent processes, which can generate unanticipated outcomes. In the absence of centralized control, order can emerge spontaneously from the interactions of individual components (Bousquet & Curtis, 2011: 48).

The most acknowledged and significant endeavor was undertaken by James Rosenau (1990), who envisioned the international system as multicentric, dynamic, and constantly evolving reality. He introduced the metaphor of turbulence, defined as "a global state of affairs in which the interconnections that underpin the main parameters of world politics are marked by great complexity and variability" (Rosenau, 1990: 78). His work represents a pivotal moment in IR by reorienting the multi-factor global perspective in contrast to the state-centric view. By employing the principles of open systems in environments with numerous actors, diverse spatial scales in intricate interactions, and nonlinear patterns, he challenges the predictability derived from structural realism within the context of anarchy (Bousquet & Simon, 2011: 51). Rosenau accentuates the decentralization and fragmentation of international politics, where micro-level subgroup dynamics impact the macro level. Micro dynamics generate patterns (such as systems of rules and authority relations) that foster order and regulation.

Complexity theory encompasses two forms of self-organization: adaptation and co-evolution (Axelrod, 1997: 153; Rosenau, 1990). Adaptation pertains to the ability of a system to adjust to both internal and external environments. Conversely, co-evolution refers to a system's capacity to evolve concurrently with its surroundings (Schmidt, 2021). The application of complexity theory and co-evolution in the international field is exemplified by Schmidt (2021), who defines a complex system as an "open system (…) comprising multiple elements (units) of various types intricately interconnected with each other and operating at various levels" (Orsini et al., 2020: 3). These systems exhibit unique features and unpredictable patterns due to self-organization and emergent properties, as observed in refugee protection (Betts, 2009, 2010), intellectual property rights (Helfer, 2009), and climate change (Abbott, 2012).

Braumoeller's (2012) study is notable for its attempt to explain changes in the behavior of great powers through systemic analysis. By transcending the traditional approach of analysis by levels that create an artificial division, Braumoeller (2012) seeks to offer a more comprehensive explanation of the actors' impact on the system and vice versa (Levy & Thompson, 2010). This systemic approach is based on the idea that interconnectedness within the system leads to the influence of two independent spheres or actors on each other (Braumoeller, 2012: 195). Accordingly, the behavior of one state can produce a change in the international system, which in turn generates a series of subsequent changes in the behavior of the remaining actors (Braumoeller, 2012: 112). This implies that great powers are not entirely free to act or modify the international arena at their will or without resistance and the need to face the emergent properties that will probably occur. Although Braumoeller's (2012) study begins with quantitative analysis and mathematical modeling, it also includes three historical cases that undergo qualitative and in-depth analysis: the polarization of Europe (1815–1832), the end of American isolationism (1940), and the end of the Cold War (1991).

Close to the systemic perspective, and specifically related to complex adaptive systems, there are some studies that draw on network literature

(Duffield, 2002). Studies on organized crime and security environments (Klein & Maxson, 2006; Kenney, 2007), the new wars in the global south (Kaldor, 1999; Duffield, 2002), or transnational health or humanitarian crises (Abbott et al., 2015a, 2015b), for example, have been approached from the recognition of loosely coupled networks and decentralized dynamics in their operation. These studies understand global governance through networked relations with actors holding different types of authority and power, integrated into formal or informal arrangements with channels of horizontal communication and coordination (Keck & Sikkink, 1998).

OTHER APPLICATIONS OF SYSTEMS THEORY IN IR

Other significant contributions to the systemic framework of international politics originate from sociology, particularly those that view the system as a global society and that challenge the state-centric paradigm. Prominent scholars such as John Burton, Dina Zinnes, and Peter Wallensteen have advanced this perspective, which seeks to depart from traditional systemic functionalist approaches. For instance, John Burton's, 1972 work, World Society, proposed analyzing global society by examining the systems and then considering the state's role. He employed a *spider's web* model, where the world is perceived as a network of global transactions, and the state is situated within this context. Wallensteen (1981) developed four models based on the functions of the state and the system of states to explain conflictive behavior, including *Geopolitik*, *Realpolitik*, *Kapitalpolitik*, and *Idealpolitik*. Additionally, Zinnes (1967) redirected the focus towards transforming systems to elucidate international violence, as Del Arenal (2007: 226) noted.

More recent studies, such as Buzan and Little's (2000), have examined the development and progression of international systems from their earliest beginnings to the present day. They argue against the prevailing notion of systems in IR, which is limited to inter-state relations, and instead propose a more comprehensive approach, including multiple levels of analysis. From highest to lowest, these levels include international systems, subsystems, units, sub-units, and individuals. Examining the interactions between these levels at different points in history makes it possible to gain a deeper understanding of society being constructed over time.

In the tradition of Niklas Luhmann, modern systems theory conceives society as a global society, which is the most significant possible social order (Albert, 2010: 44). As discussed in more detail in the following section, this theory conceptualizes social systems as fundamentally built on communicative events among persons and other social actors like organizations. The cause-effect relationship replaces the indeterminacy-determinacy relationship (Albert, 2010: 45). It views world society as one but in contestant differentiation (therefore, becoming more and more complex).

During the 1980s and the 1990s, the field's overarching narrative transitioned from a state of anarchy to governance within a global society. A greater focus accompanied this shift on networks, transnational relations, and partnerships, significantly impacting state relations. As a result, these studies have become increasingly important for understanding the complex dynamics between states in today's interconnected world.

Barnett and Sikkink (2009) highlight that states share the stage with many other actors, and trends in global politics are shaped by them and various actors and forces. Global governance has transitioned from dominated by states to the inclusion of other agents like IGOs and even private and non-governmental organizations.

From this perspective, the authority, autonomy, and agency of IGOs emerge as logical and necessary subjects of study. IGOs are increasingly seen as political actors with influence comparable to that of powerful entities such as states. A key aspect of this perspective is that the impact of IGOs extends beyond the functions assigned to them by member states or regulations based on state preferences. Instead, IGOs actively shape the social world in which cooperation and decision-making take place. They influence their environment by helping to define the issues and interests that states must address and by proposing how governance should be conducted (Barnett & Finnemore, 2004). IGOs are not merely forums for persuasion; they also engage in socialization processes (Checkel, 2005). The growing recognition of the authority and power of IGOs has, however, raised concerns about the potential uncontrollability of these entities by their creators.

Based on this short survey of the literature, it is evident that the field of international politics is shifting towards a comprehensive perspective that acknowledges the significance of diverse actors, such as IGOs, with agency, autonomy, and authority as part of a dynamic system. Initially, the straightforward systems view only considered a limited number of autonomous actors—primarily states—susceptible to control in an environment of anarchy. However, it became apparent that the evolving global landscape necessitated also to study IGOs as systems and subsystems by themselves, embedded in an intricate network where there are not only states but also other actors and influences.

A systemic perspective has been highly advantageous in the field of IR. Employing this approach from an organizational perspective can facilitate significant breakthroughs, mainly when the objective is to concentrate on investigating IGOs.

THE ORGANIZATIONAL BASIS OF SYSTEMS THEORY

Systems theory aims to serve as a comprehensive or general theory, as it posits that it is more than a mere metaphor. In other words, systems are present in various aspects of reality, including physical (such as the solar system), biological (such as the respiratory or circulatory systems), and social (such as political, economic, labor, and legal systems). This theory has exerted a significant influence and experienced considerable development in the realm of organizations, rendering them one of the most crucial systems in contemporary society due to their prevalence.

This section provides an overview of the main systemic theories related to organizations. These theories include the well-known General Systems Theory and social systemic theories such as structural-functionalism and Luhmann's theory. The social perspective of systemic theory, which emphasizes the idea that there is a vital function that tends to produce social order, is reviewed. Additionally, the conceptualization of organizations from the General Systems Theory and the paradox this entails are discussed.

General Systems Theory presents a comprehensive framework of fundamental elements in every system. Organizations are systemic phenomena that adhere to these principles. As systems, IGOs are heavily dependent on their environment, which includes other systems. The relationship between these systems is dynamic and emergent, meaning that emergencies, new effects, and dynamics are inevitable owing to the continuous change and adjustment of the interrelationships and interdependencies that arise daily. Therefore, it is crucial to recognize the concept of complex adaptive systems, in which the role of human beings in creating systems and interpreting reality is an integral aspect of systemic dynamics.

The next theory is grounded in the work of Luhmann (2005), who developed systemic theory to its most extreme implications. According to Luhmann (2005, 2006), systems exist within a dynamic and uncertain environment, and within this context, the only explanation that makes sense is that function itself is the contingency. Thus, function is not merely a factor or an assumption, as it often appears in other systems theories. By making function the contingency itself, Luhmann (2012) presents a more coherent and robust view of systems. Concepts such as autopoiesis, operational closure, and hyper-differentiation are strategies that systems employ to manage contingency. Luhmann (2005) argues that the primary function of systems is to capture or *trap* contingency, which paradoxically leads to logics of selectivity that ultimately increase complexity.

Additionally, Luhmann (2017) presents social systems as communication systems in which human beings are seen as part of the contingency. The section concludes with a reflection on organizations as decision systems, where decisions are made to control contingency. However, a chain of decisions is established in which democratization and rationalization participate in the decision-making process.

General Theory of Systems: Web of Relationships, Interactions, and Interdependencies

The principle of systems theory posits that reality is a consequence of the interactions and connections formed between various components in their encounter. These connections and interactions and the resulting interdependencies are imbued with meaning and order when situated within an environment. An environment encompasses more than just elements and their relationships; it is the source of *the function*: the interactions, at the end, tend to produce the whole. Therefore, a system can be considered a complex network of relationships, interactions, and interdependencies that tend to reproduce the system as such.

Systems must distinguish themselves from their surroundings for at least a short period. In doing so, they take on a unique identity within the environment while still being connected. They rely on the environment for survival, yet the ongoing interactions and dependencies within the system shape their order. This differentiation process is critical to a system's success, allowing it to interact with other systems and shape its environment (Kast & Rosenzweig, 1972). However, because the context in which systems exist is constantly changing, systems must adapt and adjust to survive. This creates unpredictability in the outcome of a system's efforts to maintain its distinct identity within the environment.

In the international arena, it is widely acknowledged that one of the primary responsibilities of Secretariats is to engage with various state and non-state actors through meetings, conferences, and negotiations (Ness & Brechin, 1988: 252). These interactions aim to secure support, establish technical credibility, and devise strategies to achieve a consensus. These activities are underpinned by profound systemic logic, given the complexity and diversity of the organization's environment. To survive and thrive, every system must adapt to its surroundings, forming relationships that are advantageous for the organization.

Achieving stable interactions and interdependencies is crucial for survival, even temporarily. Adaptation to environmental changes is also essential. Differentiation can be an ongoing process because the environment is so vast and powerful that it will eventually become impossible, and the system will return to the environment, ceasing to exist as a distinct entity. To avoid this, systems must continually differentiate themselves and seek new interactions that allow them to adapt and establish a new equilibrium. This process is referred to as 'complexification'. As the system becomes more complex, it becomes increasingly likely that differentiation will be exhausted, and a new one will need to be found.

General Systems Theory posits that the cycle of systems is far from static and does not simply tend toward the status quo. While stability and equilibrium are crucial components of a system, adaptation and change in response to contextual transformations are equally important. Time is also a significant variable. The environment is vast and ultimately unmanageable due to the intricate web of relationships, interactions, and elements, coupled with the relentless passage of time. The second law of thermodynamics plays a critical role here, as entropy is an unstoppable force that leads to disorder, and negentropy (the efforts to counteract or slow entropy) is inevitably limited.

The International Atomic Energy Agency (IAEA), established in 1957, was initially mandated to oversee the dissemination of nuclear resources and activities. This mandate was constantly challenged by member states needing to approve monitoring and compliance standards. In the 1970s, the Non-Proliferation Treaty led the organization to seek status as an international governing organization with regulatory and safety standard-setting capacities. While these standards could be verified, the states often imposed limitations under surveillance. Like any organization, the IAEA has adapted dynamically, maintaining high technical standards and engaging in complex negotiations to fulfill its mandate without causing major international diplomatic conflicts (Roehrlich, 2022). Its adaptation has been extreme: rather than looking to prevent the proliferation of atomic weapons (an impossible task) IAEA has been able to change its priorities to prevent nuclear disasters, something much more likely to happen. Adaptation to environment is often much more important for survival than to stubbornly pursue formal (and old or even obsolete) objectives.

In summary, the systemic order is inherently limited and transitory. Under classical systems theory, the primary tenet is fundamentally functional: the environment establishes or forces a logic (or task) that becomes a function for a particular system. Achieving such a function is necessary for survival. But the function is never clear or static. This is why systems continually select specific interactions and connections to partially close themselves from the environment and attain stability. In other words, systems emerge by selecting the connections between certain elements. To distinguish is to relate, this selection process entails energy expenditure, thereby enabling the essential dynamic logic of systems: differentiation. By differentiating, systems can govern their interactions with other elements or systems, preserving their distinctiveness. Selection represents a differentiation of relationships that maintains equilibrium and serves as a source of control and safeguard in the system's relationships with its context, other elements, and other systems that continuously influence the system.

However, the requirement for energy poses a significant challenge, as energy is finite and entropy ultimately prevails, leading to disorder as the ultimate destiny. Consequently, the environment, a broader entropic space, is considered the ultimate reality. From the system's perspective, survival, even if temporary, is the essence of existence. The struggle to differentiate, adapt, and resist entropy is essential to existence.

The fundamental premise of this perspective is that context determines the purpose or function of a system. Consequently, the principle of interrelatedness posits that the entire system is connected to the environment with openings and closings to environmental elements. The essential components for the system's survival originate from the context. In contrast, the system must transform these elements to produce the differentiation required for generating an output. These outputs are also related to the environment. In addition, the context reacts through feedback, which enables the system to assess, comprehend, or infer whether it possesses adequate resources to maintain its distinctiveness from the environment.

What is crucial for comprehension in systemic logic? Initially, it is imperative to recognize that individual elements and their collective total do not constitute the system. The system is not merely a collection of elements; selectivity is critical, as interrelation and interdependence are vital components. A system encompasses all of these aspects: the individual elements, their aggregate, the interrelationships and interdependencies that emerge among them, and their connection to the environment.

What is the advantage of possessing a well-structured internal systemic relationship characterized by equilibrium and coherence if, at the end, it fails to achieve the function? Establishing a satisfactory internal interrelationship is irrelevant if it does not align with the needed response to what the context places as the function to achieve.

A good example of an organization's constant struggle to identify and build its response to necessary functions can be seen in the UN Population Fund (UNFPA) as it seeks to address the diverse needs arising from a wide array of target populations. In other words, rather than a single function, the organization may face multiple functions, some of which may even appear contradictory. UNFPA is a subsystem of the UN, which in turn is a subsystem of the international order. From a systemic perspective, aligning functions with the environment is never an easy task for an IGO. Therefore, developing management capacities and techniques for organizations like UNFPA must take these systemic dynamics into account to achieve their goals effectively.

However, it necessary to clarify that the context is, at the end, unpredictable. Accordingly, there is no optimal method for differentiation or to know exactly what selectivity or adaptation can be optimal. It is essential to recognize that the context is uncontrollable and that there is always an inherent risk in relating elements to it. Furthermore, the context is continually evolving, and a solution that might be effective at one point in time may become ineffective at another point in time owing to changes in the context.

According to this theory's fundamental assumptions, systems cannot predict the context of movement and change. Consequently, the interaction between various elements and systems leads to constructing a mechanism known as equifinality: different actions and strategies might achieve the same end. While imperfect or infallible, this mechanism is rational and has multiple pathways to reach a common goal. In other words, no single correct or rational path exists. The changing nature of the environment and the complexity arising from interrelationships make it illogical to assume that any single solution will remain effective. Equilibrium necessitates constant adaptation and change. In addition to equifinality, another

3 ORGANIZATIONS AS SYSTEMS: IGOS COPING WITH THE SYSTEMIC... 63

mechanism, imperfect and fallible but rational under systemic conditions, can be added: homeostasis. This refers to the internal stability of a system's relationships, allowing it to adjust to environmental changes constantly. Homeostasis is closely linked to the dynamic nature of context; if the context is highly unstable, homeostasis must also be very adaptable.

Consider the case of the World Health Organization (WHO) responding to the HIV/AIDS epidemic (Jönsson & Jönsson, 2012: 142–167). It is widely recognized that IGOs initially reacted slowly during this crisis. Although the possibilities of a HIV/AIDS crisis were identified at least five years prior to 1987, it was not until then that a coordinated effort was initiated. Initially, the WHO contended that the efforts of individual countries and NGOs were sufficient to address the issue. However, it became increasingly apparent that a collaborative approach was necessary to confront the disease, involving governmental actors and various NGOs with diverse objectives and priorities.

The global challenges require a coordinated response from various organizations, including the WHO, the UNESCO, the United Nations Development Programme (UNDP), and the World Bank. To address the systemic effects of the different interventions, it became clear that an organized effort was needed at the international level. The systemic logic of the situation dictated that a coordinating agency was required to oversee the various interventions, and the WHO stepped into this role by creating the Global Fund to Fight AIDS, Tuberculosis, and Malaria (GFATM). The inclusion of NGOs in the governing body of the GFATM in 2002 reflects the importance of considering the efforts of other organizations in order to response to a changing context.

The WHO's role as a coordinating agency requires clear systemic logic that considers the interdependence of different actors. The organization was tasked with coordinating the efforts of countries and NGOs to achieve systemic effects that a single agency or interest group could not achieve. The success of this coordinated effort hinges on the WHO's ability to develop the necessary managerial and systemic capacity to effectively oversee the interdependent organizations and actors involved. However, coordinating a system of interdependent organizations and actors proved more difficult than initially anticipated.

The systematic evolution of global health governance has shifted from a coordinated approach to a flexible partnership between public and private entities. This *multi-stakeholder* governance model has brought together various actors, including NGOs, corporations, donors, and activists. This approach is grounded in systemic logic because the complex and dynamic interactions of systems can benefit from a less hierarchical and more interconnected structure. Organizations such as the Joint United Nations Programme on HIV/AIDS (UNAIDS) and the Global Fund have emerged as *meta-organizations* (Ahrne & Brunsson, 2008: 2, Ahrne et al., 2016), as they comprise other organizations as their members. From a systemic perspective, this evolution represents a more intricate and dynamic relationship between the systems and subsystems.

The WHO, UNAIDS, and the Global Fund demonstrate a crucial aspect of systems theory in organizations: the complexity of systems arises from their interactions with other systems and subsystems within their environment. A system may be a context for other subsystems and at the same time being a part of a supra-system (a system built through the interrelations of other systems). The intricate relationships and interdependencies between systems further complicate the environment, challenging the ability of a system to maintain predictability and stability. Every IGO then, has an important organizational systemic task: to equilibrate performance and resilience. At present, it must deliver its services or goods, but with one eye monitoring the environment to be capable of adapting in the future (Schemeil, 2023: 133). Or, in organizational words, it is of low value to only pursue efficiency if the effectiveness is overlooked.

The fundamental principles of General Systems Theory are applicable across diverse fields, including biology and organizational theory. Although the elements differ between the two disciplines, such as organs and cells in biology and people and organizational structures, the principles of function, interrelation, homeostasis, equifinality, and feedback remain consistent (Kast & Rosenzweig, 1972). General Systems Theory also gained considerable momentum in the social sciences through its connection to structural-functionalism, a perspective that has been both influential and subject to criticism. Although these theories are distinct, they share many similarities and are complementary.

The Structural-functionalist Approach: How Do Organizations Become a Form of Structure?

The structural-functionalist approach is rooted in the belief that individuals, in their interconnectedness with one another and the world, must establish parameters of stability and reliance on structural behaviors, relationships, and outcomes. Without this structuring, disorder would permeate, rendering impossible the existence of groups and societies. Analogous to the body, in which distinct organs cooperate for the functioning of the unified physiological system; socially, a function that contributes to the orderly operation of the collective (encompassing individuals, families, groups, and organizations) also exists. Spencer (1983) and Durkheim (1984) are noteworthy for exploring the underlying reasons and mechanisms that lead to forming a socially structured order.

The formation of social systems (including organizations) and the internalization of cultural norms (such as moral values) contribute to establishing order and stability but also engender distortions, anxieties, pressures, and domination. The challenge lies in determining the actions and processes necessary for individuals to thrive within these intricate structures. This inquiry is further amplified by the fact that humans are not entirely rational creatures and thus require shortcuts, such as institutions, to mitigate the most detrimental consequences of errors or excesses (Selznick, 1957).

In line with the principles of General Systems Theory, structural-functionalism contends that context is characterized by dynamism and unpredictability. Nevertheless, it posits the existence of an inherent force within individuals and societies that strives for order. This shared belief has sometimes resulted in convergence between the two perspectives, as evidenced by the well-known social systems theory proposed by Talcott Parsons (2005).

The connection between structural functionalism and General Systems Theory has garnered substantial scholarly attention. This literature aims to comprehend how organizations, as systems within the broader social system, persist and strive to flourish in an environment with scarce resources characterized by competition. One of the most influential perspectives is contingency theory, which posits that the context in which an organization operates is determinant and that organizations can only partially adapt. There is no singular, optimal approach to survival; instead, organizations must embrace uncertainty and prepare for unforeseen circumstances. Although contingency implies unpredictability, it can lead to stability. For example, the contingent can generate periods of stability (Gersick, 1991). Stability and change are interdependent, and systems seek to establish stability conditions within the system itself and its interactions with the environment.

Organizations, as systems, provide a framework for the context in which they operate. For instance, IGOs establish rules, norms, or regimes that stabilize shared behaviors among member states. Moreover, organizations create internal subsystems to address changing circumstances that enable them to adapt more effectively. However, this specialization also generates new complexities. An organization's structure can pose unique challenges, as evidenced by the United Nations (UN) and its numerous organizational forms. The UN High Commissioner for Refugees (UNHCR) and the Food and Agriculture Organization (FAO) face distinct challenges despite being part of the UN system. IGOs often distinguish between decision-making bodies (which are subsystems), such as member assemblies or steering committees, and the operational structures of the Secretariats and their bureaucratic departments. As differentiation increases, so does an organization's capacity to respond to its environment. However, this also increases the complexity and unpredictability of challenges that must be addressed.

The diversity of internal factors within an organization allows each component to influence the context from its unique perspective, thereby enhancing the organization's capacity to respond to contingencies. Typically, organizations are divided into various departments, such as human resources, management, and operational divisions, each with its own systemic viewpoint. A subsystem may be so differentiated that it perceives the entire organization as part of its context. For example, the FAO must consider the UN as part of its context because the FAO is a highly differentiated organization within the broader UN system. This tendency of an organization to view the broader system, or even other subsystems, as part of its context encourages the generation of additional complexity. A more diverse context increases the likelihood of encountering new and unique situations and events. Consequently, organizations are characterized as dynamic systems that differentiate into subsystems and sub-subsystems, fostering greater complexity and differentiation. This enhanced complexity and differentiation, in turn, strengthen the organization as a whole, enabling it to respond effectively to context-specific logics and adapt to contingent situations by defining itself in distinct ways.

Contingency Studies: How Do Organizations Survive in Volatile Contexts?

Organizational contingency studies were very influential in the 1960s and 1970s. According to this theory, to increase the likelihood of survival, it is far more effective to prepare for constant change rather than approaching it through a rational logic. In these analyses, size, structure, and technology are critical elements. Size is a relevant variable, but so is a highly differentiated structure, which under certain specific contexts may have a greater likelihood of success. Additionally, the impacts of technology on organizations to adapt to a contingent context are also significant. Thus, there are structural forces that organizations can utilize to adapt and survive in a contingent context.

Let us revert to the UNFPA situation within the framework of the systemic contingency theory. One of its most noteworthy accomplishments was recognizing the significance of contraceptive methods for family planning (Ness & Brechin, 1988: 257–258). However, this technological progress has elicited considerable disapproval and opposition from the Vatican. Per the precepts of systemic contingency, this is always imminent, implying that any action, no matter how carefully planned and rational, will inevitably produce unforeseen outcomes and create novel challenges, obstacles, and dynamics in the surrounding environment.

Let us now examine the matter of the sanctions regime from a systemic perspective, focusing on the connection between the United Nations, the European Union, and other non-governmental entities operating within the environment, as explored by Hazelzet (2004: 171–184). The imposition of sanctions by the European Union falls under the purview of the Common Foreign and Security Policy (CFSP), which can enforce sanctions independently or in conjunction with those established by the United Nations. The process involves various entities, including the European Commission, the Foreign Affairs Council, the Political and Security Committee, representatives from Member States, and, in cases of collaboration with the United Nations, the Security Council and its subsidiary bodies, such as sanctions committees, expert teams, and groups.

However, the dynamic interplay of relationships, differentiation, and complexity extends beyond the realm of government entities. NGOs play a significant role, including those in the business sector that operate in sanctioned countries and human rights advocacy groups such as Human Rights Watch and Amnesty International. The influence of these organizations is not limited to the initiation of sanctions policies but also extends to the later stages of monitoring and evaluation. The interactions among governmental IGOs, NGOs, companies, and their associations illustrate the fundamental systemic principle that the consequences of an organization's actions cannot be comprehended in isolation. Instead, they increasingly rely on interdependence and interaction with other systems and subsystems. The ability to manage and administer a network of complex and differentiated relationships has become an essential management competency, as Steffek (2021: 168) posits it to be the panacea for the new science of managing interdependence.

THE PARADOX OF ORGANIZATIONS AS SYSTEMS: THE NEVER-ENDING PROCESS OF DIFFERENTIATION

Thus far, this book has posited that the impact of systems lies in their interactions. This suggests that the ultimate outcomes of a system are highly unpredictable and dependent on chance, and the key is to remain adaptable and responsive. A common tactic in systems is differentiation, which entails seeking novel activities and confronting new realities with established or modified processes within the system. This is a strategy that many IGOs have utilized to endure.

Are certain IGOs capable of redesigning the international system rationally? While designing systems is possible, it requires establishing relationships between elements and accounting for the effects of interactions, the changes and dynamics of the environment, and the contingency involved. The impact of an organization, seen as a system, is more than a concrete product; it is ultimately an effect produced by the interrelationships and contingencies that occur over time. Thus, it is challenging to presuppose that the result of an organization has been planned progressively, in a linear, exact, and precise way, in a transparent and well-cared process. In particular, it is essential to consider social systems impacted by adjustments, adaptations, and interpretations of other agents in such events. From this perspective, viewing IGOs as rational, technical, and voluntary entities may not be very productive for understanding the dynamics and diversity of acting organizationally in a systemic logic.

Is it possible to reform a system rationally? While intervention in the process is possible, it is not a wholly controlled or purely technical endeavor. Instead, it is a more strategic approach that considers the need for adaptation within a specific temporal context. Organizational logic evolves over time, and what works in one moment can differ significantly in another due to changes in the context and its relationship with the organization. For example, as previously mentioned, UNAIDS' solutions evolved because, from a strictly systemic perspective, it is impossible to control all the relationships and effects generated by interactions among the parts. Therefore, designing a system is a complex task that is better approached by allowing interrelationships to naturally occur and evolve. The focus should then be on learning how these interrelationships can be guided towards specific patterns that are likely to produce certain actions and decisions, rather than rigidly striving for predetermined, formally defined results.

Therefore, it can be inferred that managing organizations from a systemic perspective entails inherent risks. While these risks can be mitigated through the implementation of normative and pertinent plans, processes, and programs, as well as the development of a strategic capacity to comprehend contingency and manage the distinctions between subsystems in the entire system, it is crucial to recognize that risks cannot be controlled entirely. It is essential to acknowledge that some literature on IGOs seems to presume that their actions can be managed rationally and technically, free from flaws and challenges. However, when viewed systemically, interventions, such as bringing war criminals to justice or intervening in a war with peacekeeping processes, prove to be inherently risky and subject to various contingencies. Rather than being a fixed and immutable objective, organizational inquiry should focus on achieving a desirable outcome while considering contingency.

Hardy (1994) accurately conveys the message by highlighting the need for a system of interrelated organizations to address a problem that affects them differently but with a unique logic for each organization. This is called an underorganized logic. For example, people looking for refuge trigger actions from a myriad of different organizations and rules across different countries. Governmental non-governmental, and international organizations are part of systemic problem (refugees), and each part of the system has its own set of needs and problems. For instance, governments may prioritize issues of sovereignty, NGOs may emphasize human rights, and IGOs may focus on specific processes and mechanisms to address the situation. Trying to perfectly organize and coordinate such a problem might be not only impossible but ineffective. This can be characterized then as an underorganized problem.

Underorganization is a complex issue that cannot be resolved by a single individual or organization. However, it also creates opportunities for stakeholders with less power or resources to enter the field, allowing new ideas and proposals for change to emerge. *Underorganization* exemplifies systemic effects that are beyond the control or design of any one entity. Success in such situations requires understanding and managing the interconnections, contradictions, and interdependencies within the system, rather than expecting to find a linear or orderly procedural design.

Complexity and Self-organizations

Structure and continuity are two intimately linked concepts and raise the question of what the role of human beings within systemic logic is. One extreme response to these questions is that the role of human beings is negligible, as relationships and interrelationships are determined by function, and therefore, their role is limited to being reactive. However, systems evolve through the adaptation and construction of complexity, which creates opportunities for expanding the range of human responses, reactions, and stimuli.

In this regard, systemic logic is predicated on the relationships and interactions among the constituent elements and the connections between systems and their environment. Essentially, these interactions give rise to consequences for the systems. However, it is important to note that systems are not independent entities but interconnected to other systems. Therefore, how can causality be discerned in a situation where the linear progression of elements does not necessarily lead to the outcomes? Instead, these are generated by interactions within a broader context in which events significantly determine the results.

How can systemic stability be grasped? What generates the equilibrium? Homeostasis is then seen as a principle in systems theory, as systems strive perpetually for equilibrium even if they cannot control it. Thus, no system can attain equilibrium independently and much less foresee it. How do they manage to create orders? At least two theories have emerged and have been utilized in organizational studies to provide explanations to these dilemmas: chaos theory and complexity theory.

The dynamics of interdependence that give rise to various relationships between elements lead to constant iteration over time. These iterations ultimately result in a feedback mechanism that stabilizes the system. When this process is applied to subsystems and larger systems, many interactions occurring at multiple levels over time may result in the formation of order. The iterations create a spontaneous order, although *spontaneous* may carry an ideological charge. Describing this process as self-organization may be more accurate because interactions between elements create interdependencies that produce iterations and repetitions. Ultimately, the order that emerges is not created by any individual or organizations alone but rather arises from interactions and iterations.

Chaos theory is one of the most widely recognized explanations for the idea of order produced by an apparently chaotic set of interactions and interdependencies. In an experiment by Lorenz (1993), he attempted to replicate a complex climate system in a laboratory setting. Through a substantial number of iterations, he discovered that the system became highly ordered and reliant on the initial conditions under which iterations were initiated. However, this order was susceptible to alterations in a chaotic manner, even in response to minor changes.

The notion of dependence on initial conditions refers to the behavior of complex, interconnected systems that generate numerous interactions and iterations, resulting in self-organizing equilibria. However, these equilibria can be highly sensitive to even minor changes in the system components or external factors, leading to significant and widespread effects. This concept is often illustrated by the famous butterfly effect metaphor, which posits that a small change, such as the flapping of a butterfly's wings, can have far-reaching and unpredictable consequences, such as the development of a hurricane in a distant location. This phenomenon is characterized by nonlinear and iterative interactions among the different elements of the system, which can give rise to significant, unexpected, and chaotic changes.

Interactions and interdependencies among numerous entities often result in the emergence of self-organizing systems that are not reliant on a specific hierarchy to function. These systems are characterized by a vast array of possible outcomes that reflect the law of entropy. Sequences and cycles are established from multiple unpredictable interactions, leading to the development of dynamic dependencies over time. However, owing to the inherently unpredictable nature of these iterations, even minor changes can have a significant effect, leading to chaotic outcomes. This concept of chaos theory could prove helpful in understanding the operations of IGOs, which frequently intervene in complex and interconnected cultural and economic systems that involve governments, corporations, individuals, and groups. The challenge for IGOs, companies, and governments is to maintain order in international arenas, such as the development of vaccines or the prevention of future pandemics. Sensitivity to initial conditions could serve as a valuable tool for analyzing the actions and interventions of these entities.

Undoubtedly, the intricate nature of complex systems is evident in the case of the actions attempted by WHO and UNAIDS. The effects generated by their policies and actions are primarily unforeseeable because of the interactions among various agents with differing objectives and structures. Consequently, although specific planned effects can be realized, numerous unforeseen consequences will arise. For example, the situation may initially be believed to be resolvable without the intervention of any IGO. However, it may subsequently be determined that coordinated action by a leading IGO such as the WHO is necessary. Alternatively, given the dynamic role of private organizations, NGOs, activists, and governments, the emerging effects may necessitate a "soft" coordination approach based on multi-stakeholder governance. From the complexity theory perspective, it is challenging to envision humans creating and managing intricate and highly interactive systems. These systems are characterized by multiple and dynamic equilibria, each driven by distinct logics that make it difficult to understand the multitude of relationships that appear random but are substantive in creating stability. These equilibria are numerous and in constant flux over time, with even slight changes in temporal conditions resulting in highly sensitive variations in the initial conditions.

This scenario offers several valuable insights into organizational management. It is imperative to recognize that minor adjustments can sometimes yield substantial consequences, and these consequences are not always straightforward; instead, they may exhibit cycles and patterns that can lead to both stability and unforeseen developments (Sherden, 2011).

The systemic theory of complexity posits that systems tend to be self-organized. It has been argued that a hierarchical vertical order cannot be sustained when interactions, iterations, and interdependencies are numerous and varied. Furthermore, the potential impact of the chaos theory (i.e., sensitivity to initial conditions, making it difficult to predict changes or high-impact effects) adds to the challenge of maintaining a structured system. In this context, self-organization refers to the order that emerges from the interdependence between elements and systems. This order is created without vertical structuring, and the elements within the system are arranged in a logical sequence guided by self-generated and self-organized rules and conditions.

Organizations as Complex Adaptive Systems

In the realm of organizational theory, the exploration and practical application of complex adaptive systems (CAS) has served as a valuable analytical framework, as it restores the role of human beings within systemic logic. Often, human beings are portrayed as mere appendages within the context of systems theories. However, human beings are regarded as indispensable components of the system under CAS because their capacity to generate equilibrium and adaptations is deemed critical.

The fundamental premise of CAS is that individuals (as one of the possible agents or actors defined by CAS theory) perceive a portion of reality, formulate information, and develop a schema that involves interpreting and establishing patterns. Ultimately, individuals require schemas to structure and make sense of reality. These schemas are particularly significant in social systems, as they influence interactions and, consequently, the interdependencies that form the foundation of any system. In social systems, where individuals communicate and express their partial perspectives and schemas, which are limited and incomplete, respectively, systemic feedback assumes a different dimension. It is a pivotal process that can change, revise, or demolish schemas over time. Schemas rely on systemic elements that involve the logic of change, such as learning, also called coevolution. Coevolution occurs through systemic logic when individuals interact and produce mutual changes by continuously communicating and exchanging ideas. However, coevolution is inherently systemic, which is uncertain because of the dynamic and ultimately unpredictable nature of the environment in which interactions occur. This uncertainty arises from the potential for chaos within human systems, which can fluctuate over time, given interdependency variations.

Human beings possess inherent complexity, and their social interactions engender a process of self-organization. This encompasses the internalization of norms and rules that many individuals adopt to such an extent that they adhere to them frequently without conscious effort. While shared norms and accepted ideas may appear stable, the potential for change, modification, or even revolution always exists.

Equilibria can emerge not only despite its complexity but also because of it. These equilibria can be partial and movable. The concept of punctuated equilibrium has been beneficial for understanding their dual dynamics: stability and change. A punctuated equilibrium consists of periods of stability and change based on contextual variations, which involve moments of transformation and then revert to stability. This logic of punctuated equilibrium has frequently been employed to explain organizational change, as it enables us to observe the entire transformation process as well as the outcomes of an intervention, mainly how it stabilizes and what effects it generates within the organization (Greiner, 1972; Tushman & Romanelli, 1985; Van de Ven & Poole, 1995).

WHO's and UNAIDS' agendas can be likened to CAS. The established governance framework comprises a network of multiple stakeholders, lacking a clear hierarchy, but sharing a belief that the collective interaction of diverse actors with related objectives will result in a beneficial systemic impact. This is achieved without necessarily requiring meticulous planning and design for each individual subsystem's action, measure, or decision. Instead, IGOs shape and modify the self-organization process.

Organizations as Decision Systems: The Luhmannian Proposal

In summary, this review of systems theories highlights some of Luhmann's notable contributions in a concise and simplified manner. Luhmann's work takes systems theory to its ultimate consequences, where function is the foundation. He presented a clear and robust definition of a function that does not rely on a specific ontological definition, making it a reality in its own right.

One of the main points of this Luhmannian theory is to resolve the category of function, in other words, to clarify that the environment or context is not a black box, nor is it an amorphous, unintelligible, or indefinable entity. To achieve this, the function—this general force that makes the environment unpredictable, dynamic, and mutable, and at the same time, the source upon which systems exist and adapt—requires a concrete and specific definition. It cannot be ambiguous, nor can it be a category that explains everything without being explained itself. The ambiguity of this function is challenging, as it can be attributed explanations ranging from the simplest and most general, such as the idea that the context is an external immanent force. This ambiguity causes a series of epistemological problems in systems theory, problems that Luhmann identifies precisely. The great problem of systems theory is that it does not resolve the dilemma that function is a key concept but is defined as something exogenous to the system's own logic. In this way, the context appears as if it were a practically metaphysical entity—a cause without a cause.

Luhmann's approach to systems theory is unique in that he constructs it from the bottom up. The underlying assumption is that elements of reality exist in an environment where contingency is an inherent aspect. As these elements interact, they select and close themselves off to the environment to contain contingencies. However, it is essential to note that contingency is dynamic and ever-changing and can never be fully captured. The selection process allows for establishing which elements of contingency are included and which are excluded. This selection process is crucial because it determines what is differentiated within the system and what infinite possibilities are left outside. Contingency is the driving force behind this process and currently exists as an open possibility. It is unnecessary to invoke metaphysical forces or logical structures to explain contingency as it arises from the event itself. Ultimately, this event is an open possibility that is constantly in flux.

The paradox that a system is more than the sum of its elements can be explained without resorting to metaphysical arguments. This is achieved through selection by interrelation and interdependence and the constant "irritation" that the environment exerts on the system. This irritation is permanent as a contingency, and the system must differentiate itself (create new selection logic) to respond to new contingencies.

Concerning this matter, it is vital to comprehend the process of selection. Interrelation encompasses two aspects: selecting first, but as selecting some other elements are excluded. It is as important what is selected as what is excluded. Consequently, certain elements are connected to some but not to others, at least for a moment: the excluded elements might become irritants forces for the previous selection attempt. In essence, the interplay between elements involves a selection process with a dual nature: the first relates to what is included in the selection. In contrast, the second relates to what is excluded.

Complexity, as Luhmann sees, arises from the selection process. This results from the impossibility of everything being interconnected, leading to interrelatedness and interdependence. In this sense, complexity can be understood as the interplay between multiple selective processes, given the impossibility of connecting everything. Selection involves distinguishing and separating the foreign and systematically preventing what is outside from entering the interaction. Time, however, poses a challenge to this process, as the contingency and the event may always emerge and require new selections that *trap* these unforeseen occurrences.

The challenging aspect of this situation is that there is no means of foreseeing or establishing which components can enter, impact, or alter the selectivity of the primary system. An internal explanation of the systemic change and stability dynamics is provided to address this issue. Stability is achieved when the system cohesively maintains its boundaries to preserve selectivity, which defines it as a system. By contrast, changes are triggered by external factors that are not part of the system.

For this reason, and not for any metaphysical cause, the environment is inherently unpredictable, and the event constitutes the essence of systemic logic. Unlike the general systems theory, for Luhmann, the environment is neither an entity nor a force, as its function is merely the occurrence of events in time. Consequently, the force of existence of systems lies in their ability to adapt and constantly differentiate themselves to exist within a selective closure, relative to the infinite possibilities of the event. Systems achieve this differentiation through their internal dynamics and constant interaction with other context elements, thereby maintaining their boundaries and survival.

Thus, to the substantive question of what constitutes function, he obtains a direct response: function is contingent upon a series of events that occur in time. Events produced by the systems themselves or all other elements that, in constant motion in time, determine the interactions, interdependencies, and selections that are available or attainable, at least for a period. How many selections are not possible now that will become possible in another event?

The functionality of a system is not necessarily dependent on its pre-established logic but rather on its ability to adapt and respond to contingencies through its interactions with other systems. The nature of contingency is unpredictable, but it can result in patterns and regularities established through the interactions of systems attempting to address it. The interdependence of a system can become so strong that it can define specific logics of contingency, at least until the next disruptive event arises.

This may be an appropriate moment to provide a clarifying example. As Betts (2010) has explained, the UNHCR has continually adapted its mandate. Rather than adhering to a functionalist perspective, it is more accurate to recognize that the organization consistently develops decision-making processes in response to contingencies arising from its environment. The UNHCR's mandate has undergone significant transformations, including expanding its scope to protect not only refugees in various locations but also displaced persons and victims of natural disasters. This expansion goes beyond the organization's original post-war European focus and now encompasses a broader range of contexts. Organizations need to *capture* these contingencies, as they are ever-present. International organizations (IGOs), like any other organization, must constantly recreate their selective processes to adapt. What was excluded in the past may become necessary to include in the present. The concept of *refugee* has evolved, with different groups being selected or excluded over time. Recognizing new categories of persons as refugees requires creating the capacity to address the new dilemmas and contingencies that such decisions entail.

IGOs are frequently perceived as highly rationalistic entities with legally binding mandates that delineate their objectives as envisioned by the states that establish them. However, it is essential to comprehend the environment in which IGOs function as they exist and operate within this context. The environment encompasses other organizations and social and political actors, all of which contribute to shaping the mandates of IGOs.

Modifications to mandates are not solely the result of decisions made by individual states; instead, they are shaped by pressing environmental problems. The UNHCR's transformation from a refugee protection agency to a relief organization for those facing various emergencies can be seen as a response to the evolving needs of its internal stakeholders as they grappled with a range of uncertainties or "irritations" over time. This adaptive process reflects the organization's capacity to respond to changing circumstances and fulfill its mandate more effectively.

In systemic logic, organizations continually differentiate themselves to endure in their environment. According to Luhmann, the source of this differentiation has been widely discussed. In response to contingencies, an order is established through structured responses, such as plans, rules, and mechanisms; to confront contingency, it is necessary to control and contain it artificially. Luhmann's perspective diverges from traditional theory in that the only means of capturing contingency is within the system. This self-reference is a logical act, implying that the elements of the system are constructed from successful responses to contingencies (Luhmann, 2006, 2017). The environment always affects the system, but the logic of the system enables it to manage these impacts and irritation.

An approach that has been effective in managing uncertainty is the core information that enables the system to refer to itself. By utilizing internal mechanisms, the system can control uncertainty. This concept is also known as structural coupling, where the system produces elements that provide limited responses to uncertainty, and the system adjusts to the event based on its own internal rules. This approach is more rational and logical from a systemic standpoint than attempting to adapt to individual events. The system's internal mechanisms are designed to constantly adapt to the environment's irritations, but they do so in a structured manner bound by the system's self-referential rules. The irrationality of adapting to each event is that it is often unpredictable, and it makes sense to handle it through the system's internal mechanisms.

Therefore, the UNHCR is responsible for addressing contingencies and making decisions based on its understanding of its mandate and mission. Definitions of terms such as "refugee," "displaced," or "stateless person" play a crucial role in shaping the organization's decisions and actions. By defining these terms in their own way, the UNHCR can delimit the problem it faces and act accordingly. This is why organizations constantly strive to refer to their solutions and make them self-sustaining.

The concept of self-reference provides a compelling explanation for how intricate relationships and interdependencies within a system possess their meaning, transcending chaotic surroundings. This self-reference attains a level of internal logic unique to the system, which Luhmann asserts is also a process of creating order and self-production. In this context, autopoiesis denotes the system's capacity to produce its logic of existence. For instance, an IGO that aims to regulate international telecommunications establishes technical and legal guidelines and norms that are considered fundamental to the logic of the communication system. The environment comprises a variety of stakeholders with diverse interests, such as governments, corporations, and agencies. However, the system's autopoietic nature captures these contingencies by selecting issues and shaping the treatment and definition of the problem. Ultimately, it is the organization itself that defines these issues and forms and, in doing so, legitimizes its authority through its internal expertise, allowing it to impose relevant rules of interaction on the environment.

Autopoiesis is derived from biology as described by Luhmann (Maturana & Varela, 1975; Maturana, 1975). This concept emphasizes the ability of systems to generate and organize their components. Luhmann suggests that systems achieve operational closure, which means that they establish their context and function by maintaining specific interrelationships and interdependencies. Although this may seem contradictory, systems close themselves off operationally to preserve their autopoietic nature. According to Deroy (2019), operational closure does not imply that systems physically close themselves off but that they strive to maintain their internal relationships and dependencies. Overall, systems are dynamic and interdependent, and their operational closure allows them to stabilize and legitimize certain relationships while maintaining their autopoietic capabilities.

To observe the concepts of self-reference and autopoiesis in action, let's consider two examples from international organizations (IGOs). First, the United Nations (UN) and how it self-referentially addresses the dilemmas faced by courts of justice in response to new contingencies. Second, how IGOs have been able to create autopoietic logics that form a network of regulations and norms. Even if a state decides to withdraw from or not participate in a particular IGO, it will find it difficult to escape the web of influences created by the rules and norms—both formal and informal—that have been established through the participation of various IGOs.

The United Nations offers a case of self-referencing through the creation of what is considered the latest type of international crimes courts: hybrid courts, which are designed to address massive human rights violations and serious crimes (Nouwen, 2006: 190). The creation of hybrid international courts (Dickinson, 2003: 295) was initiated by the United Nations, establishing a range of transitional justice mechanisms and instruments, starting with developing ad hoc international tribunals (the International Criminal Tribunal for the Former Yugoslavia and the International Criminal Tribunal for Rwanda) during the conflicts. These tribunals aimed to curb violence and hold perpetrators of genocide, war crimes, and crimes against humanity accountable. However, the United Nations later recognized the need to improve upon these instruments and overcome their shortcomings, such as their high cost, limited number of cases prosecuted, low sense of ownership among affected communities, and limited understanding of domestic cultures, laws, and legal processes (International Criminal Tribunal for the Former Yugoslavia and the International Criminal Tribunal for Rwanda).

To address these challenges, the United Nations has adopted the model of international prosecution by integrating national and international resources, laws, and jurisdictions. Hybrid courts are legal institutions with mixed composition and jurisdiction, incorporating national and international elements, and typically operate within the territory where crimes were committed. In other words, this has been a solution of a complex problems through self-reference: adapting a mechanism that has function well to a new circumstance.

In Kosovo (Serbia) and Timor Leste, where the prolonged civil war severely weakened domestic legal systems, international legal standards and personnel were integrated into the temporary administration structures set up by the United Nations: the United Nations Interim Administration Mission in Kosovo (UNMIK) in 2000, through the establishment of an international judges and prosecutors program and the United Nations Transitional Administration in East Timor (UNTAET) in 2000, with the creation of the Serious Crimes Unit and the Special Panels for Serious Crimes. Subsequently, the United Nations played a role in the establishment of other hybrid courts at the explicit request of governments, such as the Special Court for Sierra Leone in 2002, the Extraordinary Chambers in the Courts of Cambodia in 2003, the Special War Crimes Chamber in Bosnia and Herzegovina in 2005 (which was established through an agreement between the Office of the High Representative, the International Criminal Tribunal for the Former Yugoslavia (ICTY), and national authorities), and the Specialist Chambers for Kosovo in 2017 (through the EULEX Kosovo). Additionally, hybrid courts have been established in the context of peace agreements in which the United Nations has participated as a mediator or negotiator, such as the Special Jurisdiction for Peace in Colombia in 2016, the Special Criminal Court for the Central African Republic in 2015, and the African Union-backed Hybrid Court for South Sudan in 2015.

The second example pertains to the concept of autopoiesis in IGOs. Kang-Riou and Rossati (2018) contend that studying the genuine consequences of member states severing their connections with an IGO reveals that the exit process may be more intricate than initially assumed. This is due to the autopoietic capacity of these organizations and the systemic dynamics they have constructed through agreements and legal norms. These legal norms have evolved into substantive formal and informal networks that are exceedingly challenging for states to circumvent, even if they have decided to withdraw from membership or participation in an IGO. From the perspective of Luhmann, IGOs possess the fundamental capability of binding decisions. IGOs exert this influence not only within the organization but also through norms and regulations outside the organization and among a range of IGOs. In other words, IGOs can affect the international system by perpetuating their existence and the necessity of that existence by constructing a network of rules and norms that bind states within an extensive network of regulations and practices (Kang-Riou & Rossati, 2018: 278).

Systemic logic is an unyielding concept; increased self-organization is accompanied by increased differentiation. Higher levels of differentiation result in greater complexity, which, in turn, creates new relationships and interdependencies, opening up new possibilities for contingent events. The differentiation process can lead to further differentiation, as observed by Luhmann in social systems (Luhmann, 2005; Schneider et al., 2016).

The situation with UNHCR is clear in this matter: the development of its mandate has consistently been preceded by organizational structures that define the scope of its problem in terms of how the organization can act within its capabilities and restrictions. The issue of repatriation is likely the most severe and complicated environmental problem it has confronted. As a humanitarian issue with deeply political and politicized overtones, its range has been subject to substantial criticism and subsequent modification. Addressing such a severe and politicized humanitarian issue has entailed various organizational decision-making processes, ranging from highly bureaucratic approaches to defining how to act to deciding not to intervene, despite the humanitarian crisis. In response to this criticism, new decisions were made, leading to the proposal of new norms during the 1990s to deal with individuals categorized as internally displaced persons (IDPs). These individuals have been compelled to flee their homes but have not crossed international borders.

These decisions necessitated connecting new decisions, and the UNHCR was proposed to lead this effort, which implied a new adaptation of its mandate. This has also resulted in the organization's complexification and democratization (in the sense described by Luhmann): new internal units had to be created to address the activities added through the mandate or the actions to be performed (Freitas, 2004: 127). For instance, the UNHCR has established regional offices close to operations. The Division of International Protection also expanded to include the perspective that the organization should advocate for refugees and guarantee international rights.

As Luhmann posited, social systems are not merely theoretical constructs but exist in reality. These systems comprise organizations, groups, associations, and institutions, ultimately composed of individuals in communication. Individuals constitute the environment of these social systems. It is necessary to recognize that individuals are biological and psychological entities to comprehend this paradox. When they communicate, a social system exists outside the individuals themselves. Communication within this system is selective and seeks to control the environment, including the individuals who are part of it. Individuals with their own psychological and biological dynamics are the primary contingencies that social systems' selective and ordered communication seeks to regulate. Thus, the paradox that people are both the environment, and the social system is resolved: without people, there can be no social system, but the social system is a product of people's communicative interactions. The system allows for interpretation and intersubjective relationships between individuals, provided they can be bound and limited by the stable dynamics of communication. In essence, people create a social system, but over time, the system becomes distinct from the individuals and becomes the environment in which they operate.

Social systems are characterized by communication, and organizations are potent social systems because they link decisions to contingencies. This mechanism enables organizations to function as closed systems concerning their context, as they claim to connect decisions. Interlinking decisions create a potent, selective process that fosters a self-referential dynamic within organizations. In other words, each decision is connected to others, which binds to the formal and informal rules governing the relationships between the dependent decisions (Luhmann, 2012).

Like any social system, the organization exists within a temporal framework. It is situated within a particular context, where it endeavors to capture the essence of contingency but cannot do so entirely. This ongoing process involves a paradoxical increase in complexity, as the attempt to govern contingency leads to differentiation, which amplifies complexity and uncertainty (Luhmann, 2005; Schneider et al., 2016; Deroy, 2019).

Organizations are prone to creating more uncertainty by tying contingency to differentiation (primarily to people). However, more interconnected and binding decisions can open new opportunities for contingencies. According to Luhmann, two driving forces emerge organizationally: democratization and rationalization. Democratization involves the process of differentiation, wherein more individuals are engaged in achieving the goal. Consequently, an increasing number of system parts come into play to influence contingencies or situations, thereby democratizing the system's intervention.

On the other hand, rationalization strives to establish more clearly how and why decisions are correctly and appropriately connected. For instance, considering the UN and its various stakeholders, the General Assembly, one of the most complex elements due to the participation of numerous states with their agendas for making specific decisions, faces a dilemma inherent to differentiation: the difficulty of coordinating various parts of the organization. Therefore, as differentiation increases, so does democratization, which leads to the entry of more stakeholders, and in response, there is a need for rationalization.

The United Nations General Assembly established the Economic and Social Council (ECOSOC) as an additional component of the UN system. As each specialized UN agency functions as a subsystem, this suggests that each part of the organization observes the other parts of the UN and the General Assembly as part of its environment. As systems differentiate over time, the ECOSOC acquires its logic and requirements. To facilitate coordination among parties, the General Assembly created ECOSOC as a mechanism (McLaren, 1980: 140, 142). However, coordination is not automatic or entirely controllable and becomes an element of contingency. Despite decades of effort, ECOSOC has struggled to attain relevance and coordination capacity among various UN specialized agencies.

An example of differentiation is the coordination framework established to deal with humanitarian emergencies using a sectoral or cluster approach. This framework was established by a resolution passed by the United Nations General Assembly in 1991, bringing together various humanitarian organizations, both those that are part of the UN and those that are not, to address different aspects of the emergency (e.g., health, shelter, education, food security, logistics, nutrition, among others). These frameworks are designed to provide temporary assistance and strengthen a country's ability to respond to humanitarian crises (UNHCR, 2023).

The Inter-Agency Standing Committee (IASC), comprising top-level executives from 18 humanitarian organizations and led by the UN System Humanitarian Coordinator, who reports directly to the Secretary-General, is responsible for designating the sectors (UNHCR, 2023). The Resident Coordinator and Humanitarian Coordinator, along with the Humanitarian Country Team, oversee the humanitarian response through the clusters, which are activated in response to the unique needs of each situation. The education cluster is jointly managed by UNICEF and Save the Children, whereas IOM and UNHCR lead the camp coordination and management cluster. UNDP managed the early recovery cluster; the remaining 11 clusters were overseen similarly (UNHCR, 2023).

According to Luhmann, systemic dynamics are inherently characterized by constant disruptions and disturbances, which he calls *irritations*. These disturbances lead to an ongoing search for rationalization and democratization, creating new "irritations." The coordination of the United Nations within the UN is a well-known challenge, as demonstrated by the case of peacekeeping operations. A peacekeeping operation should be considered a unified endeavor with singular objectives, goals, and intentions. However, in practical applications, such an objective can be achieved only through the collaboration of various organizations and agencies, both within and outside the UN. This implies that each part of the UN involved in the operation is a system with its own distinct logic. As is known in the IGO literature, interagency coordination is one solution to this dilemma. Starting from the premise that all agencies can ultimately work towards a single concrete goal—the goal of the UN *supra-system*—it is possible to identify strategies for coordination.

According to Doring and Schreiner's (2008) findings, it is more prudent to commence from the standpoint that recognizes the dissimilarities between the agencies (the systemic elements) and seeks strategies for their divergences to be fashioned and adjusted to achieve more efficient system coordination. In doing so, each agency, as an organization, exists because of a series of factors that are unique to its organizational logic, which comprises structural, individual, and cultural elements (Doring & Schreiner, 2008: 3). Structural factors pertain to the formal rules, practices, and responsibilities of the organization. Individual factors pertain to the characteristics of individuals who make up an organization. Cultural factors pertain to shared values, self-image, and the meaning people imprint on their actions, making each organization distinct. Under systemic logic, it is essential to acknowledge these differentiated characteristics of the systems involved, comprehend them, and endeavor to address or modify them so that coordination among systems with diverse cultures, individuals, and structural dynamics can be achieved. In other words, it is astute in systemic logic to acknowledge that each part confronts its own contingencies as a means of survival. Thus, discoordination is a logical issue that must be addressed. That is, formally, an IGO like the UN is an integrated whole, a monolithic entity that decides and acts as a congruent piece. However, in practice, it is a system that operates in an environment with other systems involved (Doring & Schreiner, 2008). According to Luhmann's scheme, coordination and cooperation between systems are entirely feasible; this necessitates tying decisions and connecting different parts with linked decisions (Deroy, 2019).

As social systems, organizations entail comprehending a potent decision-making mechanism that confronts intricate environments brimming with other organizations, rules, and social systems. The perspicacity of Luhmann is of paramount importance for grasping the operations of IGOs, as it is precisely in the domain of IR that the labyrinthine relationship between governments, states, institutions, rules, legal norms, and political and geopolitical interests has been thoroughly examined. In this realm of political anarchy, an ever-increasing number of IGOs add layers of complexity, driven by a dual dynamic: an internal one characterized by self-referentiality (rules, norms, bureaucratic logics of action, group decisions aimed at establishing rules) and an external one, as IGOs, are part of a highly political, dispersed, and diverse environment teeming particular interests and relationships between agents, organizations, institutions, rules, laws, forces, and interests. This environment is intricate, complex in a systemic sense, and chaotic. However, this does not imply that decisions cannot be made to navigate it.

This perspective is shared by Koch (2012), who proposes examining IGOs through the lens of Luhmann's systems theory by recognizing them as global organizations. Once established, these organizations interact with states, nations, NGOs, and corporations within a global environment. This global focus, in a systemic sense, enables them to confront contingencies with global semantics, which are truly global. These problems are those of numerous agents, but the consequences extend beyond these agents. Consequently, global focus gives IGOs a vital characteristic of a differentiated organization compared to other organizations such as governments, corporations, or NGOs. In addition to global semantics, Koch (2012) suggests studying intra-organizational dynamics among IGOs. As global organizations, the network they establish among themselves becomes a critical element of the environment to which all other agents, including governments, corporations, and NGOs, must face and relate. The relationship environment of an IGO consists of other organizations and their relationships in a crucial manner. Ultimately, all these elements contribute to shaping world order in a real network or skein of international agents, where IGOs are increasingly critical agents. Koch (2012: 14) examines the case of the World Bank and how it has persistently expanded its network of relationships as an organization with its environment. According to Koch, the optimal form of organization allows for effectively managing relationships, interactions, and interdependencies in a game of multiple interests and diverse stakeholders.

From a Luhmannian perspective, IGOs have achieved remarkable success: their growth is undeniable, given their ability to adapt to an environment characterized by anarchy (in the sense of not being hierarchically ordered). This environment necessitates a vast network of specialized IGOs that continue to differentiate and address various sources of uncertainty, ranging from the management of migrants and the protection of human rights to security regulations (INTERPOL), communication standards (International Telecommunications Union ITU, International Civil Aviation Organization ICAO), peacekeeping operations, pandemic preparedness, and many other issues. Despite the complexity of these tasks, IGOs manage to exert influence by applying basic systemic rules such as making binding decisions, controlling multiple sources of uncertainty, creating new dynamics of rationalization and democratization, and promoting differentiation. Therefore, IGOs provide a promising avenue for applying Luhmann's systemic theory.

Concluding Remarks

Systems theory is a comprehensive and versatile theoretical framework widely applied in social and natural sciences. Its broad scope and parsimonious nature have made it a valuable tool for researchers in various disciplines, including IR. As a highly influential theory in organizational theory, the potential for interdisciplinary collaboration between IR and OT appears vast. However, as the current chapter demonstrates, this has not been as extensive as expected.

The elements of interdisciplinary productivity are evident, and the significance and role of IGOs in what can be informally or metaphorically referred to as the international system are well established in both IR and organizational theory. The international system may be viewed as a metaphor for the relationships between states, NGOs, IGOs, companies, and societies on a global scale, which self-organize without a higher hierarchical mechanism to govern them. This process is not planned, controlled, or directed by any individual actor but rather arises from the interactions and interdependencies among the system's various elements. These interactions generate systemic logics, as discussed in this chapter, and ultimately result in a particular order. States, regimes, political systems, rules, norms, international and private organizations, and social groups and institutions are the main components of these complex networks of relationships and interdependencies. Their diversity and asymmetry contribute to the emergence of order in a seemingly magical and unintended manner.

Therefore, numerous individuals, including actors and various entities, engage in IR's complex and unpredictable domain, in which states, ideologies, values, and interests intersect. As they engage in these interactions, they establish interdependencies and partial stability subject to changes in enduring uncertainty. Negotiations, agreements, conflicts, and battles are necessary and subsequently regulated to navigate such uncertainty. While systemic order is attainable, it is only temporary, and adaptation becomes a strategy for all actors involved.

States are essential components of the international system. However, they also create other systems, such as IGOs. These IGOs, like any other subsystem, must navigate their own unique environments to maintain equilibrium, adapt, and survive. To do so, they must establish relationships and dependencies with other systems. Under the systemic analytical framework, the autonomy or agency of IGOs is not about self-sufficiency; instead, it involves relational, adaptive, and self-referential logics that constantly grapple with the uncertainty of functional decision-making, processes, structures, and actions. Even if IGOs are considered subsystems under the hierarchy of states, they must operate as independent systems to achieve their objectives within a specific interdependency framework. The systemic specificity of IGOs is a crucial concept as it emphasizes the need for adaptation and differentiation, which are essential acts of intelligence that require constant construction to ensure survival. Achieving an organization's objectives is not simply a matter of will and intention; it also requires intelligence to adapt to the environment and to build strategies that enable the organization to survive and thrive.

The perception of IGOs as a systemic and organizational vision does not threaten the more traditional IR views that are skeptical and cautious about the idea of agency and autonomy of IGOs in the international arena. Agency and autonomy are crucial for IGOs to achieve their objectives. This chapter examines several instances of organizations as systems with relational logics that enable them to adjust, differentiate, and attain equilibrium to survive. Examples of such organizations include the UN, IAEA, and WHO. These organizations operate in uncertain environments, adapt to functional logic, and sometimes face conflicts in pursuing this logic.

What is functional for the organization may not be functional for another agent in the international system or a subsystem within it. From systemic assumptions, functional logic is hardly one general and universal.

Examining and empirically investigating how IGOs can effectively adjust and differentiate themselves in a highly dynamic and constantly changing international system is a crucial area of research in IR and OT.

REFERENCES

Abbott, K. (2012). The Transnational Regime Complex for Climate Change. *Environment and Planning. C, Government & Policy, 30*(4), 571–590.

Abbott, K., Genschel, P., Snidal, D., & Zangl, B. (2015a). *International Organizations as Orchestrators.* Cambridge University Press.

Abbott, K., Genschel, P., Snidal, D., & Zangl, B. (2015b). Two Logics of Indirect Governance: Delegation and Orchestration. *British Journal of Political Science, 46*(4), 719–729.

Ahrne, G., & Brunsson, N. (2008). *Meta-organizations.* Edward Elgar Publishing.

Ahrne, G., Brunsson, N., & Kerwer, D. (2016). The Paradox of Organizing States: A Meta-organization Perspective on International Organizations. *Journal of International Organizations Studies, 7*(1), 5–24.

Alba, V. C. (2020). La transnacionalización del mundo social. Espacios sociales más allá de las sociedades nacionales. *Foro Internacional, 60*(3), 1028–1221.

Albert, M. (2010). Modern Systems Theory and World Politics. In M. Albert, L. E. Cederman, & A. Wendt (Eds.), *New Systems Theories of World Politics.* Palgrave Macmillan.

Albert, M., Cederman, L. E., & Wendt, A. (Eds.). (2010). *New Systems Theories of World Politics.* Palgrave Macmillan.

Avant, D., Finnemore, M., & Kell, S. (2010). *Who Governs the Globe?* Cambridge University Press.

Axelrod, R. (1997). The Dissemination of Culture: A Model with Local Convergence and Global Polarization. *Journal of Conflict Resolution, 41*(2), 203–226.

Axelrod, R., & Hamilton, W. D. (1981). The Evolution of Cooperation. *Science, 211*(4489), 1390–1396.

Barnett, M., & Finnemore, B. (2004). *The Rules of the World: International Organizations in Global Politics.* Cornell University Press.

Barnett, M. N., & Sikkink, K. (2009). From International Relations to Global Society. In *The Oxford Handbook of International Relations.* University of Oxford. https://doi.org/10.1093/oxfordhb/9780199219322.003.0003

Betts, A. (2009). Institutional Proliferation and the Global Refugee Regime. *Perspectives on Politics, 7*(1), 53–58.

Betts, A. (2010). The Refugee Regime Complex. *Refugee Survey Quarterly, 29*(1), 12–37.

Biermann, F., Pattberg, P., Asselt, H., & Zelli, F. (2009). The Fragmentation of Global Governance Architectures: A Framework for Analysis. *Global Environmental Policy, 9*(4), 14–39.

Blauberg, I. V., Sadovsky, V. N., & Yudin, E. (1977). *Systems Theory: Philosophical and Methodological Problems.* Progress Publishers.

Boulding, K. E. (1958). Theoretical Systems and Political Realities: A Review of Morton A. Kaplan, System and Process in International Politics. *The Journal of Conflict Resolution, 2*(4), 329–334.

Bousquet, A., & Curtis, S. (2011). Beyond Models and Metaphors: Complexity Theory, Systems Thinking and International Relations. *Cambridge Review of International Affairs, 24*(1), 43–62.

Bousquet, A., & Simon, C. (2011). Beyond Models and Metaphors: Complexity Theory, Systems Thinking and International Relations. *Cambridge Review of International Affairs, 24*(1), 43–62. https://doi.org/10.1080/0955757 1.2011.558054

Braumoeller, F. (2012). *The Great Powers and the International System: Systemic Theory in Empirical Perspective.* Cambridge University Press.

Brodbeck, M. (1968). *Readings in the Philosophy of the Social Sciences.* Macmillan.

Burton, J. W. (1972). *World Society.* Cambridge University Press.

Buzan, B. (1993). From International System to International Society: Strucrtural Realism and Regime Theory Meet the English School. *International Organization, 47*(3), 327–352.

Buzan, B., & Little, R. (2000). *International Systems in World History: Remaking the Study of International Relations.* Oxford University Press.

Calduch, R. (1991). *Relaciones Internacionales.* Ediciones de Ciencias Sociales.

Capra, F. (1996). *The Web of Life: A New Synthesis of Mind and Matter.* HarperCollins.

Cederman, L. E. (1997). *Emergent Actors in World Politics: How States and Nations Develop and Dissolve.* Princeton University Press.

Checkel, J. T. (2005). International Institutions and Socialization in Europe: Introduction and Framework. *International Organization, 59*(4), 801–826. http://www.jstor.org/stable/3877829

Childers, E. (1995). Empowering the Peoples in Their United Nations. *The Ecumenical Review, 47*(3), 291–301. https://doi.org/10.1111/j.1758-6623.1995.tb03712.x

Del Arenal, C. (2007). *Introducción a las Relaciones Internacionales.* Tecnos.

Deroy, X. (2019). Niklas Luhmann and Organizations as Social Systems. In S. Clegg & M. Pina e Cunha (Eds.), *Management, Organizations and Contemporary Social Theory.* Routledge.

Dickinson, L. (2003). The Promise of Hybrid Courts. *The American Journal of International Law, 97*(2), 295–310.

Doring, S., & Schreiner, M. (2008). *Inter-Agency Coordination in United Nations Peacebuilding*. University of Konstanza.

Dougherty, J. E., & Pfaltzgraff, R. L. (1993). *Teorías en pugna en las relaciones internacionales*. Grupo Editor Latinoamericano.

Duffield, M. (2002). War as a Network Enterprise: The New Security Terrain and Its Implications. *Cultural Values, 6*(1–2), 153–165. https://doi.org/10.1080/1362517022019793

Durkheim, E. (1984). *Division of Labor in Society*. The Free Press.

Freitas, R. (2004). UNHCR's Decision Making on Internally Displaced Persons. In B. Reinalda & B. Verbeek (Eds.), *Decision Making Within International Organizations*. Routledge.

Gersick, C. J. (1991). Revolutionary Change Theories: A Multilevel Exploration of the Punctuated Equilibrium Paradigm. *Academy of Management Review, 16*(1), 10–36.

Geyer, R. (2003). European Integration, the Problem of Complexity and the Revision of Theory. *Journal of Common Market Studies, 41*(1), 15–35.

González-Uresti, L. (2021). La teoría general de los sistemas: Una opción teórica para el estudio de las Relaciones internacionales. In J. Schiavon, M. López-Vallejo, A. Ortega, & R. Velázquez (Eds.), *Teorías de Relaciones Internacionales en el siglo XXI. Interpretaciones desde México y América Latina*. CIDE.

Greiner, L. E. (1972). Evolution and Revolution as Organizations Grow. *Harvard Business Review, 50*, 37–46.

Hardt, M., & Negri, A. (2000). *Empire*. Harvard University Press.

Hardy, C. (1994). Underorganized Interorganizational Domains. The Case of Refugee Systems. *The Journal of Applied Behavioral Science, 30*(3), 278–296.

Hazelzet, H. (2004). Sanctions in Reaction to Human Rights Violations. The Impact of Non-state Actors on EU Decision Making. In B. Reinalda & B. Verbeek (Eds.), *Decisions Making Within International Organizations* (pp. 171–184). Routledge.

Helfer, L. R. (2009). Regime Shifting in the International Intellectual Property System. *Perspectives on Politics, 7*(1), 39–44.

Jönsson, C., & Jönsson, K. (2012). Global and Local Health Governance: Civil Society, Human Rights and HIV/AIDS. *Third World Quarterly, 33*(9), 1719–1734.

Kaldor, M. (1999). *New and Old Wars: Organised Violence in a Global Era* (1st ed.). Polity Press.

Kang-Riou, N., & Rossati, D. (2018). The Effects of Juridification on State Exiting International Institutions. *International Organizations Law Review, 15*, 265–294. https://doi.org/10.1163/15723747-01502002

Kaplan, M. A. (1957). Balance of Power, Bipolarity and Other Models of International Systems1. *American Political Science Review, 51*(3), 684–695.

Kaplan, M. A. (1964). Intervention in Internal War: Some Systemic Sources. In J. N. Rosenau (Ed.), *International Aspects of Civil Strife* (pp. 92–121). Princeton University Press.

Karns, M., & Mingst, K. (2004). *International Organizations: The Politics and Processes of Global Governance*. Lynne Rienner Publishers Inc.

Kast, F. E., & Rosenzweig, J. E. (1972). General System Theory: Applications for Organization and Management. *Academy of Management Journal, 15*(4), 447–465. https://doi.org/10.2307/255141

Kavalski, E. (2007). The Fifth Debate and the Emergence of Complex International Relations Theory: Notes on the Application of Complexity Theory to the Study of International Life. *Cambridge Review of International Affairs, 20*(3), 435–454.

Keck, M. E., & Sikkink, K. (1998). *Activists Beyond Borders: Advocacy Networks in International Politics*. Cornell University Press.

Kenney, M. (2007). *From Pablo to Osama: Trafficking and Terrorist Networks, Government Bureaucracies, and Competitive Adaptation*. Penn State University Press.

Klein, M. W., & Maxson, C. L. (2006). *Street Gang Patterns and Policies*. Oxford University Press.

Koch, M. (2012). *International Organizations in Development and Global Inequality: The Example of the World Bank's Pension Policy*. WIDER Working Paper Series wp-2012-103, World Institute for Development Economic Research (UNU-WIDER).

Levy, J. S., & Thompson, W. (2010). *Causes of War*. Wiley-Blackwell.

Lorenz, E. (1993). *The essence of chaos*. University of Washington Press.

Luhmann, N. (2005). The Paradox of Decision Making. In D. Seidl & K. Becker (Eds.), *Niklas Luhmann and Organization Studies*. Copenhagen Business School Press.

Luhmann, N. (2006). System as Difference. *Organization, 13*(1), 37–57.

Luhmann, N. (2012). *Theory of Society (1)*. Stanford University Press.

Luhmann, N. (2017). *Introduction to Social Systems*. Polity Press.

Maturana, H. (1975). The Organization of the Living: A Theory of the Living Organization. *International Journal of Man-Machine Studies, 7*(3), 313–332.

Maturana, H., & Varela, F. (1975). *Autopoietic Systems. Biological Computer Laboratory*. BCL Report 9.4, University of Illinois, Urbana.

McLaren, R. (1980). The UN System and Its Quixotic Quest for Coordination. *International Organization, 34*(1), 139–148.

McLaren, R. (2001). The United Nations as a Membership Organization. *International Public Management Journal, 8*(1), 115–122.

Mitrany, D. (1966). *A Working Peace System: An Argument for the Functional Development of International Organization*. Quadrangle Books.

Modelski, G. (1964). Kautilya: Foreign Policy and International System in the Ancient Hindu World. *American Political Science Review, 58*(3), 549–560.

Ness, G., & Brechin, S. (1988). Bridging the Gap: International Organizations as Organizations. *International Organization, 42*(2), 245–273.

Nouwen, S. (2006). 'Hybrid Courts'. The Hybrid Category of a New Type of International Crimes Courts. *Utrecht Law Review, 2*(2), 190–214.

Orsini, A., Le Prestre, P., Haas, P. M., Brosig, M., Pattberg, P., Widerberg, O., et al. (2020). Complex Systems and International Governance. *International Studies Review, 22*(4), 1008–1038.

Osorio, J. (2015). El Sistema mundo de Wallerstein y su transformación: Una lectura crítica. *Argumentos, 28*(77), 131–153.

Parsons, T. (2005). *The Social System.* Routledge.

Robinson, T. W. (1969). Systems Theory and the Communist System. *International Studies Quarterly, 13*(4), 398–420.

Roehrlich, E. (2022). *Inspectors for Peace: A History of the International Atomic Energy Agency.* John Hopkins University Press.

Rosecrance, R. (1963). *Action and Reaction in World Politics.* Little, Brown.

Rosenau, J. N. (1990). *Turbulence in World Politics: A Theory of Change and Continuity.* Princeton Univ. Press.

Ruggie, J. (2003). The United Nations and Globalization: Patterns and Limits of Institutional Adaptation. *Global Governance, 9*(3), 301–321.

Schemeil, Y. (2023). *The Making of the World. How International Organizations Shape Our Future.* Verlag Barbara Budrich.

Schmidt, D. R. (2021). Complexity in International Society: Theorising Fragmentation and Linkages in Primary and Secondary Institutions. *Complexity, Governance & Networks, 6*(1), 94. https://doi.org/10.20377/cgn-105

Schneider, A., Wickert, C., & Marti, E. (2016). Reducing Complexity by Creating Complexity: A Systems Theory Perspective on How Organizations Respond to Their Environments. *Journal of Management Studies, 54*(2), 182–208. https://doi.org/10.1111/joms.12206

Selznick, P. (1957). *Leadership in Administration.* Harper and Row.

Sherden, W. (2011). *Best Laid Plans. The Tyranny of Unintended Consequences and How to Avoid Them.* Praeger.

Sitter, N. (2005). European Organizations: From Negotiated Design to Overlapping Competences and Quasi-membership. In P. Van der Hoek (Ed.), *Handbook of Public Administration and Policy in the European Union.* CRS Press.

Snyder, Q. Z. (2013). Taking the System Seriously: Another Liberal Theory of International Politics. *International Studies Review, 15*(4), 539–561. https://doi.org/10.1111/misr.1206

Spencer, H. (1983). *On Social Evolution.* University of Chicago Press.

Steffek, H. (2021). *International Organization as Technocratic Utopia*. Oxford University Press.

Stephens, J. (1972). An Appraisal of Some System Approaches in the Study of International Systems. *International Studies Quarterly, 16*(3), 321–349.

Tierney, J. (1972). The Use of Systems Theories in International Political Analysis. *World Affairs, 134*(4), 306–324.

Tushman, M., & Romanelli, E. (1985). Organizational Evolution: A Metamorphosis Model of Convergence and Reorientation. In B. Staw & L. Cummings (Eds.), *Research in Organizational Behavior* (Vol. 7). JAI Press.

UN System Chief Executives Board for Coordination [CEB-UN]. (n.d.-a). United Nations System Financial Statistics Report 2021. CEB UN System Chief Executives Board for Coordination. https://unsceb.org/financial-statistics

UN System Chief Executives Board for Coordination [CEB-UN]. (n.d.-b). UN System HR Statistics Report 2022. CEB UN System Chief Executives Board for Coordination. https://unsceb.org/un-system-hr-statistics-report-2022

United Nations High Commissioner for Refugees (UNHCR). (2023). Enfoque basado en grupos temáticos. *Emergency Handbook*. https://emergency.unhcr.org/es/coordination-and-communication/sistema-de-grupos-tem%C3%A1ticos/enfoque-basado-en-grupos-tem%C3%A1ticos

Van de Ven, A. H., & Poole, M. S. (1995). Explaining Development and Change in Organizations. *Academy of Management Review, 20*, 510–540.

von Bertalanffy, L. (1956). General Systems Theory. *General Systems, Yearbook of the Society for the Advancement of General System Theory, V*(1), 1–10.

von Neumann, J., & Morgenstern, O. (1947). *Theory of Games and Economic Behavior* (2nd ed.). Princeton University Press.

Waldrop, M. (1992). *Complexity: The Emerging Science at the Edge of Order and Chaos*. Simon & Schuster.

Wallensteen, P. (1981). Incompatibility, Confrontation, and War: Four Models and Three Historical Systems, 1816—1976. *Journal of Peace Research, 18*(1), 57–90. https://doi.org/10.1177/002234338101800104

Wallerstein, I. (1979). *El moderno sistema mundial, tomo I*. Siglo XXI Editores.

Wallerstein, I. (2005). *Análisis de sistemas-mundo. Una introducción* (2a. edición). Siglo XXI Editores.

Waltz, K. (1959). *El hombre, el Estado y la Guerra*. Nova Editorial.

Waltz, K. (1979). *Theory of International Politics*. Addison-Wesley Publishing Company.

Weiss, T., Forsythe, D., & Coate, R. (2004). *The United Nations and Changing World Politics*. Westview Press.

Zinnes, D. A. (1967). An Analytical Study of the Balance of Power Theories. *Journal of Peace Research, 4*(3), 270–287. https://doi.org/10.1177/002234336700400304

CHAPTER 4

Organizations as Localized Domination Constructions: IGOs at the End of Bureaucratic Pathologies and the Beginning of Political-Strategic Constructs

INTRODUCTION

Many organizations, particularly governmental organizations and International Governmental Organizations (IGOs), are commonly perceived as entirely constrained by their legal obligations, executing only those actions authorized by their creators and financiers. Functionally, it is widely believed that any deviation from this logic is risky and should be avoided. However, the reality often diverges from this instrumental perspective. It is not uncommon for these organizations to gradually extend their mandates, sometimes informally, to undertake new actions that are determined internally, which may significantly impact the very entities that established and finance them.

The International Atomic Energy Agency (IAEA) is an intergovernmental organization established in the 1950s. Its governance structure consists of two political bodies: a Board of Directors, comprising 35 member countries, and a General Conference, where 168 members participate. The IAEA's mandate has expanded significantly over the years, with its activities and obligations extending beyond the original 1956 statute. For

© The Author(s), under exclusive license to Springer Nature   95
Switzerland AG 2025
L. Zamudio-González, D. Arellano-Gault, *International Organizational Anarchy*,
https://doi.org/10.1007/978-3-031-82392-3_4

instance, it has taken responsibility for inspecting nuclear facilities in member countries to ensure compliance with safety standards. However, despite its mandate to enhance safety in nuclear energy management, the IAEA's decision-making bodies have refused to legally grant it the authority to bind safety standards in member countries. It is a peculiar situation in which the organization is tasked with ensuring safety, but its governing bodies withhold the power to enforce compliance.

In what ways does an organization might respond to such an odd situation? One possible solution is to seek alternative means to attain comparable outcomes by leveraging and negotiating new capabilities and attributes. The International Atomic Energy Agency (IAEA) is an example of this approach, as it broadened its influence and applied its standards following the disastrous nuclear accidents at Three Mile Island and Chernobyl, even though it lacked the legal authority to do so. In other words, the political decision-making bodies of the organization deny its executive arm the ability to implement activities and formalize standards in line with the established mission. However, the technical and administrative divisions discover ways to carry out such activities, sometimes extending the scope of their mandate. The IAEA has achieved this adaptability by establishing its legitimacy not based on legal mandates but by demonstrating valuable and necessary technical capabilities to its member states.

Organizations very often need to face the challenge of reconciling conflicting and contradictory directives in practical ways. IGOs are no exception to this. For instance, the IAEA had to devise ways to reconcile its mandate to promote the peaceful use of nuclear energy to advance security and prevent the proliferation of nuclear weapons (Roehrlich, 2022).

The relationship between formal mandates and the actual and practical problems an organization faces is a critical issue. Bureaucracies do not merely comply with rules; they create conditions and use discretion to address the challenges they encounter. The IAEA is a good example. It is intended to ensure the peaceful use of nuclear energy; however, it has insufficient power to enforce compliance with standards. As a result, the organization has developed strong technical capabilities that enable it to navigate a complex environment with diverse and conflicting stakeholder interests. This allows its bureaucracy to maneuver and negotiate.

IGOs have traditionally been regarded as tools or machines that follow the instructions of their creators or designers. IGOs are believed to have a specific purpose that is thought to be clear and well-defined. In this classical view, IGOs are expected to function precisely and unwaveringly like a technical device that obeys orders. The functionalist perspective underlying this instrumental view posits that organizations exist because they effectively and efficiently fulfill their intended functions.

In Chap. 3, we observed that if systemic logic exists, the context in which an organization operates significantly influences its ability to survive and achieve its objectives. In other words, an inherent force drives organizations to acquire knowledge and utilize appropriate mechanisms to attain their goals, thereby ensuring their continued existence. Like any organization, IGOs "naturally" acquire the means and techniques necessary to perform their functions. This is in line with the functionalist logic of systemic vision. Additionally, the same phenomenon occurs in any organizational vision that adheres to the basic principles of functionalism, as outlined by scholars such as Durkheim (1912/2001) and Parsons (1951).

In the context of diverse social entities such as IGOs, the notion of them as mere instruments necessitate justifying multiple assumptions. Functionalist perspectives offer appealing and reassuring narratives to comprehend an organization. Functionalist views provide a sense of security by emphasizing that IGOs are adept at addressing problems and realizing their objectives. This is also why making predictions is relatively simple: when a failure occurs, there is a known solution to rectify the situation. Adjusting means to suit the function or modifying functions to address the issue are viable options. There are a few other available alternatives.

According to this reasoning, IGOs are developed and established primarily to achieve their objectives. Nevertheless, it can be challenging to proceed consistently along this path without examining the inner workings of these organizations. To begin, what are the elements of an organization? The answer is quite evident: organizations are, first and foremost, composed of people with unique personalities, stories, and values.

Moreover, people do not act in isolation or a vacuum; they do so in a specific context, interact with others, and face daily challenges. From a functionalist viewpoint, how do these flesh-and-blood individuals "interpret the function"? Where do they acquire the knowledge to comprehend the intended objective? Why do they submit their will to a set of organizational overarching goals? Why do they comply with those who devise and impose the organization's objectives? How do they interpret the various rules and orders they impose? How do they adapt to day-to-day concrete challenges? These questions are intended to provide a deeper understanding of organizations and their people in real, concrete situations. Individuals interacting and facing uncertainties can incorporate their knowledge, calculations, constraints, and multiple personal or group relationships as logical components of organized action.

The reliance on individuals and their connections as essential components of an organization necessitates a thorough re-evaluation of certain foundational assumptions. Specifically, can the regulations, conventions, directives, and instructions established by an organization's leadership effectively address the everyday challenges encountered by its members? For example, can an international organization tasked with mitigating the consequences of a pandemic like COVID-19 rely solely on its rules and financial resources to ensure that all employees, at every level, have access to current and sufficient information and resources to execute such a mandate effectively and without encountering obstacles? The answer to these questions is unequivocally no.

If IGOs comprise real people, they must inevitably be considered within the framework of any analysis. Furthermore, it is widely accepted that organizations shape and direct the behavior of their members, providing them with clear guidelines on how to act in various situations. However, the challenge lies in the fact that this structure is never fully comprehensive; no organization can completely capture the complex psychological and social dynamics of the individuals that make up its membership. This is grounded in systemic logic, which posits that organizations are made up of people interacting with one another, creating a web of interdependencies that lead to diverse outcomes and consequences.

Organizations typically establish norms, behavioral guidelines, and expectations related to individuals' roles within an organization. However, individuals often interpret, act upon, internalize, or strategically navigate these frameworks, which is crucial for adapting to changing circumstances and achieving their objectives. The issue, then, is that every organization exists within this duality: it is an organization with its own formal (or legal) existence, but it cannot be understood without considering the people within it who are interacting, negotiating, cooperating, and executing.

This perspective does not reduce individuals to mere elements that simply share (or are subsumed by) the organization's values and goals. They are not just organizational entities without agency, with only minimal freedom of action and decision-making. They are not impersonal bureaucrats who merely follow rules (as some unfortunate interpretations of Weber's ideal-type bureaucracy have suggested), but rather they embody diverse rationalities, groups, and coalitions, deploying various strategies and engaging in different battles among individuals and groups in pursuit of resources and power. Organizations, therefore, resemble less a monolithic, orderly, and uniform entity, and are better described by the metaphor of an arena for encounters, struggles, and contingent games (Arellano-Gault & Del Castillo, 2023).

From the perspective of an instrumental monolith, when individuals act in ways that contradict or go beyond the written roles and behavioral patterns established by the organization, it is often assumed that this leads to organizational pathologies or dysfunctions. From a functionalist perspective, individuals behave irrationally by failing to adhere to rules or adhering too rigidly to them. Under-organization and over-organization are two traditional components of the bureaucratic dysfunctions view (Merton, 1942). However, this functionalist perspective neglects to consider individuals within organizations as social, relational entities capable of decision-making, interpretation, and constructing agreements and strategies. Under the organization's view as an arena, interpreting and making sense of rules becomes the norm rather than the exception.

However, how does organizational order arise if organizations are not obedient instruments but arenas of play and interaction between diverse individuals and groups? The metaphor of the organizational arena is a construct that is the product of the multiple and unequal interrelationships that occur between people in an organization. These interactions configure, in action, relatively stable schemes of power and control because people and groups in an organization become interdependent. The organization can provide answers, create solutions, and obtain results thanks to the interdependence that individuals and groups construct and negotiate. The organization is a constructed order, but it is built not only through formal rules and functional logics but also within an arena of power and interdependencies between the people who compose it. These interdependencies can be stabilized and institutionalized.

An IGO is the product of an unequal and plural interaction, where diverse actors play the game of formal rules (structure, norms, regulations) and informal rules (leadership, capacities, resource controls) to crystallize a substantively congruent entity. Due to games, individuals and their groups deal with uncertain, diverse, and multiple objectives in highly volatile and contingent concrete circumstances. Whether it is the United Nations, the European Union, or the International Court of Justice, these diverse entities create the capacity to act meaningfully and feasibly because of the game that their members, coalitions, and stakeholders constantly play and recreate.

Understanding organizations as a construct, not as a monolith but as an arena, is a daring act that attempts to open the *black box* of IGOs. This chapter aims to introduce and understand this perspective concerning IGO studies from the perspective of International Relations (IR).

The organization of this section is as follows: initially, there will be a concise overview of the IR perspective on bureaucracies, highlighting the emergence of *International Public Administration*. This will enable us to examine the efforts made by the discipline to demystify the *black box* and to understand its fundamental principles. Subsequently, a similar process will be traced in organizational theory, where the focus is on opening the *black box* and viewing organizations as primarily comprised of the social behavior of the persons and groups interacting in an organization.

Once the topic of organizations composed of individuals who, nonetheless, do not necessarily fully control the social entity they have created has been discussed, the following section addresses the apparent paradox that the objectives of any organization are in constant dispute among various actors both within and outside the organization. In other words, delving into the *black box* of organizations reveals that individuals engage in a strategic game arena. Influencing what an organization decides and does involves playing in an arena where multiple groups and individuals seek to position themselves in such a way that their influence can materialize. These games are critical for reducing the uncertainty that any individual faces when trying to understand and act within an organization. However, it is a reality that these very games are power games. This section examines Crozier's analysis (Crozier, 1964; Crozier & Friedberg, 1980; Crozier & Thoenig, 1976), which highlights the interactions that, although they may be based on various conflicts between individuals and groups, also produce interdependence. Thus, organizations are spaces for negotiation and control, but also for cooperation and support. Moreover, the dynamics of these games explain phenomena that, from a functionalist perspective, have been considered pathologies. While these games produce counterintuitive effects that deviate from the expectation of blind and mechanical obedience to organizational orders, it is also true that without this capacity for agency among individuals within organizations, decision-making and action would be impossible.

What one perspective might view as a pathological deviation (bureaucracies failing to adhere strictly to rational norms and rules), another

4 ORGANIZATIONS AS LOCALIZED DOMINATION CONSTRUCTIONS: IGOS... 101

perspective—such as the one discussed in this chapter—can shed a different light. Individuals within organizations must navigate the dilemmas of action and execution, balancing multiple and often contradictory interests both within and outside the organization. They frequently adapt, innovate, and reinterpret norms and procedures to address challenges. While they may sometimes fail, they are also capable of implementing not the optimal solution (which may be impossible given the normative and resource constraints), but a viable and achievable solution. In this way, IGOs can manage complex realities within the constraints of time, resources, and rationality that they always face.

IGOs as International Bureaucracies

The study of the bureaucracies or administrative apparatuses of IGOs has been a significant aspect of IR since Cox, Jacobson, and Weiss highlighted in the 1970s that these organizations constitute complex political and administrative systems. Indeed, Cox and Jacobson identified two critical subsystems within IGOs: (1) the participant subsystem, which includes member states with their respective political agendas and interests, and (2) the representative subsystem, which encompasses a broader range of influential actors in decision-making processes, such as bureaucrats and experts (Cox & Jacobson, 1973, pp. 15–16). They argued that IGOs possess an instrumental dimension imposed from the outside and a strategic-political dimension in which objectives are defined through negotiations, agreements, and disagreements. Additionally, IGOs have a political-administrative dimension responsible for making viable, with limited resources and time, the aspirations set out in their objectives (Zamudio-González, 2012, p. 56). Bureaucracies, with their established codes and ethos of action, play a crucial role in any organization.

Although this text did not have the expected impact on academic literature (Codding, 1981), it offers a more nuanced understanding of IGOs, particularly regarding power relations between states and their organizational behavior and decision-making processes (Cox, 2004, p. 5). Cox and Jacobson even proposed a taxonomy of decisions within IGOs, categorizing them into seven classes: representational, boundary, symbolic, programmatic, rule-creating, rule-supervisory, and operational. The first two classes pertain to the general functioning of the organization, including internal procedures and external relationships. The following two relate to the definition of purpose. The rule-creating and rule-supervisory focus on creating and supervising rules, and the last class is centered on providing services and products offered by the organization (Cox & Jacobson, 1973, pp. 9–11).

Understanding the operations of IGOs requires examining the actions taken by their constituent members and administrative bodies to ensure the overall viability of the organization. As organizations, IGOs are composed of members and administrative bodies that can exert influence as Cox and Jacobson (1973) and Weiss (1982) suggested. This recognition leads to the understanding that IGOs require the development of an endogenous dynamic between decision-making and action. However, it is not a matter of choosing between a more political and formal approach, which has persisted in the field of IR, and a more endogenous study, which is characteristic of organizational theories. Instead, the interrelationship between the two perspectives is crucial for comprehending the functioning of IGOs.

Contemporary research has investigated how member states assign responsibilities to IGOs, introducing new avenues for intraorganizational inquiry and highlighting the significance of bureaucratic systems, actors, interactions, and values in policy formulation (Bauer et al., 2017, p. 4). Barnett and Finnemore's (1999, 2004) publications were instrumental in redefining the study of IGOs as organizations and bureaucracies (Ness & Brechin, 1988). Studies that focus on administrative inefficiencies represent an approach to examining IGOs from an internal perspective, but the paradox of bureaucratic autonomy has yet to be fully addressed (Bauer & Ege, 2017, pp. 13–15).

Recent studies guided by the Sociological Institutionalism and Principal-Agent theory have advanced our understanding of the function of bureaucratic factors within IGOs (Bauer & Ege, 2013; Biermann & Pattberg, 2012; Conceição-Heldt, 2013; Dingwerth & Pattberg, 2009; Goetz, 2014; Hanrieder, 2014; Johnson & Urpelainen, 2014; Liese & Weinlich, 2006; Nay, 2012). Sociological Institutionalism, influenced by Weber's theories and adopting a constructivist approach championed by Barnett and Finnemore (1999, 2004), underscores the impact of bureaucratic frameworks and administrative resources on political influence (Bauer & Ege, 2016). On the other hand, the principal-agent theory centers on the assignment of tasks by states (principals) to IGOs (agents) and how the latter maintains a certain level of autonomy despite control attempts (Hawkins et al., 2006).

Paradoxically, despite the limited academic interest in the study of IGOs as administrative entities, they have gained significant influence in global governance (Bauer et al., 2012; Bauer & Ege, 2016; Bauer & Weinlich, 2011; Jinnah, 2014; Knill & Bauer, 2016). The transformation is so significant that some authors argue that bureaucracy, rather than anarchy, is the defining feature of contemporary politics (Barnett & Finnemore, 1999, 2004; Bauer & Ege, 2013, p. 135; Knill & Bauer, 2016; Knill et al., 2017). Barnett and Finnemore (1999, 2004) strongly promoted the concept of bureaucratization of international politics, which refers to how IGOs utilize their knowledge, expertise, and Weberian legal-rational authority to organize and influence the behavior of states. Their work significantly impacted the study of IGOs within IR. However, there is no consensus on the extent and impact of bureaucratization in international politics; it is undeniable that the rise and dynamism of IGOs, their bureaucratic structures, and particularly their Secretariats have gained a central role in global governance.

The Secretariats serve as the technical-administrative structures of IGOs. They comprise professional officials responsible for carrying out activities and processes following the organization's regulations (Bauer et al., 2017, p. 2; Wit et al., 2020). Acting as administrative bodies within the IGOs and as counterparts to national entities, the Secretariats play a crucial and self-directed role in shaping international policy (Barnett & Finnemore, 2004; Bauer & Ege, 2017; Biermann & Siebenhüner, 2009; Busch, 2014; Christensen & Yesilkagit, 2019; Dingwerth et al., 2009; Hooghe & Marks, 2015). These structures exhibit patterned behaviors that enable a deeper understanding of why organizations achieve (or fail to achieve) their objectives beyond environmental constraints.

Voting patterns and influence dynamics, as exemplified by studies by Newcombe et al. (1970, 1977), Rai (1972), Vincent (1972), Kim and Russett (1996), and Voeten (2000), provide an avenue for exploring the impact of bureaucratic strategies and tactics on global policymaking. The role of the General Secretariat's leadership (Haas, 1990, p. 111) and the organizational loyalty of officials (Ernst, 1978; Michelmann, 1978; Peck, 1979; Scheinman & Feld, 1972; Wolf, 1973;) are also crucial in this regard. These factors allow for comprehending the significance of individuals within the organization, their interests, and convictions. Intra-organizational conflicts (Weiss & Jordan, 1976) also play a role in understanding the struggle for resources and the extension of tasks, among other issues.

At a more granular level, the behavior of EU officials, commonly referred to as Eurocrats, is relevant for gaining a deeper understanding of their functioning and decision-making processes (Hooghe & Marks, 2001; Kassim et al., 2013; Xu & Weller, 2004). Additionally, the research on soft governance, organizational design and change, regime management, overlap, and supranationalism (Abbott et al., 2015; Barnett & Coleman, 2005; Bauer et al., 2017; Johnson, 2013; Posner, 2009) can provide further insights into the structuring of these new forms of governance.

Recent studies have reinvigorated the research agenda on IGOs. The works of Bob Reinalda and Bertjan Verbeek (1998, 2004) have advocated for a more comprehensive approach to decision-making, taking into account essential variables for IR, including (1) the structural tension between IGOs and member states, (2) the need for a pragmatic synthesis between rationalist and constructivist perspectives, and (3) the application of mid-range theories that focus on specific events and factors (Reinalda & Verbeek, 2004).

Nonetheless, it can be stated that these advances have not been extensively employed in organizational theory and they are primarily concentrated on questions of institutional analysis, political relations, and rational decision-making processes as their primary contributions. In this manner, they aim to comprehend how the choices made by organizational actors are constrained or governed by rules, institutions, and rational or constructivist frameworks for decision-making based on the pursuit of predefined or formally established objectives. The field of organizational analysis has not been equally refined.

International Public Administrations

The study of IGOs could benefit from a methodological approach known as the International Public Administration (IPA), which connects the fields of IR and Public Administration (PA). Although PA has generally focused on domestic governmental organizations rather than IGOs, essential questions remain to be explored in this area. For example, what are the distinct administrative actors, processes, and structures at the international level, and how do they differ from their domestic counterparts? What is the relationship between administrative actors of different types and levels, and how do they interact with each other? Furthermore, what are the effects of administrative structures and processes on public policy? By

4 ORGANIZATIONS AS LOCALIZED DOMINATION CONSTRUCTIONS: IGOS... 105

applying key PA concepts, such as autonomy, bureaucratic style, bureaucratic entrepreneurship, administrative expertise, budgeting, and multilevel administrative coordination, researchers may gain a deeper understanding of the organizational dynamics of IGOs.

The analytical challenges of applying public administration concepts to IGOs are numerous. These organizations differ from national administrations in several key aspects. For instance, their multilateral nature, the significant influence of the international context, and the presence of multiple *principals* spread across different nations (Hawkins et al., 2006). Additionally, these administrative bodies are highly dependent on member states for resources and policy formulation. Moreover, IGOs often rely heavily on national public administrations (Abbott & Snidal, 1998; Nedergaard, 2007; Weiss, 1982). Administratively, IGOs must be particularly adept at managing multiple external relationships, which are frequently volatile and subject to constant change due to the mobility of the interlocutors themselves (for example, because of shifts in power within democratic societies) (Haas, 1990).

Indeed, IGOs often exhibit greater autonomy in their administrative functions than their national counterparts because of the inherent volatility of the state actors interacting with them. Generally, IGOs are more receptive to the influence of civil service logics to establish forms of administrative stability that enable them to steer the complex world of states. Pursuing this stability has allowed IGOs to benefit from solid and established structures, granting them certain advantages in interpreting and implementing diverse and disorganized sets of interests that member states defend or advance (Cox, 2004; Cox & Jacobson, 1973; Lyne et al., 2006). Even when member states act as unified principals, bureaucratic autonomy within IGOs refers to the extent to which the bureaucracy or its political leaders define the objectives and content of policy decisions.

The PA perspective has enabled a more open study of the entrepreneurial capacity of IGOs, which involves adopting an administrative style that actively influences international public policy. According to the IPAs' vision, the strength of IGOs lies in their capacity to define and apply rules as an authority and in their possession of critical information and expertise that is difficult to match by their national counterparts (Bauer et al., 2017, p. 185). This vision allows for a less schematic and rigid understanding of IGOs as they actively restructure their environment, an area where their national counterparts face more limitations. IGOs interact with each other in international networks, enabling them to develop multilevel management structures based on cooperation and persuasion rather than the hierarchical imposition commonly found in national public administrations.

According to Bauer et al. (2017), international bureaucracies differ from traditional national bureaucracies due to their more complex contexts and adverse institutional settings, which limit their financial and human resources. Despite these challenges, many international bureaucracies actively participate in policy formulation by relying on their unique ability to manage information. This allows them to significantly influence other actors and strategically modify their organizational environment, taking advantage of structural changes and interactions with multiple actors (Bauer & Ege, 2017, pp. 20–21).

In the contemporary discourse on international bureaucracies, considerable attention has been directed toward determining these organizations' autonomy and operational scope concerning the states that constitute them. From the perspective of the PA of IGOs, it becomes evident that IGOs possess agency and organizational capabilities (Christensen & Yesilkagit, 2019, p. 947). Given the substantial influence these organizations exert on international policy formulation and implementation, it is essential to recognize them as active participants in the international arena.

One fundamental concept in the field of IPA is bureaucratic autonomy. This refers to the independence of administrative organizations from the influence of other political actors, particularly member states (Christensen & Yesilkagit, 2019, p. 948). Bauer and Ege (2016) made significant contributions to the study of the bureaucratic autonomy of IGOs by focusing on observing formal administrative structures, resources, and competencies of secretariats. They developed indicators to measure bureaucratic capacities and determine whether an international organization possesses organizational autonomy. They start from the premise that international bureaucracies exert influence and possess specific conditions that give them autonomy. They view this autonomy as a combination of two aspects: the ability of IGOs to "develop independent preferences" (autonomy of will) and the ability to execute their decisions (autonomy of action) (Bauer & Ege, 2016, pp. 6–7, 2017, pp. 11–16, 23–28).

Following Ege's (2017) work, this context presents a typology of four classes of IPAs: autonomous, ideational, politicized, and status quo manager bureaucracies. Autonomous IPAs enjoy both types of autonomy, which makes them influential actors throughout the policy cycle. Ideational

IPAs possess independence of will, but they have a limited capacity for action. Politicized IPAs have the capacity for action, but principals dictate their will. Meanwhile, the status quo IPAs lack both types of autonomy and they are limited to performing technical or supervisory functions (Ege, 2017, pp. 559–560).

In contrast, Wit et al. (2020) stress the character of bureaucracies as autonomous entities that surpass governments' directives. They pinpoint the international structure, functions of bureaucracies, and organizational independence as factors that shape the influence of these bureaucracies. They assert that the intricate nature of global governance and the demand for specialized knowledge have generated a niche for IGOs, allowing their bureaucracies to occupy a significant role in this expanding and multifaceted domain (Wit et al., 2020, pp. 60–63).

The bureaucracies' responsibilities depend on their autonomy level and can involve agenda-setting, policy development and application, as well as the shaping of regulatory frameworks. Knill et al. (2017) extend this examination by introducing the concept of administrative styles, which encompasses the standard routines and procedures that define the behavior and decision-making processes of bureaucracies (Knill & Bauer, 2016, p. 1059). They identified three policy stages during which international civil servants may adopt various roles: policy initiation, formulation, and implementation (Christensen, 2020, p. 950).

According to Knill et al. (2017, pp. 43–69), there are two ideal leadership styles: entrepreneurial and servant. The entrepreneurial style is characterized by intense advocacy for bureaucratic policies, while the servant style is focused on complying with state mandates and interests. These styles are shaped by internal factors, such as the political ambition of a bureaucracy, and external factors, such as institutional challenges (Bauer et al., 2017; Knill et al., 2017, pp. 65–67).

Christensen (2020) advocates for an approach that integrates political and administrative dimensions, examines mechanisms of political control within bureaucracies, and emphasizes the negotiation processes in public service (Christensen, 2020, pp. 954–957). This perspective on the inherently political nature of IGOs is particularly useful for understanding the thorny issue of state-building. Transitional governments overseen by the UN provide valuable case studies for examining the practical significance of state-building in diverse and often challenging political and social contexts. Observing how an international organization administers a state, reconstructs its legislative and judicial branches, and ultimately transfers power back to the people at the conclusion of its mandate, warrants further study within the fields of International Relations, Organization Theory, and Public Administration (Chandler & Sisk, 2013).

The ongoing debate regarding international bureaucracies centers on their autonomy level and their impact on policymaking. Although it is acknowledged that these organizations are distinct from national bureaucracies due to various contextual factors (Bauer et al., 2017), there is a lack of exploration regarding the internal operations and functioning of IGOs. The paradox of bureaucratic autonomy, which is considered a necessary evil for accomplishing tasks and fulfilling mandates while posing a risk to organizational goals, remains an open issue (Bauer & Ege, 2017, pp. 13–15). The challenge for international bureaucracies lies in the diversity of their styles and nature, an essential next step in this study area.

In summary, the concept of IPAs presents a fruitful area for the study of IGOs, particularly regarding their independence, management style, proficiency, budget allocation, and relationship in multilevel contexts. These aspects represent both the difficulty and chance to enhance the comprehension of their impact on global public policy.

IGOs as Organizations: Spaces of Constructed Order

Enhancing the idea of an organizational perspective on IGOs appears to be a worthwhile interdisciplinary endeavor. International Public Administration (IPA) studies have suggested linking the discipline of public administration with IR to illustrate the productive cross-fertilization between disciplines. The next logical step is clear: while the formal objectives and the normative or legal definition are essential features of any IGO, they alone are insufficient elements to understand what the organization and its persons are deciding and why there are acting as they do. Organizations possess their endogenous logic which is critical to their existence. However, this endogenous logic is not necessarily always aligned with the formal or abstract aspects of their missions or functions. To make an organization viable, individuals must develop, design, and execute behaviors in an arena where strategies, practices, routines, and intelligence are required to render feasible the abstract goals set forth in the mission or legal purpose. It is important to note that there can be no organization without individuals, and therefore, there can be no organization without friction, conflict, or the constant risk of error.

4 ORGANIZATIONS AS LOCALIZED DOMINATION CONSTRUCTIONS: IGOS... 109

Why do organizations exist? If they are not just obedient tools for their creators' will, how do they manage to provide the benefits of the collective action on which their promises are based? How do they legitimize themselves as essential and pervasive entities in contemporary society? Organizations have become constant actors in forming social order in the current era, as it is impossible to imagine the world without them. Clegg (1990) argues that organizations are one of the most salient characteristics of modernity: we born, grow, learn, achieve, fail, die, make war or peace, and experience all other aspects of life within, through or in relation to them.

The main challenge then is that organizations are not merely passive entities that blindly follow orders or are tools to achieve objectives straightforwardly. Instead, organizations are dynamic entities that possess their agency and actively shape their goals, logics, and dynamics. They are social constructs composed of individuals whose behavior is influenced by organizational structures and practices, which in turn are shaped by the values, beliefs, and interactions among individuals. Thus, the relationship between individuals and organizations is reciprocal, and they influence each other continuously.

Organizations are comprised of flesh and blood persons, as demonstrated by the notorious Inter-American Development Bank (IDB) scandal. In March 2022, the board of directors of the IDB received an unusual email. Conversations about the email commenced in the corridors of IDB headquarters in Washington. The email accused two prominent figures at the regional lending institution—the president and a senior official—of having an illicit romantic relationship, which is prohibited by the organization's bylaws. The email presented sufficient evidence to confirm these allegations, indicating that the president had breached the IDB's rules and regulations. The email incorporated statements from the president's ex-wife concerning extramarital affairs with an IDB employee.

After several months, a law firm presented the findings of an investigation commissioned by the organization. The investigation failed to uncover any evidence of embezzlement of funds from the organization due to a potential conflict of interest stemming from the president's relationship with the incumbent senior official. However, the firm also noted in its report to the board that there may have been an inappropriate relationship between the president and another subordinate, based on an image provided by the incumbent senior official`s ex-husband. Following the presentation of the investigation's results, the Board of Directors of the IDB had to determine whether to act against the president, so they convened the Board of Governors to select a new member.

The president's allegations of suspected wrongdoing have another human and organizational political implications, given that the president is a U.S. citizen. This has caused concern among IDB members, as it violates the long-standing tradition established in 1959, where the president was always a Latin American national. The suspicion is growing that this change in the custom of appointing a president may have triggered the scandal and subsequent investigation. Consequently, some individuals in the IDB's Washington corridors have expressed their belief that, in fact, persons from the government of Argentina may have orchestrated the entire situation, as per the jocular phrase that "all this has a porteño perfume" (Paybarah, 2022).

Upon evaluation of the investigation, the Board of Governors of the IDB concluded that the president had engaged in an inappropriate relationship with a female subordinate, which violated the organization's rules. Consequently, the Board of Governors, comprising ministers of the economy, finance, or central bank managers from the 48 member countries of the IDB, voted nearly unanimously to terminate the president's employment (El Cronista, 2022; Jiménez, 2022).

The primary takeaway from the IDB case is unambiguous: organizations are, at their core, made up of persons. Persons possess unique lives, beliefs, relationships, and emotions intrinsic to their actions and decisions. According to Weberian bureaucratic doctrine, these human elements must be impersonalized and subject to discipline (Weber, 1922/2019. However, individuals are fundamentally human in practical applications, and their virtues or vices can have significant organizational consequences. Moreover, personal factors can generate political and administrative ramifications rather than being inconsequential or concealed. In other words, despite the appearance of organizations being *impartial*, the profoundly personal factors are interwoven within the rules, norms, and organizational structures themselves, and they can be leveraged politically, as evidenced by the IDB case.

Interactions among individuals within an organization can lead to unforeseen paths and effects. The very people who create and sustain organizations are unable to fully control what they do and what they achieve, at least not completely. This is a profoundly social paradox from which no organization—whether private, governmental, or international—can escape.

The intricate dynamics of contemporary societies have led to the recognition of the significant role played by organizations in almost every facet of life. As Coleman (1982) highlights, organizations have evolved into distinct entities with their own legal and social personalities. While individuals engage with one another, increasing interactions occur through the mediation of an artificial entity, the organization. For instance, if an employee of an international organization provides service to an individual or group in a specific country, both parties, the official and the recipient, are genuine entities with names and surnames. However, the nature of their interaction and its consequences are understood and legitimized by a third, non-personal actor, the international organization. As an abstract, formal entity, the organization's rules and resources form the basis for the interaction between real individuals. In this context, the names, histories, and local realities of the individuals involved are less relevant than the framework of their interaction, which is always shaped by the presence of the non-visible yet *real* third party, the organization.

This is because the individual offering the service as a member of an IGO does not act formally and socially in a way that aligns with their personal interests, values, and overall human qualities. Instead, they represent a role and must adhere to the rules and expectations of the organization as members. This peculiar situation is genuine, even if it is assumed that the organization's managers represent it. Managers are still individuals with first and last names. They are transformed into organizational entities that embody their goals based on their formally assigned role.

Organizations, as powerful entities, can represent a negation of the individual persons who make up the entity. This is due to the transformation of flesh-and-blood individuals into abstract persons who discipline themselves to act as employees or members rather than as the individuals they indeed are. While this transmutation is often seen as accurate, it is essential to consider whether there is a separation between the corporate actor and the actual social being. This separation is more of an abstraction, and transmutation is impossible as individuals incorporate their elements, such as values, beliefs, feelings, ideas, routines, customs, traditions, and emotions, which alters how the corporate actor must play. The dream of organizational control implies that the assumption and legitimization of this transmutation are possible; however, in practice, individuals learn to play the game of transmutation, acting based on never-complete formal roles and constantly changing in a dynamic reality.

A case that exemplifies formal/informal dynamics is the European Union. The bureaucracies that constitute it are believed to have political and moral relationships with the countries from which their members hail. However, the question remains whether their primary allegiance lies with the nation they originate from or the organization they belong to. Moreover, if decisions about the people in question adversely affect their country or government, to whom do they owe greater allegiance: their country or the EU? Christensen (2020) explored these questions.

Although the third actor, the corporate actor, is a creation, legal, and social artifice, it can induce people to modify their behavior and impose values, meanings, and ways of interpreting reality. In contemporary societies, the corporate actor is legitimized and institutionalized and has even been fetishized. This is evidenced by the fact that they are treated as entities with rights, attributions, faculties, and responsibilities as real people who make decisions and act autonomously.

Organizations possess significant power within their structures and often extend beyond their boundaries. IGOs may even coordinate across state lines on various issues such as migration, health, military affairs, and global economic and social development. These organizations' expectations are often ambitious, far surpassing what an individual can achieve alone. This underscores the critical role of instrumental legitimacy in the existence of organizations. These entities are composed of individuals but are assumed to be controlled and transformed into rational, impersonal entities that adhere to their designated organizational roles. However, closer examination reveals a more intricate reality.

Ultimately, when organizations are composed by persons, they come to the organization with a unique set of *baggage*, including stories, values, and emotions. A role-assignment process is necessary to transform these intangible aspects into tangible performance, where each role entails a set of actions, guidelines, and specific expectations. The role or position within an organization is the key to transform real people into organizational people. Consequently, the actions and decisions permissible within an organization are determined by the position, which can be formally defined but it is also influenced by the social dynamics, relationships, and knowledge shared among individuals. While people create the organization, the organization also shapes the people, albeit asymmetrical, as individual employees or persons affected by organizational actions, often possess fewer resources to oppose organizational decisions or effects than the "corporate actor" known as the organization.

4 ORGANIZATIONS AS LOCALIZED DOMINATION CONSTRUCTIONS: IGOS... 113

This interaction between individuals and organizations creates a tight interconnection; it is impossible to comprehend this interaction without considering the organizational logic that generates it, and individuals cannot be fully understood socially without the organizational logic in which this interaction takes place. The relationship between individuals and organizations is fundamentally unequal, as individuals typically possess fewer resources and lack the capabilities and resources organizations possess. A notable contemporary example is the harsh critique that the World Health Organization (WHO) has received regarding the transparency and accountability of its actions during the H1N1 pandemic. The WHO's role has been crucial during the pandemic and the recent COVID-19 pandemic. However, individuals, groups, and even national governments can demand accountability from WHO as an organization with asymmetric resources to induce certain policies across local populations and even nations.

Furthermore, the WHO is composed of multiple organizations, some regional, which are part of the *parent organization* but act autonomously and in a decentralized manner. When it is said that the WHO fails in some issue, does it fail as a single IGO? Or the failure did come from one of its components? or does it fail in one of its decision-making mechanisms (such as the Assembly)? Without defining an organization with absolute precision as a cohesive and unique entity, how can a diverse and complex organization like the WHO be held accountable? (Deshman, 2011).

Organizations possess the authority and capabilities to influence individuals within and outside their boundaries. It is often assumed that this power is solely attributed to the organization itself and not the individuals who comprise it at specific moments and conditions. However, maintaining a definitive distinction between the two is challenging in practice. The legitimacy of organizations is closely connected to the idea of impartiality.

The capacity of IGOs to exert power and shape reality through the values they promote is exemplified by the World Bank's definition of corruption. In a notable speech (World Bank, 1996), the director of the World Bank characterized corruption as a disease that needed to be confronted. Although simple, this definition reduced the various types and logics of corruption to a colloquial expression, ultimately leading to biased actions and policies. Critics argue that the World Bank's anti-corruption logic was a covert way of promoting free trade and privatization policies in developing countries (Arellano-Gault, 2020). While IGOs have the power to influence behaviors through their legitimizing aura, it is essential to remember that individuals who exercise that power are still concrete people with their personal views and beliefs.

Organizations are an indispensable aspect of contemporary societies; however, they also generate feelings of anxiety. This is because these artificial entities possess instruments of influence that can be coercive and opaque. Furthermore, they can become sources of domination, control, and subjugation, as evidenced by instances such as United Nations peacekeeping operations that are imposed with violence, mobilized populations, or borders that are established and enforced. This paradox is a fundamental aspect of organizational theory, as organizations are necessary for achieving primary social and collective objectives and they are a source of significant problems. As agents, organizations can impose and move interests and values under the guise of their technical capacity and impersonal actions. In addition, they possess increasingly significant power sources through technologies such as surveillance and control techniques, which are supported by generative artificial intelligence.

Thus, the issue raised by IR concerning the power and influence capabilities of IGOs is pertinent and significant. Particularly when considering that these organizations are composed of individuals who follow their own interests, operate within arenas of strategic power, and engage in decision-making, negotiation, and bargaining. When IGOs are viewed as full-fledged organizations accountable for critical agendas such as human rights, the relevance of these concerns cannot be overstated. As evidenced by the studies conducted by Øby Johansen (2020), who analyzed the rules and norms of IGOs, including the European Union, the United Nations Office of the High Commissioner for Refugees, and the International Criminal Court, none of these organizations had robust accountability mechanisms in place. Similarly, Hirschmann (2020) examined several human rights violations committed by IGOs, particularly those involved in UN peacekeeping. Given the complexity of IGOs, which often comprise numerous offices, departments, and areas, and sometimes even organizations within other organizations, defining specific responsibilities for successes or failures of actions, has become increasingly challenging and costly. As a result, the lack of clarity in assigning responsibility has implications: individuals within organizations learn to exploit such ambiguities in the strategic games in which they participate.

Indeed, to establish more effective systems of accountability, direction, control, and management for IGOs, it is crucial to conduct research that views these organizations as arenas rather than monolithic entities.

IGOs: Strategic Games and Organizational Battles

Understanding any organization requires grappling with a paradox: while individuals establish organizations through formal acts, routines, and the internalization of rules and procedures, they also adapt to and adopt the organization's values, generally accepting its directives as guiding principles for their behavior. However, transforming this formal structure into a functioning reality demands ongoing decisions and actions, which occur in constant interaction with a myriad of other individuals and groups, all within an uncertain environment. This dynamic process necessitates political and strategic acumen to ensure the organization operates effectively. The paradox lies in the fact that the formal existence of the organization, though fundamental, is not sufficient on its own. Individuals may adhere to the organization's values and directives, but they must also adapt—and sometimes bend—these principles to ensure the viability of collective action.

This paradox stems from the fact that daily organizational life occurs in response to various situations and contingencies. To act and make decisions, individuals must interpret the circumstances within the framework of a formal organizational structure that demands the attainment (or, at the very least, the pursuit) of specific objectives or formal ends. These ends are often abstract and broad in scope, failing to consider the contingencies that must be addressed to achieve them. Organizations require individuals to act in certain ways and interact with each other in specific ways to accomplish their objectives. To do so, they possess the ability to influence, impact, and even coerce (in certain cases) individuals to behave in particular ways and define what is considered *normal, appropriate, or efficient* in a manner that aligns with the organization's standards.

IGOs possess framing capabilities as they define international problems in a specific manner, thereby limiting and even closing alternative ways of defining the same problem through other actors or groups. This is exemplified in Chap. 5, in which the concept of organizational sensemaking is analyzed. Who, then, controls whom in such situations? The organization acquires a unique aura, as it can represent collective objectives. Collective objectives may be challenging to achieve if individuals do not relinquish their agency. However, if people do not utilize their agency to interpret and mobilize wills in pursuit of the objective, achieving them will also be inviable.

116   L. ZAMUDIO-GONZÁLEZ AND D. ARELLANO-GAULT

Lastly, to bring this cycle of opposing views to a conclusion, when individuals use their agency, they may disobey orders, misconstrue instructions, or disregard organizational norms. Bending rules is a deliberate action that can make specific actions feasible. However, if done carelessly, it can be considered a breaking of rules or even an act of malice. This intricate pattern of contradictions partly explains why various studies refer to *pathological* acts that ultimately obstruct accomplishing an organization's purpose.

According to a widely held interpretation, people can be a source of disruption or deviation from the ideal functioning of an organization, which is undoubtedly a mechanical vision of an organization. This view has been applied to various areas of analysis, including IGOs. It is often assumed that these entities are inherently orderly and highly rational; however, this overlooks that they are built and sustained by individuals and their relationships. As a result, the agency of individuals, groups, or practices can *distort* an organization from its intended purpose. The solution proposed by the functionalist views of organizations is to minimize the impact of individual and group agencies on the collective rationality of the organization. However, this approach is limited and has been challenged by empirical evidence.

The functionalist perspective has been widely discredited and abandoned in organizational studies for a long time now. In his influential work on bureaucratic phenomena, Crozier (1964) posited that this view had largely lost its relevance, particularly considering unsuccessful attempts to address the distortions caused by human agency, such as bureaucratic pathologies.

The Bureaucratic Phenomenon (Or Why Bureaucracies are More Competent Than Assumed)

In his seminal work The Bureaucratic Phenomenon, Crozier (1964) grapples with a simple question: Why do dysfunctional organizations persist—and even reproduce themselves—in contemporary society? Furthermore, if human beings are rational and capable of achieving ambitious goals through organizations, why do they continually fall prey to bureaucratic dysfunctions? Unless one assumes that human beings are inherently irrational and unchangeable, it is challenging to account for the recurring dysfunction and pathological characteristics of bureaucratic anecdotes across different countries and organizations. Alternative approaches may be necessary to explain organizational failures more satisfactorily.

It is essential to recognize the dissatisfaction that some experts on IGOs have recently expressed. The bureaucratic shortcomings outlined by Barnett and Finnemore (2004) encompass a range of problems with severe repercussions, such as reluctance to act during the Rwandan genocide. Their explanation is rooted in the straightforward premise that bureaucracy often leads to irrationalities or dysfunctions by deviating from its formal objectives. These bureaucratic pathologies result in contradictory actions in which the organization's intended purpose is overshadowed. This type of analysis is grounded in a substantial tradition initiated by prominent sociologists, including Merton (1942), Selznick (1948), and Gouldner (1954).

The question arises as to why these irrationalities occur in almost all organizations fundamentally based on identifiable bureaucracies. One approach to answer this question is to assume that there is a general contradiction, a failure of rationality, which must be addressed. However, there is another possible explanation: what if bureaucratic failures are not just pathologies but an outcome of organizational rationality itself? These failures may be a byproduct of practical and operational dilemmas faced by real people within the institutional framework of the legitimacy of organizations seen as instruments. This is worth considering in more detail.

According to Crozier (1964), organizations are fundamentally driven by human behavior, and they are subject to continuous social dynamics. Observations reveal that organizations are composed of various groups that engage in continuous interactions while grappling with uncertainties, such as how objectives can be achieved, who interprets and operationalizes goals or expectations, who within the organization understands the causal chains of an organizational problem, how decisions are made, where resources and processes are needed to take action, how objectives that depend on different actors positioned in various parts of the organization can be achieved, and how to satisfy the external stakeholders of the organization who often have conflicting objectives. These examples represent only a tiny portion of people's uncertainties in organized actions. While formal rules, structures, and processes can provide guidance, they cannot fully resolve these uncertainties. People within organizations eventually recognize that addressing these challenges involves interacting with other groups and individuals, which involves communication, influence, symbols, negotiations, bargaining, and exchanges. This is a game that is partly structured by the formal rules of the organization (such as structure, hierarchy, and resources), but where these formal rules themselves become currency for interactions.

Uncertainty serves as a source of power (Crozier & Friedberg, 1980). Those who control an uncertain area utilize it as a negotiation tool, leveraging it to gain advantages in the organizational arena. Consider the International Telegraph Union, established in 1865 and now known as the International Telecommunication Union. As telecommunications advanced, the technical areas of the organization provided various advantages to its members. The above is due to specialized knowledge required in telecommunications which enables the organization to dominate the uncertain area of technical expertise. As a result, technical areas defend their position as indispensable actors within the organization, although they depend on the political management areas within the same organization which have direct contact with interstate governance bodies where vital decisions are made (Peters & Peter, 2012).

The administration of political management encompasses a particular domain of uncertainty that involves direct interactions with the highest decision-making bodies of the International Telecommunication Union (ITU). These areas wield power and control and are significant in their capacity to govern distinct and essential aspects of organizational uncertainty. This interdependence exists because both areas rely on each other at different times for various reasons. While this interdependence may not always be balanced or stable, it still exists. By managing areas of uncertainty, each party leverages its knowledge and position to protect control over these domains. Defending these areas is crucial to exercise influence within an organization. Technical expertise is now considered critical for many IGOs in establishing their legitimacy. Some individuals argue that IGOs have discovered a way to protect themselves and play a political game in their favor, creating a network of technocratic organizations (Steffek, 2021).

The common belief is that organizations are rational and goal-oriented and use their resources to attain objectives by coordinating individuals' efforts. However, this impersonal bureaucratic logic, inspired by the work of Weber, is only a theoretical framework in which people must determine how to achieve objectives that may or may not be attained. For instance, an organization tasked with alleviating the suffering of migrants in desert or jungle areas must decide how to proceed when faced with hundreds or thousands of migrants in real settings and amorphous situations.

Furthermore, the operational logic may differ depending on whether migrants are persecuted or victims of natural disasters or if they include a significant number of infants (Geiger & Koch, 2018). Despite the existence of general instrumental rules for most adult migrants, they may not be applicable with precision in all cases. Organizational rules and norms are almost always incomplete. And following them strictly cannot guarantee success. Therefore, individuals in organizations must interpret and construct their bases for action, which depend on what other areas and groups can do or decide. Conversely, other areas and groups base their actions on what an individual or group can do or decide.

Therefore, according to Crozier, the actions of individuals within organizations can be better understood as a game. A game in which different actors and groups understand that it is necessary to play with rules, interpretations, solutions, and possibilities, as the outcomes and decisions are the result of this interaction, solutions, and possibilities, as what they ultimately decide is a product of this interrelation. Consequently, what is accomplished will have consequences that some actors must confront, either as a reward for success or punishment for failure. Of course, the cycle continues: who determines success or failure? Who defines what constitutes legitimate punishments or rewards? These are areas of uncertainty that are a significant power source to whoever controls them. They represent critical pieces in a game. The organizational game is rational and situational; it defines and frames legitimate actions and meanings that enable individuals to act based on certain assumptions and negotiated agreements.

In the case of IGOs, as discussed before, the definition of the organization's components is crucial. An IGO consists of its decision-making and representation mechanisms for member states, its Secretariat, its technical and political management areas, among others. Under the framework of strategic games, each part seeks to control areas of uncertainty in search for grasping opportunities to act with some guidance and viability. Understanding who controls which areas is key to grasping the power dynamics within an organization. These areas are also contingent: at certain times, specific areas of uncertainty become more important. Consider the case of the Agenda for Democratization (Boutros-Ghali, 1996) promoted by Boutros Boutros-Ghali at the United Nations during the context of the third wave of democratization following the Cold War. In February 1991, the General Assembly requested a report from Pérez de Cuéllar on the measures taken by the organization to support new and restored democracies. Pérez de Cuéllar prepared the report based on the organization's expertise in assistance in decolonization contexts, specifically electoral verification and assistance (Haack & Kille, 2012).

The new Secretary-General, Boutros Boutros-Ghali, sought to restore the United Nations' power in a crucial area, driving a democratization agenda and establishing standards and actions for all member countries. This was accomplished by introducing the Agenda for Democratization, which established a critical operational triad for the UN and its member states along with the Agenda for Peace (Boutros-Ghali, 1992) and the Agenda for Development (Stiglitz, 1998). By embedding democracy deeply within the UN's technical operations, Ghali overcame resistance from governments who believed that the UN should not intervene in this issue, which was otherwise considered a cultural matter (Haack & Kille, 2012). This example demonstrates how organizational actors learn to navigate the power dynamics that are both situational and relational, seeking to gain new spaces of uncertainty. Of course, other actors may seek to defend or gain control over different arenas of uncertainty. This is in line with the concept of the organizational game proposed by Crozier.

Perennial uncertainty is, therefore, the sword of Damocles that every individual or group faces in the organizational environment. But the surprise is that uncertainty is not only something to be endured; it can also be used strategically. Since uncertainty is perennial and can be triggered by various situations or events, those who manage to control these sources of uncertainty (by defining, interpreting, or being accountable for them) wield power. Those who do not control any area of uncertainty will struggle to play the organizational game effectively. Uncertainties create opportunities for negotiation. In other words, individuals and groups can employ defensive or offensive tactics: defensive to protect the controlled area of uncertainty, or offensive to reduce or impact the area of uncertainty controlled by another group or department. For example, in an IGO responsible for a peacekeeping operation, the group that manages to secure better agreements with the conflicting parties can likely claim to have achieved the mission's objective. But which agreements are considered just or legitimate, and which are not?

Under certain circumstances, not all negotiations for settlement within an IGO can be considered valid or morally defensible. As there is no universally accepted definition of a *favorable outcome*, various groups occupying different organizational positions may exploit formal avenues, such as rules, agreements, and hierarchies, to initiate discussions and negotiations within the organization itself to potentially alter the existing agreements

4 ORGANIZATIONS AS LOCALIZED DOMINATION CONSTRUCTIONS: IGOS... 121

or modify the criteria used to assess the validity of actions or decisions. In this manner, the organizational game involves navigating uncertainty while leveraging it to gain an advantage over rival groups.

Let's take the example of UNOPS. The United Nations Office for Project Services is a service organization within the UN (Dijkzeul, 2012, pp. 195–217). Designed as an organization that offers management services, it constantly competes for relevance and resources, making it a unique entity in the universe of UN organizations. Precisely because of its unique profile, it is an organization that systematically faces suspicion of pushing to be too independent. Its area of uncertainty—its exceptional design and technical administrative expertise—is broad and unparalleled. An apparatus that operates more like a business model to provide services efficiently and effectively has its advantages, but as seen in the overall organizational strategic game of the UN, it also faces challenges due to the power it gains by controlling such a potent and unique area of uncertainty. Throughout its history, when it transitioned from being a Project Execution Office (PED), its growth and efficiency became a concern and a source of internal struggles within the UN. Some specialized UN agencies protested the unfair competition posed by the Office and, above all, the concern about the lack of control the UN itself could exert over such a specialized organization. In the language of strategic games, the area of uncertainty controlled by the PED was too large from the perspective of other parts of the organization, and therefore had to be counterbalanced. The PED was then restructured as the Office for Project Services (OPS) to specify its expertise as distinct from that of the specialized UN agencies: its capacity was limited to capacity development and managerial services as part of the UNDP (United Nations Development Programme). However, the power struggle within the organizational arena continued. Thus, in 1992, a proposal was made to reform it and transfer it to the Secretariat of the Department for Development Support and Management Services (DDSMS).

That movement, seemingly innocuous from a general perspective, was, however, a radical transformation in the language of strategic games—a move to control the arena of uncertainty under OPS's jurisdiction, which had been a source of significant conflict. Although framed in entirely technical and neutral language, the proposed change caused considerable distress among OPS staff. The organizational culture within the UN dictates that the Secretary-General is not questioned, at least not officially (Beigbeder, 2021, p. 203). OPS had to adapt to this new game: the organizational defensive/offensive game began by trying to specify, as technically and thoroughly as possible, the types of reforms needed, how they would be implemented, and the specific effects expected. This initiated a process of back-and-forth negotiations, justifications, and the involvement of additional actors in the discussion. For instance, the ACABQ (Advisory Committee on Administrative and Budgetary Questions) had to enter the game, requesting further technical and organizational explanations and justifications.

OPS itself fought to demonstrate that the new structure endangered its technical expertise and strength. The reform process then had to be slowed down to *technically strengthen* the proposed changes. This gave OPS time, which it used to diversify its actions and establish itself as a necessary technical support in more areas, including peacekeeping and peacebuilding operations. In other words, it modified its area of uncertainty by offering its management capacity to more areas, thereby increasing the significance of its uncertainty relative to other areas. This strengthened the impression that a poorly designed change to OPS would have significant negative consequences for more parts of the organization. This risk was acknowledged by other organizational entities (likely due to their own areas of uncertainty), and they managed to slow down the proposed changes by the Secretariat. This provided time and options to propose a different solution: a separate project and services office with a clear identity, linked to the Secretary-General, and managed under its authority. Thus, UNOPS was born, under the logic of a strategic organizational game that is common to any type of organization.

The perspective that these games may lead to dysfunctions or pathologies is valid, albeit in a limited sense. Particularly, this may be the case when the objectives or goals of the organization are clear and attainable without ambiguity or uncertainty. However, in most, if not all, IGOs, achieving objectives often necessitates specialized actions from a variety of expertise. This expertise must then be coordinated, as the division of labor implies specialization of capabilities. Consequently, each area or group becomes specialized and interdependent. These dynamics occur in an environment where dynamic and uncertain realities are encountered.

Organizing is not merely about execution; it is about creating the conditions for coordination, communication, and cooperation—issues than never come automatically: they must be built and agreed among several actors and groups. From an abstract and normative perspective, one might assume that simply stating an organizational goal is sufficient to produce coordination and cooperation. However, an organization entrusted with a goal is a social construct composed of multiple interconnected parts. Many IGOs, for instance, define their objectives through processes of negotiation and bargaining among various governments (represented by their delegates). Each government pursues its own goals and faces its own organizational dilemmas in both foreign and domestic policy. States and their representatives protect various values, such as sovereignty and economic and geopolitical interests. The mandates they create are often the result of negotiated and bargained agreements, which can embody values and functions that are frequently incompatible or even contradictory. Once these mandates are established, it is the responsibility of the IGOs (and their departments) to interpret, operationalize, and make them feasible.

When an IGO formulates and implements a specific objective, it is logical to consider the political context and discourse framework within which the objective is set. This marks the beginning of the organization's history, during which it must determine which components can achieve the objective and what resources, tools, and knowledge they possess. It is also essential to consider whether these resources are distributed equally throughout the organization and how agreements can be reached to facilitate coordination and responsibility sharing among different parts of the organization. It is unrealistic to believe that simple rules and instrumental logic can resolve complex issues and achieve organizational objectives. Games, negotiations, resistance, and conflicts that arise are essential for action and cannot be avoided.

The organizational sphere encompasses more than just strife and competition. There are organizational centrifugal forces, but also, centripetal ones. It is crucial to recognize that the cohesive force of organizations lies primarily in the interdependencies that interactions engender. Although organizational dynamics are situational and ever-changing, specific principles and regulations have been established to cope with perpetual uncertainty. By accepting and replicating effective interdependencies, stability is fostered, albeit partially, because agents and groups may continually seek to redefine them. Consequently, while interdependencies remain dynamic, they serve as a foundation for organizations to establish alliances, cooperate, and reach agreements. Thus, organizational games are dynamic and capable of creating stability, ultimately facilitating action and decision-making to achieve organizational objectives and those of the groups and individuals that comprise them.

Empirical evidence suggests that the actual organizational history differs from the perception of people mechanically following structures with congruent objectives. Instead, it reveals a dynamic process involving constant communication and debate between individuals and groups. They seek to comprehend the necessary actions, goals, and means to achieve the formal objectives of the organization, which are not only recognized by its members but also by external stakeholders, such as states, in the case of international organizations. The observed organizational history deviates from the straightforward application of rules and regulations to accomplish objectives.

Consider the case of the Association of Southeast Asian Nations (ASEAN) (Reinalda, 2020, pp. 221–240). The ASEAN was established in 1967 as a cooperative network of states without a central Secretariat. Initially, the organization was designed to facilitate dialogue and cooperation among nations in a region marked by political and economic tensions. ASEAN has evolved into a forum for multilateral discussions and agreements, necessitating increased coordination, cooperation, and follow-up mechanisms. As a result of the complex interdependencies in security and economics that have emerged between countries, ASEAN has become more specialized and has had to develop new structures and bodies to manage the new areas of uncertainty that have arisen. Initially, ASEAN's primary function was to organize meetings and oversee agreements. However, the strategic game has created new interdependencies that have evolved and solidified over time, creating new organizational dynamics.

Consequently, ASEAN has had to adapt its organizational structure to accommodate the evolving needs of its member states. Initially, ASEAN's minimal organizational needs were met through ad hoc arrangements. However, as the organization's mandate expanded to include security issues in the 1970s, member countries established an ASEAN General Secretariat with their own staff.

By the 1990s, this administrative body had become crucial to ensuring the organization's existence. This, as in any strategic organizational game, involved granting a certain degree of autonomy and discretion to its leadership and management bodies: their coordination and organizational capacities empowered certain groups within the organization through the areas of uncertainty they began to control. Who knew how to monitor agreements? Who had the most comprehensive understanding of the negotiations and the conditions in each country? The management and leadership bodies of ASEAN gained areas of uncertainty by virtue of their control and knowledge, as well as through their connections and relationships. What these organizational groups controlled were areas of uncertainty always in relation to the areas of uncertainty controlled by other groups or actors. Power is situational and relational. It stabilizes because it is played out in the organizational arena, an arena of constructing and reconstructing interdependencies. In ASEAN's case, this game led the various national actors to be willing to bear the cost of a Secretariat (and its staff) with decision-making and action capacities, endowed with the relative autonomy that the specialization of issues entailed. The ASEAN Secretariat thus began to function as a global negotiator: its role involved intervening, with its own agenda and expertise, in the relationships between countries, focusing on the global interests of those countries rather than just on bilateral or multilateral relations. This is evident in the Secretariat's role in supporting and advising the different member countries, with legitimacy gained through its specialized capacity as an organization.

Interdependence is an essential aspect of organizational functioning. However, it is also a complex game wherein the diverse capabilities and tactics of each group or area are evaluated to some extent, as they are developed in an environment where abstract and impersonal rules are considered the minimum legitimate benchmark for any organizational action or decision. Just as operators manage areas of uncertainty, so do managers, but not only because they enjoy certain hierarchy. It is also important to understand the position that actors such as managers need to defend and reproduce in every organization. Formal positions imbue the game with meaning, not because they dictate what people do but because they provide the basis for legitimate arguments on which people justify their actions and decisions. This is exemplified in the case of the UN Secretary-General, whose responsibilities outlined in the Charter do not fully encompass his leadership expectations (Haack & Kille, 2012, p. 31). While the Charter states that the Secretary-General should bring the attention of the Security Council to any matter that, in her/his opinion, may threaten the maintenance of international security (Art. 99), there is little in the Charter that reflects her/his position as one of the six core areas of the organization. In practical terms, the job of the Secretary-General is to serve as the chief administrative officer (Art. 97), attend meetings, prepare the annual report to the General Assembly (Art. 98), and appoint staff (Art. 101).

While some authors focus on the limited autonomy and leadership of the Secretary-General (Benner et al., 2007; Traub, 2006), others analyze her/his strong administrative capabilities (Finger & Mungo, 1975; Sutterlin, 2003), his moral authority (Kille, 2006), his dual mandate of political and administrative roles (Jeong-Tae Kim, 2006), her/his role as a normative entrepreneur (Johnstone, 2003), or specifically her/his strategic political position within the organization (Dorn, 2004; Rikhye, 1991). Simon Chesterman (2007), in *Secretary or General? The UN Secretary-General in World Politics*, reflects this debate on the role of the Secretary-General and her/his ability to act independently of the states that appointed her/him.

It is evident that the interpretation of rules is a double-edged sword: it constantly requires making exceptions to adapt actions to specific situations and circumstances. However, while this is necessary, it also involves taking risks, opening new arenas of struggle and opposition, and potentially facing the consequences of failure or setbacks due to a lack of results. Interpretations that lead to exceptions or the manipulation of events also generate conflicts, as they create possibilities for advantages and privileges, which may rouse counter-reactions from other groups, either to defend those privileges or to challenge them.

If a manager within an IGO necessitates to create a standard operating procedure to address the distribution of medicines and food to various refugee groups across different countries, such standardization, although founded on the principle of equal treatment, may result in difficulties for field-operating groups. These operational groups have limited discretion to address specific challenges in the context in which they must act (which may differ significantly from another group's context in a different geographical location). This may lead to potential consequences if they must make exceptions to address their situation, whereas refraining from doing so may result in a hierarchical reprimand. However, they may also be accountable for the outcomes if they do not make exceptions.

Furthermore, certain operational groups may possess greater negotiation leverage to sanction their exceptions, resulting in divergent consequences and quantity. In other situations, some operational groups might succeed in insulating their decisions, thereby concealing their expertise from the organization's upper management. This isolation may be viewed as a bureaucratic flaw from a normative standpoint, but it is consistent with the underlying logic of the organizational game. However, isolation cannot be absolute, as there is inevitable and necessary interdependence between individuals and groups in any organization. Consequently, this game can be understood as a continual exchange of offensive and defensive maneuvers that distinct actors and hierarchical levels must engage in to act with a reasonable degree of assurance that their actions are rational and grounded in probability. The game can sometimes be disruptive but often leads to cooperative outcomes once an equilibrium is established. In this standardization example, the application of a standard is ultimately achieved through a consensus on the allowable interpretations and practical exemptions required to comply with it.

The organizational landscape is highly dynamic and characterized by interactions between individuals and groups in an environment of high uncertainty. However, the basis for generating equilibria that can become stable is through interaction, which creates diverse interdependencies among the parties involved. It is important to note that stability does not necessarily equate with optimality or efficiency. These terms are subjective and can vary depending on the situation and individuals involved. Equilibria are achieved through the interdependence that groups and individuals involved perceive and accept, at least temporarily and partially. It is essential to recognize that trade-offs may benefit certain groups or coalitions more than others. The game is continuous and never independent of negotiations, power structures, rules, and balances reached and legitimized. A balance may be perceived as inefficient, unfair, or *dysfunctional* by certain actors or groups. It is essential to avoid evaluating the goals of an organization in an abstract, neutral, and decontextualized manner. The goals of an IGO are often the product of negotiations and agreements and they are, therefore, neither transparent nor free of contradictions. Members of the organization must interpret them to achieve them. However, the primary objective of an organization is to create conditions for coordination and cooperation in an environment where the interdependencies between agents and stakeholders are crucial to enabling any form of action.

Under Crozier's (1964) perspective, the dysfunctions that arise in organizations are not due to the gap between an ideal state proposed by Weber and the persons in reality; persons that *fail* or act irrationally. Instead, these failures or dysfunctions are rooted in the social, political, and organizational dynamics of an organization, and in the relationships between individuals who face uncertainty and resort to strategic actions to protect themselves. Although an equilibrium deemed *dysfunctional* by certain actors or groups may exist, this does not mean such an equilibrium is not a viable and potentially desirable solution under specific circumstances. The organizational game does not strive for the optimal solution but rather for feasibility in pursuit of a satisfactory outcome.

Organizational Order: Between Chaos and Interdependence

The dynamics of the game involve interaction among individuals in search of a precious element of understanding and interrelation: reciprocity. But how is reciprocity achieved in a context where goals are contested among different groups, resources are scarce, and the technologies to achieve various objectives and utilize various means may be limited or uncertain? Uncertainty is perennial in organized action. Acting in an organized manner is poorly explained by the metaphor of a linear rational process where singular goals are pursued through precisely established means. A more realistic depiction is one in which various actors and groups seek to impose a particular sense of what the goals and values to be pursued should be, requiring individuals to navigate this complexity

Organizations are human creations designed to achieve results; this is the powerful image that justifies and legitimizes them. In part of the International Relations literature, there is a great hope that IGOs will behave exactly like this: as obedient instruments to achieve the grand objectives of the international order. However, IGOs, like any organization, are constituted by formalized and abstract objectives or mandates that rely on the day-to-day actions of individuals with values and emotions, within power relations and conflicts, and are constantly tested in confronting a concrete reality that is dynamic and changing.

Certainly, numerous organizations rely on the bureaucratic form of the organization, at least partially. Bureaucracies, as a form of organization, have served as powerful social rhetoric. In the face of the uncertainty and volatility of human relationships, the impersonal nature of bureaucracies allows individuals to envision a world that is mainly ordered and structured (Du Gay, 2000). By controlling for the heterogeneity of individuals, even artificially, the order in interactions becomes more probable. The bureaucratization of the contemporary world has served as a powerful social force that has enabled the creation of massive corporations and organizations facilitating the orderly interaction of individuals across different cultures, periods, and geographic locations (Bromley & Meyer, 2015).

However, while *impersonalization* is a significant source of contemporary organizational order, it is equally limited in comprehending the daily processes through which individuals construct organizations. Although individuals can discipline themselves to adhere to the impersonal logic of purposes, decisions, and processes, this approach has inherent boundaries. Effectively coordinating efforts, resolving dilemmas and conflicts, and adapting to changes and emergencies requires more than merely following the rules and explicit norms defined by an organization. In practical applications, individuals navigate this dual dynamic by employing various tactics and strategies in the real world, where people's values and diversity play a crucial role in addressing unique and specific situations. The issues of discretion and individual capacity within IGOs have long been a topic of concern in the field of IR. The presence of discretion, as assumed in functionalist logic, is believed to lead to inefficiencies and potential problems. In contrast, the absence of discretion, as posited in the view of organizations as an arena, undermines the very existence of an organization. This dilemma presents a significant challenge for the study of IGOs as organizations.

It is crucial to recognize that IGOs are, at their core, composed of individuals behaving, as they do in any other type of organization. However, the organizational game must be concealed to some extent in a world that values impersonal rationality. The functionalist belief in the ideal of organizational rationality serves as the basis for legitimacy and accepting that coordination between groups and individuals requires negotiation, bargaining, and confrontation undermines this socially or politically expected legitimacy. Formal rules, written processes, and established goals are insufficient for navigating dynamic and changing realities full of specificities. Consequently, individuals within organizations must maintain the pretense of adhering to formal rules and impersonal logic while simultaneously constructing foundations that make these formal logics applicable to real situations. This ability to juggle formal and real logics can result in diverse and imperfect solutions, exemplifying the schizophrenic nature of modern organizations.

Research on IGOs has demonstrated that individuals involved at different levels and structures in these organizations experience vibrant and situational political and organizational games. Nevertheless, this dynamic is often disregarded or merely considered a pathology. All organizations, whether governmental, private, social, or judicial, are venues where individuals and groups engage in actions, negotiations, construction, and reconstruction of interdependencies. Likewise, IGOs are composed of people who must adapt formal rules and abstract objectives to diverse and uncertain situations while adhering to these guidelines.

This organizational contradiction has not escaped analysis in the context of IGOs. One of the most famous interpretations is that of organizational pathologies. Organizations, including international ones, often fail to prevent the distortion of their formal objectives and goals due to inherent flaws and contradictions. Although organizational literature following Crozier (1964), as mentioned above, has largely abandoned the perspective of bureaucratic pathologies or dysfunctions, it remains a concept used in various areas of administrative analysis and International Relations.

Let's revisit the case of the World Bank (WB) and the complex process of incorporating an anti-corruption policy as a key decision-making axis (Park & Weaver, 2012, pp. 92–117). As part of its mission to support development, particularly in countries with the greatest needs, President Wolfensohn, in the early 1990s, proposed and promoted a sustainable development agenda alongside a strong anti-corruption policy. Achieving this required disrupting certain circuits of the Bank's deeply economistic culture. By creating a specialized vice presidency focused on sustainable social development, the aim was to introduce this criterion as a critical factor in the Bank's decision-making processes.

A groundbreaking shift from conventional economic and technical reasoning was introduced, akin to that of a financial institution. Alongside the environmentally conscious agenda, the well-known phrase *corruption as a cancer* emerged, which implied an additional critique of the decision-making process within the organization. The underlying issue is profound: from an organizational perspective, the WB was tasked with promoting development support and intervention packages aimed at countries adopting "good governance practices". However, its capabilities and internal logic were insufficient to incorporate these new agendas in a coherent, comprehensive, and systematic manner. Criticism from both within and outside the institution has grown, suggesting that such interventions, controls, and supervision might hinder the countries they were intended to help. Opposition to these measures increased both internally and externally. From a functionalist perspective, which tends to view deviations as pathologies, can this resistance and conflict be explained as mere resistance to change? Or does it indicate pathology or dysfunction when internal actors disagree with the objectives and reforms initiated from the top of the organization?

Drawing from the standpoint presented in this chapter, the question at hand is dynamic. The strategic games played within any organization extend beyond mere resistance and may encompass proposals for change, reform, and innovation. Decisions made by the top-tier hierarchy do not solely dictate these transformations; instead, they unfold gradually over time, with various groups and individuals collaborating to create spaces for negotiation, adaptation, and reinterpretation. The literature on organizational change has long emphasized the disparity between the proposed reforms and their actual outcomes (Poole, & Van de Ven, 2004). Intentions alone are insufficient, and practical results are crucial for determining the functionality. Organizations are continually shaped by the diverse individuals who comprise them as they face new challenges every day. As Tsoukas and Chia (2002) noted, organizations emerge through the ongoing reweaving of beliefs and habitual behaviors to accommodate new experiences derived from interactions. This phenomenon can be observed in the case of the WB, where the departure of Wolfensohn and the arrival of Wolfowitz precipitated new crises. The well-established green policy agenda of the Bank was dismantled without further negotiation or explanation, and the anti-corruption agenda suffered due to the president's conflicts of interest (as discussed earlier in this chapter).

To comprehend the dynamics of organizational change it is necessary to understand the spaces of power and interdependence within the organization. Change is often negotiated and legitimized, resulting in outcomes that may differ from those initially intended or formally proposed. This does not necessarily indicate pathology but emphasizes the importance of the reactions, intentions, and projects of the organization members and groups. The success of change (whether positive or negative) depends more on a specialized understanding of organizational logics, such as negotiations, leadership, and feasibility building, rather than on abstract functionalist laws that pre-determine the outcome of organizational actions.

Overcoming the conceptual limitations and contradictions associated with bureaucratic pathologies or dysfunctions requires acknowledging a complicated truth: conflicts and apparent bureaucratic inefficiencies, resistances, or rigidities cannot be removed like a tumor in an aseptic manner. Negotiation and bargaining are essential components of daily life in the real world. Conflict is an integral part of the need for interaction, as it allows the creation of meaning that individuals can internalize and use to guide their actions in uncertain situations. When considering that individuals within organizations possess agency, these acts of negotiation and bargaining can be regarded as both intelligent and rational, as they contribute to the formation of the stable and credible power structures necessary for action. The apparent errors or inefficiencies that may arise can represent concrete solutions to the dilemmas posed by the situation. While these solutions may be perceived as irrational by external actors, they may be highly logical or even inevitable for those directly involved in the organization's specific networks of beliefs, skills, and capabilities grappling with a concrete reality rather than an abstract or formal one. To view power and conflict as pathologies is to adopt a narrow perspective that ignores the diversity of ways in which individuals within an IGO establish a purpose, understand objectives, and make sense of the definition of problems or situations that need to be addressed. Empirical research on IGOs quickly reveals that individuals possess diverse approaches to these matters.

This diversity, rather than detracting from it, enables the organization to flourish and attract individuals dedicated to following abstract guidelines and regulations while simultaneously grappling with resource limitations and conflicting demands from various stakeholders. For organizational stakeholders to exert their influence and exhibit agency, they must possess a crucial element: the capacity to maneuver within spaces of freedom. Crozier (1964) emphasized that organizations require effective governance, as they are not mere mechanical entities designed to transform individuals into uniform, interchangeable components of collective action.

Breaking away from the conventional understanding of bureaucratic pathologies has allowed the organizational theory to blossom. This shift in perspective has opened a different avenue of analysis, wherein it is essential to comprehend the concrete mechanisms through which each organization achieves a state of equilibrium, where power, conflict, and agency are distributed unequally and inequitably among its various stakeholders, including directors, managers, and even operators. These stakeholders are engaged in a constant game of controlling and reconstructing the areas of uncertainty that dominate their environment. However, as interactions generate heterogeneous and unequal interdependencies, these games can lead to equilibrium and stability. Agreements, negotiations, the definition of legitimized rules and norms, and the establishment of structures and processes all contribute to making the organization a rational and capable entity that can achieve diverse and far-reaching objectives. However, the same dynamics can lead to failure. The organization's stability and instability, crystallization and modification of games, and transformation of organizational life are all interconnected. As Tsoukas and Chia (2002) call it, this becoming is characterized by schizophrenic logic, as games, bargaining, agreements, and constantly redefined interdependencies imply conflict. This conflict, a web of games that must be skillfully subsumed to maintain the illusion of rational and impersonal organizational action, is a fundamental aspect of organizational life.

The functionalist perspective on the pathologies of bureaucracy accurately identifies the contradictions that individuals experience in the face of the impersonal nature of societal power. However, this view likely underestimates the extent to which these contradictions are inherent in the social process of human agency and that they cannot be eliminated by applying more instrumental rationality. Instead, conflict and power play crucial roles in shaping human behavior and organizational action.

The above-mentioned assertion does not suggest that numerous activities, behaviors, frameworks, and organizational procedures are not contradictory or result in errors or blunders. Nevertheless, it is not as straightforward and confined as positing that these elements can be surgically excised neither administratively nor institutionally by labeling them as pathologies.

Organizations are inherently contradictory entities, as they are complex, dynamic systems shaped by human agency and they need to navigate uncertainty around the world. The pursuit of freedom in this context is closely tied to managing uncertainty, and this freedom is achieved through a social and political process of negotiation and strategic maneuvering, in which power dynamics play a central role. Despite the seemingly stable nature of organizations, they are constantly engaged in a political battle to achieve goals and objectives. The key to organizational success lies in the dynamic construction of interdependence, which establishes equilibrium. However, these trade-offs are not always rational or fair for everyone involved, and they are ultimately situational agreements that arise from the resolution of interdependence equilibria derived from organizational games. Therefore, it is more beneficial to consider these pathologies not as harmful or deviant but as an inherent aspect of any organization.

Concluding Remarks

IGOs are both objects of study and a complex reality. They are characterized by a duality in which they serve the entities that create and lead them while also creating their own dynamics as social constructions. This duality is typical of any organization. However, the specificity of IGOs lies in their legal and normative creation, not only by individuals or groups but also by transcendent institutions such as nation-states. Additionally, it is crucial to consider the context of multiple political regimes, systems, and agendas of great importance, such as trade, health, migration, and war.

As Herbert Simon eloquently stated, organizational theory posits that an organization is fundamentally a collection of individuals and their behaviors (Simon et al., 1991). This fundamental reality emphasizes the crucial role that interactions and interdependencies among individuals play in comprehending an organization. It is important to note that these relationships are not only formed daily but also evolve and change over time, giving rise to dynamic and persistent patterns that shape an organization's logic and stability. Understanding an organization requires thoroughly examining its micro-, meso-, and macro-dynamics.

Macro-dynamics, encompassing institutions, laws, rules, and formal political environments, aim to provide meaning and establish ultimate goals and values. Conversely, micro-dynamics involve real-life interactions and interdependencies of individuals influenced by both macro- and micro-dynamics. Meso-dynamics, characterized by interrelations and interdependencies among groups and coalitions, serve to coordinate parts of the organization and between organizations. Ultimately, a comprehensive understanding of an organization requires examining these three levels of dynamics.

The dynamics of IGOs are remarkably intricate, encompassing the micro-, meso-, and macro-levels. The normative vision of IGOs is quite powerful, with a prevailing macro vision. The International Order is a heavy metaphor sustained by powerful legalistic discourses, norms, and diverse international regimes, imposing high expectations of order, effectiveness, efficiency, and technical capacity on IGOs. Given these high expectations, IGOs that operate under deeply meso- and micro-logics of conflict, games to control uncertainties and performances, and fabrications are quickly perceived as risks, failures, and even pathologies under macro lenses. This is unfortunate because, as we have seen in this chapter, human and group performance in an organization is conflictive, dynamic, and involves construction and learning. What one literature labels as pathologies, another understands it as the indispensable consequences and dynamics of social relations. Contradictory yet indispensable, conflict and organizational games are necessary for an organization to exist.

This chapter has facilitated an exploration of a critical paradox in the study of IGOs. The discipline of IR has grappled with this dilemma by examining the inner workings of these organizations, utilizing theories such as constructivism and principal-agent theory. However, further progress is necessary to delve deeper into meso and micro-analyses, which focus on the intra-organizational dynamics that shape the decisions and actions of IGOs. The rationality of organized action extends beyond pursuing formal objectives and goals. Individuals within organizations devise strategies, reach agreements, and imbue their actions meaningfully. Labeling these decisions and actions as discretionary or disruptive of the minimum order necessary for the IGO to fulfill its state-mandated mission is an approach that sidesteps comprehending the intricate relationship between the agency of individuals and organizations and their capacity to render action effective and achieve desired outcomes. Furthermore, the existence of the complex reality in which multiple interests and limited predictability of the concrete effects of actions must be considered. Additionally, it is essential to consider the constraints imposed by the limited and uncertain nature of the available technologies and administrative tools to modify reality.

Studying IGOs as complex, multi-faceted entities rather than as single, uniform entities, is a promising and necessary approach in both the fields of IR and IPA. Using organizational theory tools can enhance the analysis of IGOs, making them more sophisticated and accurate. However, the micro- and meso-perspectives proposed by organizational theory can be challenging when studying IGOs' broader role in the international order. As more research on IGOs is conducted, this difficulty may be overcome, leading to a deeper comprehension of the various roles of IGOs as instruments and gears of the international order and their social constructs that create complex dynamics of interpretation and interdependence.

References

Abbott, K. W., Philipp, G., Duncan, S., & Bernhard, Z. (Eds.). (2015). *International organizations as orchestrators*. Cambridge University Press.

Abbott, K. W., & Snidal, D. (1998). Why states act through formal international organizations. *Journal of Conflict Resolution, 42*(1), 3–32.

Arellano-Gault, D. (2020). *Corruption in Latin America*. Routledge.

Arellano-Gault, D., & Del Castillo, A. (2023). *The promises and perils of compliance*. De Gruyter.

Barnett, M., & Coleman, L. (2005). Designing Police: Interpol and the Study of Change in International Organizations. *International Studies Quarterly, 49*, 593–619.

Barnett, M., & Finnemore, M. (1999). The politics, power and pathologies of international organizations. *International Organization, 54*(4), 699–732.

Barnett, M., & Finnemore, M. (2004). *Rules for the world: International organizations in global politics.* Cornell University Press.

Bauer, M., & Ege, J. (2013). International bureaucracies from a public administration and international relations perspective. In R. Bob (Ed.), *Routledge handbook of international organization.* Routledge.

Bauer, M., & Ege, J. (2016). Bureaucratic autonomy of international organizations' secretariats. *Journal of European Public Policy, 23*(7), 1019–1037.

Bauer, M., & Ege, J. (2017). A matter of will and action: The bureaucratic autonomy of international public administrations. In M. W. Bauer, C. Knill, & S. Eckhard (Eds.), *International bureaucracy: Challenges and lessons for public administration research.* Palgrave Macmillan.

Bauer, M., Knill, C., & Eckhard, S. (Eds.). (2017). *International bureaucracy: Challenges and lessons for public administration research.* Palgrave Macmillan.

Bauer, M., & Weinlich, S. (2011). International bureaucracies: Organizing world politics. In B. Reinalda (Ed.), *The Ashgate research companion to non-state actors.* Ashgate.

Bauer, S., Andresen, S., & Biermann, F. (2012). International bureaucracies. In F. Biermann & P. Pattberg (Eds.), *Global environmental governance reconsidered.* The MIT Press.

Beigbeder, Y. (2021). Fraud, corruption, and the United Nations' Culture. In D. Dijkzeul & D. Salomons (Eds.), *International Organizations Revisited. Agency and Pathology in a Multipolar World* (pp. 191–221). Berghahn.

Benner, T., Mergenthaler, S., & Rotmann, P. (2007). *International bureaucracies: The contours of a (re)emerging research agenda. Paper presented at the German Political Science Association (DVPW) IR section conference,* July 14. Technical University Darmstadt.

Biermann, F., & Pattberg, P. (2012). *Global environmental governance reconsidered.* MIT Press.

Biermann, F., & Siebenhüner, B. (2009). *Managers of global change: The influence of international environmental bureaucracies.* The MIT Press.

Boutros-Ghali, B. (1992). An agenda for peace: Preventive diplomacy, peacemaking and peace-keeping. *International Relations, 11*(3), 201–218.

Boutros-Ghali, B. (1996). *Agenda for democratization.* UN Department of Public Information.

Bromley, P., & Meyer, J. (2015). *Hyper-organization. Global organizational expansion.* Oxford University Press.

Busch, P. (2014). Independent influence of international public administrations: Contours and future directions of an emerging research strand. In S. Kim, S. Ashley, & W. Lambrigh (Eds.), *Public administration in the context of global governance.* Edward Elgar.

4 ORGANIZATIONS AS LOCALIZED DOMINATION CONSTRUCTIONS: IGOS... 137

Chandler, D., & Sisk, T. D. (Eds.). (2013). *Routledge handbook of international state building* (pp. XIX–XXVII). Routledge.

Chesterman, S. (Ed.). (2007). *Secretary or general? The UN secretary-general in world politics*. Cambridge University Press.

Christensen, J. (2020). Representative bureaucracy, international organizations and public service bargains. *Public Administration, 98*, 408–423. https://doi.org/10.1111/padm.12625

Christensen, J., & Yesilkagit, K. (2019). International public administrations: A critique. *Journal of European Public Policy, 26*(6), 946–961.

Clegg, S. (1990). *Modern organizations in the postmodern world*. SAGE.

Codding, G. A. (1981). Influence in international conferences. *International Organization, 35*(4), 715–724.

Coleman, J. (1982). *The asymmetric society*. Syracuse University Press.

Conceição-Heldt, E. (2013). Two-level games and trade cooperation: What do we now know? *International Politics, 50*(4), 579–599.

Cox, R. (2004). Foreword: International organization in an era of changing historical structures. In B. Reinalda & B. Verbeek (Eds.), *Decision making within international organizations*. Routledge.

Cox, R., & Jacobson, H. (Eds.). (1973). *The anatomy of influence: Decision making in international organization*. Yale University Press.

Crozier, M. (1964). *The Bureaucratic phenomenon*. Chicago University Press.

Crozier, M., & Friedberg, E. (1980). *Actors and systems: The politics of collective action*. Chicago University Press.

Crozier, M., & Thoenig, J. C. (1976). The regulation of complex organized systems. *Administrative Science Quarterly, 21*(4), 547–570.

Deshman, A. (2011). Horizontal review between international organizations: Why, how, and who cares about corporate regulatory capture. *European Journal of International Law, 22*(4), 1089–1113. https://doi.org/10.1093/ejil/chr093

Dijkzeul, D. (2012). Not just states or the secretary-general, but also staff: The emergence of UNOPS as a new UN organization. In J. E. Oestreich (Ed.), *International organizations as self-directed actors: A framework for analysis*. Routledge.

Dingwerth, K., Kerwer, D., & Nölke, A. (Eds.). (2009). *Die organisierte Welt: Internationale Beziehungen und Organisationsforschung*. Nomos.

Dingwerth, K., & Pattberg, P. (2009). Actors, arenas and issues in global governance. In J. Whitman (Ed.), *Global governance*. Palgrave Macmillan.

Dorn, A. (2004). Early and late warning by the UN Secretary-General of threats to the peace: Article 99 revisited. In S. Albrecht & D. Carment (Eds.), *Lanham conflict prevention from rhetoric to reality, Vol. 1. Organizations and institutions*. Lexington Books.

Du Gay, P. (2000). *In praise of bureaucracy*. SAGE.

Durkheim, E. (1912/2001). *The elementary forms of religious life*. Oxford Univ. Press.

Ege, J. (2017). Comparing the autonomy of international public administrations: An ideal-type approach. *Public Administration, 95*, 555–570. https://doi.org/10.1111/padm.12326

El Cronista. (2022). Más escándalo en el BID: los directores votaron por unanimidad echar al presidente de la entidad, Mauricio Claver-Carone. *El Cronista*. https://www.cronista.com/economia-politica/mas-escandalo-en-el-bid-los-directores-votaron-por-unanimidad-echar-al-presidente-de-la-entidad-mauricio-claver-carone/

Ernst, M. (1978). Attitudes of diplomats at the United Nations: The effects of organizational participation on the evaluation of the organization. *International Organization, 32*(4), 1037–1044.

Finger, S., & Mungo, J. (1975). The politics of staffing the United Nations Secretariat. *Orbis, 19*(20), 117–145.

Geiger, M., & Koch, M. (2018). World Organization in migration politics: Tie International Organization for migration. *Journal of International Organizations, 9*(1), 25–44.

Goetz, K. H. (2014). Time and power in the European commission. *International Review of Administrative Sciences, 80*(3), 577–596.

Gouldner, A. (1954). *Patterns of industrial bureaucracy*. Free Press.

Haack, K., & Kille, K. (2012). The UN Secretary-General and self-directed leadership. In J. Oestreich (Ed.), *International organizations as self-directed actors*. Routledge.

Haas, E. B. (1990). *When knowledge is power: Three models of change in international organizations*. University of California Press.

Hanrieder, T. (2014). Gradual change in international organisations: Agency theory and historical institutionalism. *Politics, 34*(4), 324–333.

Hawkins, D. G., Lake, D. A., Nielson, D. L., & Tierney, M. J. (Eds.). (2006). *Delegation and agency in international organizations*. Cambridge University Press.

Hirschmann, G. (2020). *Accountability in global governance*. Oxford University Press.

Hooghe, L., & Marks, G. (2001). *Multi-level governance and European integration*. Rowman & Littlefield.

Hooghe, L., & Marks, G. (2015). Delegation and pooling in international organizations. *The Review of International Organizations, 10*, 305–328.

Jiménez, M. (2022). IDB ousts its president for violating bank policies in his relationship with a female employee. *El País*. https://elpais.com/economia/2022-09-26/el-bid-destituye-a-su-presidente-por-violar-las-reglas-del-banco-en-su-relacion-con-una-empleada.html

Jinnah, S. (2014). *Post-treaty politics: Secretariat Influence in Global Environmental Governance*. The MIT Press.

4 ORGANIZATIONS AS LOCALIZED DOMINATION CONSTRUCTIONS: IGOS... 139

Johansen, S. Ø. (2020). *The human rights accountability mechanisms of international organizations.* Cambridge University Press.

Johnson, T. (2013). Institutional design and bureaucrats' impact on political control. *The Journal of Politics, 75*(01), 183–197.

Johnson, T., & Urpelainen, J. (2014). International bureaucrats and the formation of intergovernmental organizations: Institutional design discretion sweetens the pot. *International Organization, 68*(1), 177–209.

Johnstone, I. (2003). The role of the UN Secretary-General: The Power of Persuasion Based on Law. *Global Governance, 9*(4), 441–458.

Kassim, H., Peterson, J., Bauer, M. W., Connolly, S., Dehousse, R., Hooghe, L., & Thompson, A. (2013). *The European commission of the twenty first century.* Oxford University Press.

Kille, K. (Ed.). (2006). *The UN Secretary-General and moral authority. Ethics and religion in international leadership.* Georgetown University Press.

Kim, J. (2006). The UN Secretary-General walking a two-scope rope: An analytic approach to the secretary-generalship. *Korea Review of International Studies, 9*(2), 65–88.

Kim, S. Y., & Russett, B. (1996). The new politics of voting alignments in the United Nations General Assembly. *International Organization, 50*(4), 629–652.

Knill, C., & Bauer, M. W. (2016). *Policy-making by international public administrations: Concepts, causes and consequences.* Taylor & Francis.

Knill, C., Enkler, J., Schmidt, S., Eckhard, S., & Grohs, S. (2017). Administrative styles of international organizations: Can we find them, do they matter? In M. Bauer, C. Knill, & S. Eckhard (Eds.), *International bureaucracy. Challenges and lessons for public administration research.* Palgrave Macmillan.

Liese, A., & Weinlich, S. (2006). Die Rolle von Verwaltungsstäben in internationalen Organisationen. Lücken, Tücken und Konturen eines (neuen) Forschungsgebiets. *Politische Vierteljahresschrift, 37,* 491–524.

Lyne, M., Nielson, D. L., & Tierney, M. J. (2006). Who delegates? Alternative models of principals in development aid. In D. G. Hawkins, D. A. Lake, D. L. Nielson, & M. J. Tierney (Eds.), *Delegation and agency in international organizations.* Cambridge University Press.

Merton, R. (1942). *Social theory and social structure.* Free Press.

Michelmann, H. J. (1978). Multinational staffing and organizational functioning in the Commission of the European Communities. *International Organization, 32*(2), 477–496.

Nay, O. (2012). How do policy ideas spread among international administrations? Policy entrepreneurs and bureaucratic influence in the UN response to AIDS. *Journal of Public Policy, 32*(1), 53–76.

Nedergaard, P. (2007). *European Union Administration: Legitimacy and efficiency. v. 69 of Nijhoff law specials.* Nijhoff.

Ness, G. D., & Brechin, S. R. (1988). Bridging the gap: International organizations as organizations. *International Organization, 42*(2), 245–273.

Newcombe, H., Ross, M., & Newcombe, A. G. (1970). United Nations voting patterns. *International Organization, 24*(1), 100–121.

Newcombe, H., Young, C., & Sinaiko, E. (1977). Alternative pasts: A study of weighted voting at the United Nations. *International Organization, 31*(3), 579–586.

Park, S., & Weaver, C. (2012). The anatomy of autonomy: The case of the World Bank. In I. J. E. Oestreich (Ed.), *International organizations as self-directed actors: A framework for analysis*. Routledge.

Parsons, T. (1951). *The social system*. Free Press.

Paybarah, I. (2022). Trump nominee is voted out as head of Inter-American Development Bank. *The Washington Post*. https://www.washingtonpost.com/politics/2022/09/26/trump-nominee-is-voted-out-head-inter-american-development-bank/

Peck, R. (1979). Socialization of permanent representatives in the United Nations: Some evidence. *International Organization, 33*(3), 365–390.

Peters, A., & Peter, S. (2012). International Organizations: Between technocracy and democracy. In B. Fassbender & A. Peters (Eds.), *The Oxford handbook of the history of international law*. Oxford University Press.

Poole, S. M., & Van de Ven, A. (2004). *Handbook of organizational change and innovation*. Oxford University Press.

Posner, E. (2009). Making rules for global finance: Transatlantic regulatory cooperation at the turn of the millennium. *International Organization, 63*(4), 665–699.

Rai, K. B. (1972). Foreign policy and voting in the UN General Assembly. *International Organization, 26*(3), 589–594.

Reinalda, B. (2020). *International secretariats: Two centuries of international civil servants and secretariats*. Routledge.

Reinalda, B., & Verbeek, B. (Eds.). (1998). *Autonomous policy making by international organizations*. Routledge.

Reinalda, B., & Verbeek, B. (Eds.). (2004). *Decision making within international organizations*. Routledge.

Rikhye, I. (1991). Critical elements in determining the suitability of conflict settlement efforts by the United Nations Secretary-General. In L. Kriesberg & S. Thorston (Eds.), *Timing the de-escalation of international conflicts*. Syracuse University Press.

Roehrlich, E. (2022). *Inspectors for peace. A history of the International Atomic Energy Agency*. John Hopkins University Press.

Scheinman, L., & Feld, W. (1972). The European Economic Community and national civil servants of the member states. *International Organization, 26*(1), 121–135.

Selznick, P. (1948). An approach to a theory of organization. *American Sociological Review, 8*, 47–54.

Simon, H. V., Thompson, & Smithburg, D. (1991). *Public administration*. Transaction Publishers.

Steffek, H. (2021). *International organization as technocratic Utopia*. Oxford University Press.

Stiglitz, J. (1998). An agenda for development in the twenty-first century. In B. Pleskovi & J. Stiglitz (Eds.), *Annual World Bank conference on development economics 1997*. World Bank.

Sutterlin, J. (2003). *The United Nations and the maintenance of international security: A challenge to be met*. Praeger.

Traub, J. (2006). *The best intentions: Kofi Annan and the UN in the era of America world power*. Farrar, Straus, and Giroux.

Tsoukas, H., & Chia, R. (2002). On. Organizational becoming: Rethinking organizational change. *Organization Science, 13*(5), 567–582. https://doi.org/10.1287/orsc.13.5.567.7810

Vincent, J. E. (1972). An application of attribute theory to General Assembly voting patterns, and some implications. *International Organization, 26*(3), 551–582.

Voeten, E. (2000). Clashes in the assembly. *International Organization, 54*(2), 185–215.

Weber, M. (1922/2019). *Economy and society. A new translation by K. Tribe*. Harvard University Press.

Weiss, T. G. (1982). International bureaucracy: The myth and reality of the international civil service. *International Affairs, 58*(2), 287–306.

Weiss, T. G., & Jordan, R. S. (1976). Bureaucratic politics and the World Food Conference: The international policy process. *World Politics, 28*(3), 422–439.

Wit, D., Ostovar, A., Bauer, S., & Jinnah, S. (2020). International bureaucracies. In F. Biermann & R. Kim (Eds.), *Architectures of earth system governance: Institutional complexity and structural transformation*. Cambridge University Press. https://doi.org/10.1017/9781108784641.003

Wolf, P. (1973). International organization and attitude change: A re–examination of the functionalist approach. *International Organization, 27*(3), 347–371.

World Bank. (1996). *People and development: Annual meetings address by James D. Wolfensohn, Presidential speech*. World Bank Group. http://documents.worldbank.org/curated/en/135801467993234363

Xu, Y., & Weller, P. (2004). *The governance of world trade: International civil servants and the GATT/WTO*. Edward Elgar.

Zamudio-González, L. (2012). *Introducción al Estudio de las organizaciones internacionales gubernamentales: la pertinencia de una agenda de investigación interdisciplinaria*. Centro de Investigación y Docencia Económica.

CHAPTER 5

Organizations as Machines of Meaning: IGOs as a Result of Bounded Rationality and Meaning Producers

INTRODUCTION

Consider a hypothetical city's fire department, whose primary responsibilities include responding to emergencies and safeguarding both individuals and their properties. This organization must be ready to deploy its resources promptly to address any emergencies effectively. It is also expected to engage in preventative activities, such as educating the public and organizations about potential hazards and aiding in the development of their protective strategies. However, imagine a scenario where, upon receiving a fire alarm, the department must first secure the necessary resources to respond. This entails persuading other individuals and organizations to provide the essential support. Only after acquiring these resources can the department swiftly act to manage the emergency.

The situation described above is like that experienced by the World Health Organization (WHO) (Kelley, 2008). The WHO is an international governmental organization (IGO) that serves as a coordinating agency with states that are primarily responsible for their own policies. As a result, the role of the WHO is limited to coordinating efforts, developing alliances and agreements, providing technical support, and monitoring potential threats. Its budget is primarily funded through mandatory contributions from member states (approximately 16% of the total), with the

© The Author(s), under exclusive license to Springer Nature Switzerland AG 2025
L. Zamudio-González, D. Arellano-Gault, *International Organizational Anarchy*,
https://doi.org/10.1007/978-3-031-82392-3_5

143

remainder coming from voluntary contributions from member states and foundations. It is important to note that a significant portion of these budgets is often earmarked, which reduces the flexibility of the WHO in forecasting its own need for resources. In an emergency, this complex structure of resources and authorities can lead to a high level of uncertainty in the organization.

Managing an IGO and leading it toward its objectives demands an enormous ability to overcome the uncertainty inherent to its design and the vicissitudes that constantly arise. In management terms, these organizations must constantly create and recreate conditions so that, even in the most unusual circumstances, they possess the capacity to act. Health emergencies do indeed arise, and the WHO must act accordingly. However, what does it mean to act? Rushing out as firefighters do, with all the necessary elements at hand to confront an emergency, is an inaccurate metaphor. The design and mandate of the WHO entail coordination capabilities, and the creation of agreements and alliances between governments, their agencies, and other national and international actors such as foundations, research centers, and pharmaceutical companies, among others. Only then can the defined action be considered adequate. In other words, organizations must frequently strive to create the minimum conditions necessary for their actions to be possible, feasible, and legitimate. Coordination is one of the formal obligations required of many IGOs, which, before launching into action, must invest time and resources–often considerable and valuable–to adapt to the preferences and goals of other actors (Schemeil, 2023: 230). The performance of an IGO rarely involves acting as if its goals are exclusively or entirely under its control. Therefore, the assumption that evaluating and judging these organizations by their actions or results is a linear and straightforward process, is a fallacy. In the world of organizational action, and more so in the world of IGOs, the straightest path between the two points often proves to be otherwise.

As discussed in the previous chapter, every organization and every person within it faces a constant battle against uncertainty. There is uncertainty about objectives: What exactly are they? Who decided them and why? How viable or achievable are they? Is there consensus about them both within the organization and among the various stakeholders? There is also uncertainty regarding the means: What means can be used and how effective can they be? Who has the knowledge and capabilities to use and control them? How precise are they and what is their potential to generate undesired consequences? Are they affordable, can they be used immediately, or, on the contrary, does it require time and resources to acquire them? Similarly, there is uncertainty regarding available technologies: Is it precisely known how to use the means and how the means will lead to the objectives? Are such knowledge and skills readily available, or is there a need to research first and develop capabilities? There is also, alas, uncertainty about the social relationships that sustain an organization: Do the involved people cooperate, coordinate, or compete among themselves? Are the links and shared understandings among those who make up the organization accurate, and do they help the objective or the use of the means? Are the levels of understanding among individuals optimal, or do they need to be developed and modified to be useful? Do the people in leadership positions have the capabilities and attributes to achieve coordination and manage conflict productively?

Given the inevitable uncertainties that accompany organizational phenomena, the central question that arises in the study of IGOs is how individuals within these organizations manage the multiple uncertainties they face. Individuals in any organization, including IGOs, create clever and skilled ways to cope with unavoidable uncertainty. It is important to note that the organizational phenomenon is not focused on finding and possessing optimal or ideal levels of information and knowledge to make decisions and take actions with complete certainty. It is irrational and empirically unsustainable to attempt to obtain complete and perfect information in an environment with perennial uncertainty. Instead, it is rational to experiment with and legitimize practices, heuristics, routines, and habits that provide clarity and certainty in facing diverse and situational scenarios. This can be achieved by limiting, structuring, and avoiding uncertainties.

Organizations rely on habits, norms, and institutions to reduce uncertainty among their individuals. Bounded rationality, applicable at both the individual and organizational levels, is a crucial instrument for decision-making and action in an inherently unpredictable environment. Nevertheless, while enabling action, these bounded rationality strategies are also double-edged swords, as they introduce various biases that actors acquire and defend to simplify, delimit, and direct reality.

As discussed in Chap. 2 regarding constructivism, reality is shaped by social interactions and the meanings individuals attribute to these interactions. To act, one must first define and construct a vision of reality that provides a framework for understanding the situation. This process of defining reality involves endowing it with meaning and legitimacy and directing one's actions towards achieving a desired outcome. However, while offering a degree of certainty, using bounded rationality strategies does not guarantee infallible results. The environment is dynamic and can change, leading to the transformation of a previously constructed understanding. Consequently, what was once logical and practical may no longer be sufficient or productive in response to changing environmental conditions.

In the context of this subject, it can be asserted that IGOs not only construct meaning about reality but also utilize strategies based on bounded rationality to overcome uncertainty. This chapter examines these rationalities and endeavors to demonstrate how these entities, cognizant of the intricate and unforeseeable nature of their surroundings, employ bounded rationality strategies to act and make decisions in a world that eludes predictability. By establishing norms, protocols, and institutional frameworks, IGOs strive to confine their range of potential actions, thereby furnishing a structure for comprehending and guiding reality.

These approaches are not free from their own difficulties, and it is evident that they create tensions and challenges for organizations. The bounded rationality tactics, including heuristics, practices, habits, incentives, and other factors, offer an artificially constructed stability by constraining individuals through rules, norms, and processes. Limiting their perspective causes them to focus on certain elements or factors of reality while ignoring others that are deemed unimportant. Consequently, the construction of any process or solution is inherently limited by bounded rationality. IGOs legitimize solutions, communicate processes and norms, and attempt to delimit reality to act. However, by defining reality in a specific and arbitrary way, IGOs face the limitations of their definitions and biases. Moreover, if these definitions become rigid, they can solidify through path dependence. Constructing reality and defining it heuristically also creates conditions for learning, change, innovation, and breaking down past biases.

Adopting a vantage point of bounded rationality and the construction of organizational meaning will enable us to comprehend why functionalist theories that perceive the bureaucratization of IGOs as unavoidable may be inaccurate. Instead of being an inevitable functional destiny, bureaucratization results from heuristics and practices of bounded rationality that crystallize over time. However, empirical research on any organization reveals that its stability stems from solutions, habits, and rules that address powerful and critical uncertainties. These resolutions do not necessarily represent the optimal or ultimate solution, but they provide a sense of logic that allows the organization to function. Changing rules, meanings, and institutions requires the development of new rules, meanings, and habits, as well as the ability to face uncertainties under new heuristics and practices.

As discussed in earlier chapters, the present endeavor commences with a theoretical examination of the relevant literature on International Relations (IR). The aim is to elucidate the strategies of bounded rationality that IGOs employ to fashion their own reality, thus imbuing meaning to their actions and objectives. Following this, scholarly research from the domain of organizational theory is integrated and demonstrated to hold promise for investigating IGOs.

Sensemaking in IGOs: From Constructivism to the Ambition of Global Governance

According to this book, International Relations (IR) predominantly view IGOs as instruments that serve or *must* serve the states, especially the most powerful ones. From an organizational perspective, schematic approaches such as the principal-agent model are provided (Finnemore & Sikkink, 2001; Hawkins, 2004; Oestreich, 2012), which, while helpful, oversimplify organizational dynamics at the meso- and micro-levels, as discussed in the previous chapter. At the same time, numerous IR studies have demonstrated that IGOs use various tactics and strategies to navigate diverse and variable stakeholder contexts. Reducing these complex relationships and interdependencies into principal-agent schemes may be a costly oversimplification.

The absence of an approach that examines organizations as sites for internal negotiation, cooperation, and interaction among actors to define the interests, values, and objectives to be attained is noteworthy. The classical work of Graham Allison (1971) represents a significant advancement in this regard, as he presents analytical lenses for understanding the intersections between political frameworks and the organizational logics of bureaucracies and government agencies. According to Allison, states make decisions and act in fields of interaction characterized by routines, schemes, power games, and strategic games, all under various uncertainties and both domestic and foreign policy agendas. Taking Allison's models into account when studying IGOs is beneficial because it helps to comprehend how decision-making occurs in a world that emphasizes rationality but recognizes that participating in such a game requires navigating organizational and political arenas.

Under Allison's models, it would be much easier for the discipline of IR to incorporate ideas suggesting that International Governmental Organizations (IGOs) require autonomy and discretionary margins to make and act on decisions. IGOs utilize and need organizational tools that allow them to engage in the political-bureaucratic games of the networks they operate within. IGOs deploy not only rational or technical strategies but also capabilities of influence and sense-giving that enable them to frame a highly dynamic reality into one that is more manageable and comprehensible. Organizational identity and culture are also key elements for IGOs. Therefore, it has become increasingly accepted within the discipline to study the tools that actors within IGOs use to cope with internal and external pressures, uncertainty, ambiguity, and competition for resources, among others (Barnett & Coleman, 2005).

IGOs require strategies and tactics to navigate complex and diverse environments. To do so, they construct their reality in a particular way, forming a structured sense and directing their actions based on their perception of reality. Given that knowledge is constructed by subjectivity, and it is actively developed by individuals, groups, and organizations, this discussion can be approached from a constructivist perspective of IR (Brechin & Ness, 2013; Haas, 2002). Individuals interpret and make sense of their social environments through their experiences, social interactions, and cognitive frameworks. Constructivism in sociology and organizational theory posits that social structures, norms, and values are not inherent but are constructed and maintained through the interactions and cultural practices of individuals and groups.

According to Haas (2002), constructivism posits that the constituent elements of international reality are ideological and material. Ideological factors possess normative and instrumental dimensions that convey individual and collective intentionality. As a result, various actors and groups have created meanings to define and act accordingly in the international arena. In this manner, constructivists examine the mechanisms and consequences through which actors, particularly states, interpret the complexity and, from this, how they identify, define, and redefine their interests and identities. From this perspective, IGOs are perceived as bearers of specific sets of norms defined and attended to by states, not only because they align with their rational interests but also because of their capacity to shape identities and establish a logic of appropriateness (Duffield, 2007). The logic of appropriateness serves as the central causal mechanism for constructivism. It implies that different agents not only consider questions of rational calculation but also of feasibility and what, from a particular perspective, can be deemed necessary, right, or reasonable. From this perspective, the framework of identities and norms or the structure of intersubjective meanings in which IGOs participate and around which states develop, and act have significant implications for comprehending international politics (Checkel, 1998; Finnemore & Sikkink, 2001; Hopf, 1998; Wendt, 1992).

According to constructivists, international governance can be understood by examining socialization, persuasion, discourse, and the formation and reproduction of norms (Haas, 2002). These processes are often intricate, involving numerous actors who interact over time and contribute to altering the perceptions of national identity, international agendas, and political dynamics to achieve the interests of various governments (Adler, 1997; Price & Reus-Smit, 1998; Risse et al., 1999; Ruggie, 1998; Wendt, 1998, 1999). Nevertheless, some essential discussions have arisen from this perspective. On the one hand, specific authors contend that adherence to international norms or rules diminishes the discretion of various state actors and compels them to honor their commitments. However, others argue that this view is overly simplistic because it neglects that international norms are derived from social processes, which feature the feedback effects of local agents on global structures (Finnemore & Sikkink, 2001; Kaufmann & Pape, 1999). Moreover, highlighting local cultural variations and elements in the effects of norms disregards the influence or impact of global ideological trends (Finnemore, 1996a, 1996b; Finnemore & Sikkink, 2001).

The conventional notion in the field of IR, which posits that states are the primary actors and IGOs are mere instruments, is called into question using this approach. While constructivism challenges this idea, it also acknowledges the presence of power imbalances in international politics and that IGOs adapt their actions and decisions to these power dynamics. They do so strategically and tactically intend to gain influence. IGOs recognize that they are part of, and sometimes even able to shape, the decision-making arenas of various groups and coalitions. This leads these groups to act under certain constraints and norms that are not only obligatory but also considered fair, reasonable, and legitimate.

The significance of this issue lies in the fact that it presents a contrasting perspective on IGOs as entities capable of devising their procedures to form cognitive frameworks and meanings about the world as well as methods of interacting with actors beyond states. Consequently, although IGOs depend financially or operationally on states, they function independently and prioritize their interests. As a result, IGOs adapt and organize themselves, allocating resources, powers, tactics, and strategies to shape their reality in a specific manner. For instance, as Barnett and Coleman (2005) assert that IGOs employ tactics such as acquiescence, compromise, avoidance, defiance, manipulation, and strategic social construction to secure resources in internal and external pressure situations. However, the range of tactics is extensive and can be expanded to encompass broader models, including bureaucratization and international regimes.

BUREAUCRATIZATION: BETWEEN PATHOLOGIES AND TECHNICAL LEGITIMIZATION

IGOs are complex entities that employ various strategies to promote their goals. Doing so aims to create a more manageable and predictable environment. One of the most effective strategies that IGOs can employ is to establish a permanent bureaucracy that coordinates and mobilizes resources and influence to achieve their desired outcomes technically and instrumentally. However, it is essential to note that IGOs are not limited to this strategy alone, as they can draw upon a range of other strategies to achieve their goals.

The concept of Weberian bureaucracy posits that bureaucracies are the most effective and legitimate form of organization because of their fundamental characteristics, such as order, *impersonalization* of power, the importance of technical expertise, and the ability to establish stable social relations over time. In this regard, IGOs are composed of several bureaucracies. While not everything within an IGO is bureaucratic, decisions made in critical spaces such as Assemblies are carried out by administrative bodies or bureaucracies. This means that bureaucratic bodies are permanent fixtures in administrative and political games within any organization. Executing decisions, as recognized in the literature on international public administration, involves interpreting, influencing, and managing unintended consequences. Bureaucracies possess significant power because of their legal rationality and exclusive expert knowledge (Barnett &

Finnemore, 1999), enabling them to make action possible, operate, and decide in the field while also facing the real consequences of their decisions, which often require quick discretionary responses from bureaucratic bodies. Therefore, it is unsurprising that international bureaucracies have become a fundamental aspect of analyzing IGOs as part of the network of actors on the international stage.

International organizations such as the World Bank (WB) and the International Monetary Fund (IMF) are recognized for their technical sophistication. This recognition serves as a form of legitimization, as these organizations often claim neutrality or technical expertise to navigate politicized contexts. While they must operate politically to survive, their legitimacy is based on the perception of them remaining neutral or technical (Barnett & Finnemore, 1999; Boli & Thomas, 1999; Polzer, 2001). In essence, the defense of neutrality is often a political position.

Many IGOs are legitimized by the argument that they operate under solid technical criteria, with specialists in substantive issues shaping reality. By defining criteria and operationalizing problem-solving, IGOs often significantly impact the lives of individuals and communities. For example, the United Nations High Commissioner for Refugees (UNHCR) operationalizes categories such as *refugee* or *stateless*, which can have concrete consequences for those who do not fit within these definitions. Ultimately, the actions of IGO bureaucracies, such as the UNHCR, can have a significant and tangible impact on the lives of individuals and the situations they aim to assist.

Technical and professional bureaucracies define and shape the means of action to achieve the objectives assigned by the political structures of the organization. Aspects such as measuring the population living in extreme poverty or creating manuals to define conflicts of interest or corruption exemplify their efforts to address international situations (Barnett & Finnemore, 1999).

In discussing the pathologies of bureaucracies in Chap. 4, we have examined the inherently political nature of their technical functions. The fundamental act of categorization and classification is a hallmark of bureaucratic processes and has significant implications for those who are classified. According to the argument of Scott (1998), classification is an exercise of power that disproportionately affects the most vulnerable individuals.

Within IGOs, bureaucratization can have significant consequences for their members. Bureaucratization refers to documenting every decision or action and adhering to pre-established patterns and procedures. How an IGO organizes its internal operations is crucial. While bureaucratization can bring certainty and legitimacy by reducing discretion, it can also create a vicious cycle in which the focus shifts from achieving desired ends to modifying procedures. This phenomenon, known as the *displacement of ends*, was first identified by Merton (1942). In the IR field, the bureaucratization of IGOs is a constant concern, and it is essential to understand and address this issue.

REGIMES OR THE DREAM OF GENERAL LEGITIMATE SHARED RULES

Another way to consider the tactics used by IGOs to shape and influence their environment is through the concept of regime. Krasner (1983: 3) defines regimes as "principles, norms, rules, and decision-making procedures around which actors' expectations converge in a given area of international relations". They are intricate normative systems that require substantial time to develop, disseminate, and gain acceptance (Brechin & Ness, 2013; Barnett & Finnemore, 1999).

Regimes are sets of processes and norms developed, implemented, and sustained by various actors and organizations. These regimes are shaped and reproduced by actors who accept and internalize the logics of these regimes (Anaya-Muñoz, 2017a). The regimes are strengthened and reinforced continuously and progressively, as well as new or modified regimes and socialized norms and values (Brechin & Ness, 2013; Barnett & Finnemore, 1999). According to Scott (2008), IR regimes are institutional processes involving actors, collective activities, discourses, and norms combined to address collective action problems. As a result, the logics of action and organizational meanings, or cognitive and interpretative frameworks, are developed within this network of actors. International regimes are arenas in which organizations confront internal and external pressures, leading to common actions. Organizations within these regimes often share values, interests, visions, and decision-making processes.

Regimes are valuable tools for comprehending the rules, agreements, and procedures that attempt to address specific international issues, such as climate change, environmental degradation, human rights, and the prohibition of torture or chemical weapons (Anaya-Muñoz, 2017b). However, some traditional constraints have also emerged from a governance perspective, including the number of actors and power disparities within regimes. In regimes, decision-making is based on agreements. However, some actors, such as non-governmental organizations (NGOs), certain nation-states, and other groups, may have limited resources to participate and express their goals and interests. Moreover, other actors can influence regimes by providing culturally acceptable rationales and internalized processes within regimes. In this societal model, certain actors may be more affected by material and immaterial factors, values, norms, and other influences (Anaya-Muñoz, 2017b). It is also essential to consider other non-state actors that have gained increased resources and power, as well as IGOs and transnational private companies.

Regimes are inherently dynamic, resulting in interactions within and among them that can change unexpectedly or even in directions not originally intended by their creators. This is because regimes are inherently social and organizational, with members acting differently in response to specific situations (Anaya-Muñoz & Saltalamacchia, 2019). According to Koch and Stetter (2013), there are three metaphors for differentiating the roles of IGOs: as instruments, settings, or as more independent actors. In the context of regimes, IGOs can assume any of these roles, making it challenging to accurately capture the interaction forms.

Compliance with a system involves adhering to its rules and norms, which can be achieved by implementing internal programs or procedures. By following established regulations, individuals and organizations gain legitimacy, providing access to the essential resources necessary for survival.

United Nations (UN) conventions are instruments utilized by regimes within this analytical framework. While their efficacy and impact are subjects of ongoing debate, they play a significant role in the broader process of multilateral governance, fostering social learning and contributing to the development of new conceptual frameworks (Haas, 2002; Hawkins, 2004). Additionally, these conventions produce local effects such as heightened national interest and increased governmental capacity to address political and technical issues through agenda-setting, awareness-raising, broadened participation, monitoring, knowledge generation and dissemination, target-setting, norm development and dissemination, and administrative reforms (Haas, 2002; Risse et al., 1999).

Network Governance: The Deep Web of IGOs, Actors, Governments, Regimes

From an alternative standpoint, grounded in the constructivist theory of IR, the institutional, discursive, and inter-subjective processes of socialization, education, persuasion, and norm internalization, which form the basis of international governance, have been scrutinized (Haas, 2002). Governance emerges as a particularly crucial factor, as it is posited that the development of governance networks transpires through intricate procedures involving numerous actors who interact over time and contribute to altering national interests, identities, and international agendas.

Drawing from a broader perspective, it is apparent that IGOs have come into existence to coordinate these networks, whereby there are entities comprising other organizations (Ahrne & Brunsson, 2008). The authors refer to these as meta-organizations (Benjamin et al., 2011).

The concept of governance is fraught with ambiguity and has been defined in various ways in literature. Kjaer (2004) explores the concept of governance, acknowledging its etymological origin and defining it as guiding or directing. However, there are differing conceptions of the term, such as that by Rosenau (1995): global governance encompasses systems of rules at all levels of social activities–from the family to international organizations– which produce transnational effects. On the other hand, Hyden (1999) posits that governance is primarily about the rules of the game, measures, and regulations for exercising power and resolving conflicts. Furthermore, for governance to be fully understood, it must be examined through an organizational lens to discern the causal chains that supposedly link the form of governance to its effects or outcomes, as Arellano-Gault et al. (2014) suggested.

Kjaer (2004) posits that governance encompasses rules and network-based organizational structures wherein diverse actors collaborate, negotiate, coordinate, and resolve disputes. Moreover, Kjaer (2004) thoroughly examines various definitions, underscoring that they all share the commonality that in the organizational logics of governance, the state is not the primary actor but rather one among a group of actors with differing interests, thereby accentuating the significance of non-governmental organizations, IGOs, and other social and political entities.

In the context of global governance, IGOs and intergovernmental agreements are essential components in comprehending the intricate international landscape. The development and effectiveness of global governance are contingent on the necessity for states to collaborate and tackle shared challenges, formulate agreements, and establish standard rules in the face of globalization and persistent interaction. Organized networks of actors facilitate the negotiation of global agreements to address cross-border issues, such as financial crises, climate change, and pandemics.

Global governance, as both a tool and inter-organizational structure, presents a potential response to transnational problems that cannot be resolved at the national or regional level. Global problems require a myriad of agents and agents to act. Global governance currently involves diverse actors, institutions, and mechanisms. Although IGOs are the quite visible actors in this landscape, it is crucial to recognize the distinctions between different IGOs, as Barnett and Duvall (2005) emphasize, in the configuration of global governance. The range of activities carried out by IGOs is vast, encompassing issues such as mediation, economic development, environmental protection, peace promotion, combating organized crime, and many more. How IGOs interact with other actors and organizations is also highly variable, ranging from dyadic relationships such as collaboration between the UN and the North Atlantic Treaty Organization (NATO) in joint peace process interventions in the Balkans during the 1990s to clusters of non-governmental organizations and actors addressing humanitarian emergencies or multi-actor networks such as the WHO during the COVID-19 pandemic.

Moreover, there are considerable variations in the capacities, performance, and discourses of these organizations. McFarlane (2013) elucidates that in certain regions, there are organizations that concentrate on security issues, such as the African Union. Conversely, other regional organizations, such as the Organization of American States (OAS), adopt a cautious and limited approach to security concerns while acknowledging the principle of non-intervention in internal affairs (Pellicer, 2022). Further, the relationship between regional organizations and the UN presents challenges for authority, legitimacy, and coordination. Regional organizations contend for roles, credit, and resources and possess differing norms, interests, and institutional cultures (McFarlane, 2013; Brechin & Ness, 2013).

Global governance presents both theoretical and practical challenges that must be addressed. A significant aspect of this challenge is the configuration of networks that can create power asymmetries and influence capacities. However, a fundamental issue is how these networks form epistemic communities, construct meaning, and establish frameworks to interpret reality. These frameworks are crucial in shaping how we understand and approach global governance challenges.

Governance actors comprise States, IGOs, NGOs, and social movements, which often result in asymmetries of power owing to differences in resources or influence. Shaffer (2005) examines the World Trade Organization (WTO) as a central actor in global trade governance and how powerful countries such as the United States or large entities like the European Union utilize the organization to exert their influence. Despite being a networked organizational model, certain actors coopt IGOs to promote specific interests and discourses.

Global governance mechanisms are characterized by multiple levels and interactive processes influenced by actors with more significant resources. This influence can lead to biased participation and indirectly limit the choices, actions, and understanding of other actors (Brechin & Ness, 2013; Shaffer, 2005). Consequently, it is crucial to assess the relative direct and indirect participation of affected parties in alternative institutional settings (Shaffer, 2005).

Considering this, questions arise as to whether governance models ensure spaces where actors have agency or whether, in reality, deliberation and the parameters of action and interpretation are limited by the actors who define the discourses, symbols, and beliefs that influence the rest of the nodes in the network. This reflection is particularly relevant for actors, such as NGOs, who often lack sufficient resources compared to transnational corporations. Indeed, scholars such as Aart Scholte (2013) and Lipschutz (2005) have argued that NGOs rarely participate in substantive decision-making and seldom contribute to the structural conditions of the topics in which they participate.

Lipschutz (2005) posits that global governance underpins a *neoliberal governmentality*, wherein states and specific IGOs exert power through discourses and practices that preserve the social and economic order. As a result, despite their critical stance towards these dominant discourses and practices, they inadvertently adopt neoliberal logic without effecting substantial changes in power structures. Therefore, integrating local social actors is crucial for resistance and critique. Social movements have significantly impacted global governance by influencing its development and bringing attention to social and environmental concerns. Although these movements lack clear organizational structures, they have facilitated international cooperation in various sectors. For instance, they have expanded international human rights legislation and advocated environmental protection through conferences and UN-related initiatives (Haas, 2002).

Undoubtedly, specific IGOs possess considerable influence, as Lipschutz (2005) elaborates on the World Economic Forum (WEF) as a case in point. This organization serves as a hegemonic project where business and political leaders convene to deliberate and promote globalization, although its legitimacy and representativeness are subject to question. This raises issues concerning the colonial and postcolonial contexts of governance models. Muppidi (2005) emphasizes the significance of comprehending global realities as socially constructed phenomena and explores the interconnections between global governance, power dynamics, and social relations. Consequently, the process of globalization entails both forces of integration-harmony and disintegration-chaos. Additionally, Roy (1998) contests the constraints of national communities as catalysts for political action, advocating alternative forms of political association that transcend national boundaries.

According to Barnett and Duvall (2005), there are two opposing standpoints regarding the role of IGOs in preserving or diffusing power. The authors argue that both perspectives are valid. Realist and institutionalist theories suggest that IGOs maintain the status quo by being dominated by powerful states. However, critical constructivist theories propose that IGOs can also serve as agents of inclusion and empowerment (Barnett & Duvall, 2005). IGOs utilize both compulsory and institutional power to influence the ability of actors to control their destinies. Compulsory power refers to forcing other actors to comply with specific actions using material and ideational resources. In contrast, institutional power involves guiding, directing, and constraining actions through the rules and procedures of the institutions themselves (Barnett & Duvall, 2005). Additionally, IGOs may diffuse power by being influenced by global cultural values such as democracy and technocracy. However, it is essential to note that these values can work against democracy.

Global governance has a substantial impact on world order. Barnett and Duvall (2005) contend that there are four types of power: coercive, institutional, structural, and productive. Coercive power entails direct control by one entity over the actions and circumstances of another. Institutional power refers to the indirect control of distant actors by institutional rules and procedures. Structural power pertains to the mutual constitution of the capabilities of actors through their structural positions. Finally, productive power focuses on the production of subjects through diffuse social relations.

By contrast, Weiss and Wilkinson (2013) emphasize the significance of recognizing the shortcomings of international organizations and global governance by examining their glaring failures. They illustrate the inability of global humanitarian instruments to safeguard vulnerable populations, pointing to past calamities, such as the Rwandan genocide in 1994 and the Somali Civil War in 1993. Furthermore, the lack of a solid global regulatory framework to oversee financial transactions and innovations has had consequences, as evidenced by the Global Financial Crisis of 2008 (Weiss & Wilkinson, 2013). Frequent breakdowns of governance mechanisms and regulatory regimes are apparent and tangible. Moreover, the rise of potent non-state actors, such as private military companies, terrorist organizations, and credit rating agencies, exemplifies the objectives pursued within networks and the disparities in capabilities and, consequently, influence.

Adler and Bernstein (2005) investigate the interdependent relationship between power, knowledge, and global governance. The authors posit that power is contingent upon knowledge and that its potential for productivity is accompanied by the development of formal and informal institutions that help establish the meanings necessary for effective global governance (Adler & Bernstein, 2005; Barnett & Finnemore, 1999; Haas, 2002). According to the constructivist theory, global governance is supported by material capabilities, knowledge, legitimacy, and equity. Consequently, epistemes and intersubjective knowledge are crucial for shaping actions and constructing social realities.

Episteme is characterized as a form of collective knowledge that encompasses human dispositions and practices and plays a significant role in shaping social reality (Adler & Bernstein, 2005). This shared understanding impacts issues such as authority, epistemic validity, practical reasons, and effective practices in global governance.

After evaluating the insights gained from the review of the challenges faced by IGOs in shaping their highly diverse and chaotic environments, it is essential to incorporate additional organizational tools. What strategies and tactics can IGOs employ to influence their environment, defining and framing it to enable decision-making and action?

BOUNDED RATIONALITY IGOS: HEURISTICS AND TACTICS FOR ACTING AND NOT DYING IN THE ATTEMPT

IGOs consist of individuals who, ideally, work together to achieve common goals. According to Weaver and Nelson (2016: 921), these individuals create psychological and symbolic frameworks that positively and negatively facilitate coordinated action. The authors raise the question of why the UN failed to implement a robust peacekeeping mandate and force that could have prevented the devastating 1994 genocide in Rwanda and why the IMF promoted capital account liberalization in the 1990s despite mounting evidence that such openness led to a damaging financial crisis. According to the authors, the answer lies in individuals within IGOs constructing a framework of norms, beliefs, symbols, and arguments that enables them to act. They interpret their situation and generate centripetal forces, such as agreements and shared values, which shape their understanding of reality and the functioning of the organization. These psychological forces can lead to biases within organizations. Weaver and Nelson argued that the slow response of the UN to the Rwandan genocide in 1994 and its failure to recognize the situation in the Democratic Republic of Congo in 2003 as a post-conflict were critical factors that contributed to the adverse outcomes in both cases. For instance, the UN's delayed recognition of the situation in the Democratic Republic of Congo as post-conflict resulted in ineffective procedures and policies, such as organizing elections, which proved unhelpful in addressing the situation (Weaver & Nelson, 2016: 930).

Organizations ought to be at the center of the study as they are composed of individuals behaving. It is crucial to comprehend their behavior and the rationale behind them. Both psychological and interpersonal elements influence the behavior of individuals, with the latter being the primary focus. The individual serves as a critical organizational variable as its behavior is shaped by interaction with others. This shared understanding enables coordinated and cooperative interactions that are essential for the functioning of organizations.

Positioning individuals as organizational variables entails unleashing Pandora's box of perspectives. Those who view organizations as rational entities with objectives and unified actions may find such a view as a metaphor, illusion, or increasingly untenable assumption (Allison, 1971). In his book, The Administrative Behavior, Simon (1947) sought to understand how individuals, through their actions, form agreements and understandings that enable collective and coordinated efforts. While these agreements and understandings are always incomplete, they are sufficient to transform individuals into cohesive and unified groups.

Metaphors such as *Homo economicus* oversimplify the complex reality of organizational construction. The individuals responsible for building these organizations are limited in their rationality. Moreover, these individuals create organizations that are inherently characterized by bounded rationality. For instance, Simon (1947) critiques traditional management theories, questioning their universal rules, such as the belief that unity of command is always preferable or that clear hierarchies are achievable. The notion that an organization's goals must be universally accepted and understood by all members is another rule that Simon argues is merely an administrative proverb or common-sense view.

Organizations are essentially the result of interactions among individuals. In other words, the specific and contextual behavior of these individuals creates the patterns and stability that characterize all organizations. Simon's response is intriguing because it posits that organizational order emerges from individuals lacking complete information and optimal resources to determine and set collective objectives or goals; they cannot be certain that the means at their disposal are sufficient. Considering these limitations, individuals devise innovative and intelligent persuasion and interaction strategies to circumvent the persistent uncertainty, which they must confront and make decisions.

IGOs: Constructs of Multiple Negotiated Rationalities

Simon formulated a theoretical framework rooted in bounded rationality. This perspective seeks to comprehend the consequences of "the capacity of the human mind for formulating and solving complex problems is very small compared with the size of the problems whose solution is required for objectively rational behavior in the real world" (Simon, 1957: 96). Bounded rationality is based on the premise that individuals pursue ends that synthesize the values, beliefs, and preferences of specific groups and individuals. Achieving these ends always entails interaction with the environment, which is complex because of its size, its countless events, and the presence of other individuals pursuing their own ends. Successfully attaining an end requires navigating the complexities of reality, including changes, transformations, and counterreactions from the environment or other individuals. An ideal human being, modeled on the concept of *Homo economicus*, would possess complete information, allowing them to evaluate all alternatives and their potential outcomes. However, people with inherently incomplete information, doubts, and affectations in preferences and beliefs must make decisions within this context.

Acquiring information and knowledge can be expensive. Developing clear goals based on preferences and beliefs is costly. How much time and resources should be invested to gain comprehensive information about all possible alternatives? The same applies to preferences and beliefs: must they be perfectly ordered and consistent in every situation or scenario? Are there any contradictions, doubts, and paradoxes among preferences and beliefs? How can values be established in a consistent manner given limited resources, such as time? To obtain complete information on values, allocating time, energy, and resources of all kinds is necessary. This implies an almost unlimited supply of energy, especially when decision logic involves risks, as effects are probabilistic, and alternatives are stochastic. The question remains: How are decisions made when the available alternatives are not entirely settled? Part of the answer is that organizations develop a framework of heuristics and assumptions that allows individuals within the organization to make decisions, even when information is incomplete, and their own rationality is bounded. Weaver and Nelson (2016: 930–931) emphasize the importance of the IMF in the oversimplified view of the relationship between credits, debt, and payments and the need for a universally applied model of the effects of fiscal policies and the creation of balance of payment dynamics. This universal model has often been applied with harmful consequences, but it is complicated to change. Limited rationality can create solutions but can also lead to blindness.

Achieving complete rationality is unattainable, as is possessing perfect information. The most effective approach for dealing with these limitations is to seek additional, better information while recognizing that an optimal level will never be reached. In addition to rationalistic strategies, it is necessary to establish conditions for reasonable decision-making and action, such as satisficing, as proposed by Simon (1947). Many decisions and behaviors do not occur under the conditions of complete rationality, and alternative conditions are required. The significant contribution of the concept of bounded rationality lies in revealing how individuals and organizations do not adhere to the logic of complete rationality but instead operate and make decisions under a different dynamic that is equally effective in practical applications. The model followed by individuals is more practical and effective because it acknowledges the real-world conditions in which they make decisions.

Consider the example of the International Commission against Impunity in Guatemala (CICIG), established in 2007. The CICIG, an organization created by the UN, faced disputes over its purpose even before its inception. Its mandate was to effectively confront the pervasive impunity in the country by independently investigating and prosecuting it, but this proved unattainable. The reason for this was that to operate, the CICIG needed to gain approval from the Guatemalan political system, which was sensitive to its sovereignty and insisted on maintaining control over criminal proceedings within its territory. Initially, the CICIG entered the country with the ambiguous objective of combating political impunity and criminality. However, it subsequently evolved into an organization that achieved notable results in the fight against corruption. It was a more concrete objective and one for which it had technical capabilities, including police, legal, and financial resources. In this capacity, the CICIG could carry out independent investigations and collaborate with national authorities as an *accompanying denouncer*, meaning it could not prosecute but could support the prosecuting authorities (Zamudio-González, 2020). The CICIG did not wait for ideal conditions, total resources, or precise agreements. Instead, it defined its role, redefined its approach to action, and interacted with its context to exist and operate effectively.

Since individuals are not entirely rational, organizations are not devoid of irrationality. Organizations are creatures of limited rationality, formed based on feasibility and acceptability, making decisions, and establishing structures for action through agreements that provide stability. However, they always operate under the assumption that their collective actions have meaning and are cognizant that this is a risky endeavor.

IGOs: People Acting, Deciding, and Behaving

Individuals who make up an organization, ranging from high-ranking officials to entry-level employees, typically possess incomplete information, limited resources, and an uncertain outcome from their efforts. Rather than devoting their finite energy and resources to the pursuit of absolute certainty, they smartly establish schemes, rules, and practices that create a sense of order and shared vision. These frameworks for collective action include accepted norms, assumptions, and habits, which are then reinforced and solidified as organizational decision-making and action patterns. Although these rules, heuristics, and practices do not eliminate uncertainty, they provide a means to navigate it reasonably and intelligently. This is achieved through communication, repetition, and legitimization of specific practices, which can potentially become standardized and stabilized within the organization.

Bounded rationality is a double-edged sword that can lead to errors and failures. Organizations can fall into self-deception by assuming that practices or routines that were functional in the past will continue to be effective in different situations in the future. For instance, the UN assumed that the agreement reached between the warring parties in Rwanda in 1994 was sufficient and that genocide was unlikely to occur. However, past practices and routines are not always reliable resources. While organizational order and stability are built and agreed upon, they can also become a source of resilient stability that is no longer effective in a changing environment.

This paradox is inevitable and must be continuously confronted. Organizations exist because they build argumentative pathways that shape and frame complex reality to artificially make it understandable and thus enable action. They simplify to cope with the chaos and unpredictability of the environment. Such simplification is inevitable and necessary. However, it is also a source of self-deception, and resistance to change. It can even lead to myopia, as the organizational agreement that creates a style, an organizational culture, a congruent psychological environment that allows for decision and action, can become a straitjacket, reducing the possibility for the organization to learn and change under certain circumstances to better achieve its objectives.

Rationality, an inherently limited human capability, is susceptible to failure. Although agreements, habits, and customs can assist, they may also have detrimental consequences. However, the logic of bounded rationality is deeply rooted in social dynamics, which results in its persistence. Bounded rationality thrives on the premise of existing rationality and commitment to improve and enhance it continually.

In various ways, people have developed logics of bounded rationality, establishing constant relationships and transactions with their context. This implies a gradual narrowing of the context. Thus, the fundamental strategy is to limit what is observed and abstracted, artificially differentiating it, namely, by focusing. Focusing brings significant benefits: it provides order and perspective. However, much is also lost, as other options, alternatives, and possibilities are no longer considered. In this regard, operations and procedures are developed to cope with this complexity, such as reacting quickly, albeit at the cost of precision; stereotypes are created to generalize and categorize, which facilitates decision-making and action. But by discriminating, other options or alternatives are also lost. Without the ability to narrow down, it would be extremely difficult to handle complexity, and thus, acting and making decisions would also be complex. At the same time, generating reductionist typologies has costs, which again highlights the importance of the transaction as a substantive operation in interaction.

Simon suggested that although attaining optimization in organizational decision-making is a challenging endeavor, its second-best alternative is both feasible and logical: *satisficing*. This concept, a portmanteau of *satisfy* and *suffice*, involves seeking alternatives, new information, and forms of action up to a certain point where a particular aspiration is achieved. This aspiration is learned through habit, practice, and experience and can change over time due to various agreements, accidents, and learning. Organizations make decisions, act, and undergo change every day through this process. Nevertheless, these changes may not always be rational, planned, organic, or uncertain, with implied resistance.

Organizations are inherently limited in their rationality and derive effectiveness from their ability to fulfill their needs. They engage in various actions and then justify and legitimize them, often utilizing heuristics to structure their understanding of reality. Over time, they learn how to navigate their environment, sometimes adapting to existing norms, sometimes challenging them, and sometimes implementing small changes. The International Maritime Organization (IMO) is a prime illustration of these dynamics (Stiles, 2012: 168–194). This IGO, established in 1949, evolved from a narrow regulatory body to a broader institution. Its creation was met with skepticism from states that were hesitant to grant significant enforcement powers to an organization overseeing international maritime activity. However, its inception was motivated by the need to collect and analyze information, maintain records, and assess contexts without conferring enforcement authority.

The IMO was initially established with a small workforce of 300 individuals. However, as maritime activities became increasingly complex and international commercial relations evolved, the need for a more comprehensive regulatory framework became evident. One proposed solution was to create a multilateral regime in which powerful states could develop regulations to benefit all. Rather than striving to acquire greater regulatory authority, the IMO supported this decision. Attempting to force more power on the organization may not be favorably received by other states. Instead, the IMO capitalized on its technical expertise and supportive nature, positioning itself as an organization that provides advice and expert information to countries seeking to enhance their mechanisms.

Over time, the IMO has grappled with whether it should transition into an organization with stronger regulatory, oversight, and punitive capabilities. This shift would require the generation of supervisory rules, necessitating a new role for the organization. The IMO's continued success has been rooted in its limited rationality logic: an organization with technical prestige that prioritizes consensus and the provision of expert advice. However, transitioning into an organization with punitive capabilities and intense supervision would introduce numerous uncertainties regarding internal capabilities and the potential impact on the neutrality and technical reliability of the organization.

Despite these challenges, the IMO has expanded its autonomy, authority, and influence while simultaneously limiting uncertainty. This ensured their stability and continued existence. The IMO's approach to negotiating with its environment has been critical to its success, allowing it to maintain its position as a respected and reliable organization within the maritime community.

IGOs and Their Bounded Rationality Strategies

Bounded rationality theory posits that organizations create psychological environments through rules and mechanisms that influence the behavior of individuals, ultimately shaping the expected behaviors within the organization. These psychological environments are widely recognized as the logics behind the influence of employees. Experienced individuals can discern distinct psychological environments in various organizations. Following this, Simonian machinery is found to be situational and contextual, as each organization is unique and requires the establishment of a specific psychological environment tailored to individuals, their roles, activities, and the conditions they face. Therefore, efficiency criteria vary among organizations, even though they may appear very similar. While this theory can be applied to any organization, its outcomes are highly contextual and dependent on specific circumstances. It is not feasible to create an all-encompassing theory of organizations based on this concept, as each organization possesses unique characteristics and nuances.

The development of a theory grounded in real individuals and their actions results in an organized action theory built upon the premise that individuals possess limited rationality, diverse values and principles, cognitive constraints, and contexts of uncertainty. The focus of this theory is to interpret how these individuals construct coordination schemes that are both effective and efficient despite their bounded rationality. People are inherently impressionable and can quickly adapt to their habits. They may also be docile, accepting external influence because it allows them to navigate an uncertain context. Thus, individuals not only grapple with uncertainty but also employ various psychological and behavioral mechanisms to simplify complex situations, weighing the costs and benefits of such efforts.

Organizations often develop mechanisms to simplify complex situations, as suggested by Luhmann in Chap. 3. By reducing complexity, individuals can focus their attention and employ mental shortcuts, known as heuristics, to achieve their goals and those of the organization. Consequently, organizations are complex systems that integrate multiple logics of influence to create a cohesive psychological environment. This environment capitalizes on the willingness of individuals to be influenced and employs strategies to achieve outcomes through satisfaction and stability. This perspective also calls for reevaluating the concept of organization and its distinction from organizing, an ongoing process that occurs in real time in response to day-to-day circumstances.

Schemeil (2004: 77–89) investigated the World Trade Organization (WTO) and World Meteorological Organization (WMO) for their ability to construct a psychological environment of bounded rationality that facilitates the resolution of highly political and technical issues. These organizations are focused on international cooperation and often face political debates regarding trade and meteorological information. A technical solution alone could lead to significant political disagreements, whereas relying solely on political debate would result in substantial time and friction costs for these regulatory bodies. Instead, both organizations prioritize consensus building, allowing states and companies to resolve their conflicts while balancing the interests of political actors and experts. The former group seeks to understand and acquire technical knowledge, whereas the latter develops negotiation and persuasion skills. Their decision-making processes, for instance, combine voting elements with constraints that facilitate consensus-building through bargaining. These mechanisms have been proven to be effective in achieving satisfactory outcomes.

The concept of *reverse consensus* refers to deciding after some time unless there is clear opposition. According to Schemeil (2004: 87), both organizations have established a middle ground of *consensual knowledge*, which demonstrates their ability to solve problems effectively (Haas, 1990). This suggests close cooperation between the heads of the organization (politicians) and the heads of the bureaucracy (technicians and scientific groups). Organizations with limited rationality can reduce uncertainty by adopting consensual and negotiated organizational forms (in this instance, the complex relationship between politicians and experts and the interactions between states and companies). These forms allow for adjustments and learning, enabling organizations to refine their decision-making processes and improve their effectiveness.

The proposal for a distinct organizational logic, incorporating the concept of bounded rationality within both prescriptive and descriptive organizational theories, is situated in the middle ground. This perspective acknowledges that each organization is unique, and, subsequently, each case must be examined in its specific situation and context. Although general rules exist that can be studied generically, it is crucial to understand organizations within their context. The General Systems Theory discussed in Chap. 3 advocates for a comprehensive theory of organizations; however, the implications of this proposal indicate that it is not feasible to establish such a theory because of the complexity and variability of human decision-making processes. Consequently, when considering the design and reform of organizations, it is essential to recognize limitations to fully comprehend the consequences of change initiatives. These projects invariably impact individuals with bounded rationality in various ways, making it difficult to predict the overall effect of such interventions.

IGOs and Sensemaking: The Important Question Is, What Situation Are We Facing?

IGOs, as entities composed of individuals, confront uncertainty and situational challenges by interpreting reality and seeking to frame it. To do so, they establish a psychological environment, as referred by Simon: This entails creating a shared environment within the organization that sets forth the minimum frameworks and references for individuals to be guided in their everyday actions through values, hierarchies, practices, and routines. Thus, individuals within the organization give significance to their actions; they assume that due to the frameworks provided by the organization, they will possess the knowledge necessary to interpret the situation they are facing. It is crucial to give meaning to reality to act and face uncertainty with confidence, order, and security.

Consider the case of the International Union for Conservation of Nature (IUCN) (Lehmann, 2019: 161). Established in 1948 to promote the conservation of the world's species, the IUCN faced the daunting task of effectively organizing its efforts to achieve this goal. To this end, the organization focused on acquiring knowledge and information to prevent the extinction of species. It is worth noting that the IUCN is an IGO that does not primarily consist of nation-states as its main constituents but derives its legitimacy from a narrative of nature protection. However, since the 1970s, several trends have challenged the *raison d'être* of the organization, such as the growing importance of developing countries that prioritized utilizing natural resources for their development. This shift in perspective fundamentally altered the IUCN's approach, leading to a new organizational sense, discourse, adaptation of norms and expertise, and incorporation of new stakeholders, including indigenous communities, local populations, and NGOs from developed and developing countries. A significant change involved the integration of the private sector (Lehmann, 2019: 168).

Considering the new sustainable development paradigm, it was necessary for an organization focused solely on conservation to collaborate with private companies and adopt a new agenda that emphasized market mechanisms, development standards, and environmental regulations. This shift in the focus of the organization was met with mixed reactions, with some arguing that it allowed the neoliberal agenda to infiltrate the IUCN, transforming conservation from an end to a means subordinate to development and business interests. The international community continues to grapple with the question of the primary focus of the organization on conservation as an end, conservation in service of development, or conservation as part of broader market-driven realities that require normative intervention. The implications of these different perspectives extend to the actions and outcomes of the organization.

The process of creating organizational sensemaking and *sensegiving* has been established and is widely recognized (Rheinhardt & Giola, 2021; Urquhart et al., 2024). Karl Weick initially proposed this theory in the field of organizations, and it has been validated through numerous case studies. This interpretive theory emphasizes the importance of the life experiences and reactions of an individual in shaping their understanding of reality.

According to this logic, individuals first make sense of their situation to comprehend their current circumstances, which in turn directs their preferences and objectives. Identifying the nature of a situation is crucial in the decision-making process. Weick (2001) argues that decision-making and action are intrinsically connected, with action shaping preferences and providing a context for individuals to understand the situation and make informed decisions. In other words, individuals commit to a course of action based on their understanding of the situation and their expectations of the outcome. Therefore, creating organizational sensemaking involves assigning meaning to interpret and understand the reality being faced. This process shapes preferences through action and leads to a commitment to a course of action informed by an understanding of the situation and anticipated outcomes.

Organizations are fundamentally shaped by the way they interpret reality. They comprise individuals who engage in intersubjective logics to establish a commitment to action, cooperation, and coordination. As a result, organizations can generate coordination, cooperation, and sensemaking beyond their own boundaries. For instance, as described by Finnemore (2001), UNESCO has consistently endeavored to promote the idea that states should support the creation of specialized science policy organizations. This global organization has advocated that states bear the responsibility to direct and even control decisions and programs that connect various actors, such as businesses, universities, research centers, and government agencies, intending to foster scientific activities as a critical development component. The success of this sensemaking approach can be seen in the widespread emergence of state bureaucracies specializing in science policy, which view science and scientific knowledge as a public good that must be supported through rational and organized means (Finnemore, 2001: 583).

Sensemaking theory posits a profoundly dynamic and profound process that begins with the premise that individuals within an organization must make sense of their reality to decide and act, with no possibility of doing so without preconceptions of reality. Therefore, making reality intelligible is an internal commitment of individuals and a commitment to the logic of interaction with others. According to Maitlis (2014), a choice is not a calculation based on utility but a matter of social logic. The organization relies on the ability of individuals to make sense of reality and their capacity to support this process.

The European Commission's policies for addressing the challenges and opportunities of Artificial Intelligence (AI) have been structured in a cumulative and negotiated manner, as demonstrated by Malmborg (2022). In response to global fears and uncertainties surrounding AI, the Commission began to make sense of the situation with its first document in 2018, the High-Level Expert Group on Artificial Intelligence (AIHLEG), which proposed Artificial Intelligence for Europe. This document outlines the policy for the EU and its members, leading to the subsequent publication of various policy documents. The Commission emphasizes that AI is an inevitable technology that needs to be harnessed and regulated. Unlike more pessimistic or conservative perspectives, the Commission has utilized rhetoric and arguments to advocate flexible regulations that allow harnessing AI. The organization aims to demonstrate that risks can be confronted and controlled by positioning AI as a risk rather than an uncertainty. The position of the Commission provides an interpretive framework of heuristics and arguments that define what the organization and other agents can do and what is deemed acceptable and legitimate. Essentially, this framework serves as a guide for how to act in the face of a defined situation.

Similarly, it is commonly believed that people make choices and act, yet it is also crucial to recognize that these choices can be difficult to change once made. This is because the reasons for changing them must be explained, which involves altering the existing commitments. Making a choice is not merely an intellectual exercise; it has public consequences that can make it challenging to modify. Commitment, both as a form of interaction and because of that interaction, arises from interpretation and its influence on action. Interpretation shapes actions that align with a particular vision of reality, creating a sense of certainty and stability (Cristofaro, 2022).

For instance, Von Billerbeck (2020) examines how international organizations such as the UN, NATO, and the WB have established strong identities that are flexible enough to enable them to act autonomously in addressing diverse and contradictory issues. This flexibility and ambiguity provide room for maneuver, allowing these organizations to respond to environmental changes and conflicting requests from their member states despite their formal mandates or obligations.

Organizations function as platforms for the practical application of rationalization. However, transforming the logics of visibility, involvement, and cognition into a shared dynamic among numerous individuals within an organization does not occur rationally, linearly, or straightforwardly. The theory of sensemaking assists in comprehending the resilience and resistance to change exhibited by organizations. Individuals not only grasp the objectives of an organization but also engage with them, as this is how they make sense of the world. This can significantly impact how organizations respond to changes and unforeseen circumstances. In terms of meaning, Weick's research delves into the repercussions that arise when a particular meaning within an organization collapses, leading to the entire organizational process descending into chaos. When meaning crumbles, organizations face considerable obstacles, as the prevailing interpretation no longer contributes to the collective understanding of reality. At the same time, the organization must establish a new method of comprehending a specific reality. However, this is a multifaceted process, as transformation and dynamics entail deeply ingrained, solid, and socially accepted logics. As a result, modifications to meaning can be remarkably intricate, influencing the logics of reciprocity and opening the possibility of conflicts and errors.

Sensemaking: The Creation of Solid Organizational Commitments

Sensemaking theory is conceived in organizational studies as a dynamic process through which individuals interpret reality and make it intelligible. However, this flexibility is counterbalanced by the fact that once a sense has been constructed and legitimized, it can become a cage, as it becomes difficult for an individual to change choices, and people may defend and rationalize the sense they have constructed, making the cage even more closed and inflexible.

The interpretation of inflexible and inefficient bureaucracies, as studied under the logic of bureaucratization, is altered by the notion that the very need to interpret and give meaning to reality leads organizational actors to establish a strategy. This strategy provides meaning and makes situations that they face comprehensible. However, these strategies tend to solidify and become inflexible. When the context changes, the established meaning impedes any possibility of adjustment, closing off the possibility of finding new interpretations, even if it means failing or being unable to adapt to new circumstances. The paradox is that flexibility and rigidity are inextricable aspects of organizational phenomena.

Sensemaking entails the construction of an interpretive network in which individuals endeavor to determine the nature of the situation and devise an appropriate (more than the optimal or pure normative) solution. In this process, individuals collaborate, share commitments, and demonstrate their actions and choices. Consequently, questions have emerged concerning the appropriate course of action in particular circumstances, the desired role of each actor, the interpretation of that role, and the comprehension and acceptance of the roles of others.

The Iron Cage that Weber so greatly feared acquires an additional meaning with sensemaking: giving meaning to reality within an organization constructs networks of interpretation and commitment that bind individuals and create specific expectations. These expectations are sustained by rationalizations that gradually solidify until they become a kind of self-fulfilling prophecy. This is the type of paradox that Weick has studied in various organizations: sensemaking brings clarity and dynamism to commitment, enabling organizations to exist. It is also a wager, one that is rationalized and allows for order and reciprocity, but it can be difficult to modify if the utility of the constructed meaning is in question or is outright failing. When change does occur, it is carried out through action, and people bring it to life. However, these actions can turn into a circular cage, as altering interpretation with a different logic of intelligibility is not easy. This is because meaning paradoxically serves to provide coherence and order to the organization, but it can do so through a rigid mechanism. In this way, the possibility that it becomes a specific cage in the face of changes in the context is perpetual.

The UNHCR offers an approximate idea of sensemaking cages. The UNHCR faces constant friction between protecting the rights of refugees and respecting the sovereignty claims of member states. When the organization was established, it was neutral and impartial, intending to protect human rights (Reichel, 2019: 201). However, it has evolved to address various major conflicts worldwide over time. The new organizational sense became humanitarian, aimed at protecting, solving, creating services, adapting flexibly to new conflicts, and establishing mechanisms for lasting solutions. This sensemaking has resulted in diverse consequences. For instance, the neutrality of the organization has been questioned, leading to friction with states that demand sovereignty. One of the fundamental principles in protecting refugees—the principle of non-refoulement—has also been a challenge. As a result, the UNHCR has had to take various actions with political implications and negotiate with various parties about the conflict in Yugoslavia (Goodwin-Gill, 1999). The constant interrelationship between mandates, changing realities, and capabilities always requires adjustments and modifications of sensemaking for organizations to meet the challenges imposed on them. However, organizational sensemaking is never closed, as it provides an understanding of reality. Nevertheless, it can also bias and generate disputes inside and outside the organization to redefine or change this sense.

Sensemaking theories postulate that individuals navigate their environments by interpreting and making sense of various situations. These situations are often complex and uncertain, necessitating the determination of the nature of the situation at hand. To do so, one must ask: What situation are we currently facing? This question makes current reality intelligible. The success of this process can vary, and different approaches to interpreting reality or a particular situation may be more effective in some circumstances than others because they are contingent upon the relationships and interactions a person has with others in various situations.

Sensemaking theories assume that people navigate the world by interpreting situations. Situations are diverse and uncertain for the purposes of acting and making decisions, so the first thing that must be done is to answer the question: What situation am I facing? This question is key to making that reality intelligible. It can be inferred that this way of making reality intelligible can be relatively successful or fail completely. The very ways of interpreting reality or the situation that a person faces change from one situation to another because they depend on the relationships and the people with whom one interacts in different circumstances.

Let us take the example of the apparent self-imposed blindness that the World Bank and the IMF experienced during the economic crisis in Mexico in 1994 and 1995. Woods (2004: 109–122) suggests that a phenomenon known as groupthink (Janis, 1972) distorted the actions of both organizations. Groupthink is a phenomenon that typically occurs in small decision-making groups, especially in situations of stress and the need to reach a consensus to act. In other words, decision-making groups within organizations require cohesion. However, too much cohesion can lead to effects of self-constructed blindness and arrogance, which give people a limited and narrow perspective, allowing them to make biased decisions under the guise of great legitimacy. In this case, the success of the Mexican government in presenting an aggressive and rapid economic reform had many supporters in both organizations. When signs of a crisis deepened in Mexico in 1994, the decision-making groups in both organizations prepared to make sense of the situation. The quickly reached consensus was that a crisis was not very likely, and that the Mexican government could resolve it. There was no further search for additional or contradictory information, nor any search for an alternative plan in case of crisis. In a logic of self-imposed blindness, aiming for a quick consensus that would not disrupt decisions made years earlier, both international organizations might have fallen into groupthink. This ultimately led to an agreed and consensual but incorrect understanding of what was happening. Intelligent, well-prepared, and experienced people in both IGOs created an organizationally sustained veil to avoid understanding other possible interpretations of the situation. Organizational sensemaking is a double-edged sword: without the ability to make sense of the organization's actions, the ability to act would be very limited. But rigid and inflexible organizational sensemaking can lead to various disastrous scenarios, even (or especially) in highly specialized and technical organizations (Arellano-Gault, 2020).

People are not bound to behaviors but rather to relationships, which gives rise to phenomena such as self-reference. In organizations where people are led to believe that the world is a competitive jungle where only the strongest survive, the prediction will become self-fulfilling, as individuals assume that the appropriate way to interact with others is through competition, demonstrating their superiority over others, resulting in some individuals being eliminated while others thrive.

An organization at the other end of the spectrum asserts that the actual situation is cooperation, altruism, coordination, goodwill, rationality, or shared value. However, what is observed is that individuals behave following expectations and are anticipated to cooperate, coordinate, and work together in a manner that is consistent with human values. Consequently, these actions lead to the achievement of the desired organizational outcomes.

The prophecy becomes self-fulfilling because the organization constructs a network of relationships that replicates the dynamics on which shared meaning bases the ability of individuals to rationalize and comprehend reality. How does this operate within the confines of the microprocess? This plays a second theory, the institutionalist theory, which contends that established incentives and values are essential to individuals acting in A or B ways. Incentives are the driving force behind behavior. On the other hand, sensemaking theory reinterprets this by highlighting a micro rather than a macro logic; as individuals interpret reality, they make maintained pledges because they have become public and shared and even defended.

This visibility begins to make certain logics irrevocable; in other words, to avoid inconsistency, the process of binding behaviors and generating expectations starts. From this point of micro-institutionalization, as Weick calls it, these expectations are not merely expectations because they factually end up serving their purpose. The organization is successful because its interpretation of reality is the most appropriate. Given that reality is so dynamic and complex, it is likely that these expectations will be fulfilled, not only because they stem from an interpretation of reality but also because there is a high level of adherence to this logic or a self-fulfilling prophecy.

When establishing an interpretation of reality, one inherently biases it. In other words, commitments are made to a particular way of viewing reality, determining the nature of commitments. Explaining reality is carried out through microscopic, concrete acts enacted in organizational action, as these acts focus solely on specific elements of the interpreted reality while ignoring or disregarding the rest. Thus, only what falls within the framework of the interpretation is observed and considered, as well as what conforms to the logic of intelligibility that shapes the organization. This is advantageous because it allows organizations to become stable and enduring regardless of changes in personnel or positions. Organizations are networks of commitments and interpretations that persist as individuals come and go.

The sensemaking vision aims to comprehend how IGOs make sense of decision-making and actions from the inside. As per Kleine (2013), decision-making within an IGO, such as the European Union (EU), is not solely determined by generalized models or networks of interest. Instead, it involves interpreting the meaning of actions based on formal rules and political logics (Ruano, 2023). Moreover, feasibility generation is required for the decision-making process. Kleine believes informal decision-making processes are crucial for mega IGOs like the EU.

Given that the EU must balance its actions according to the agendas of member states, informal governance practices are critical for accommodating the negotiations and interests of these states (Kleine, 2013: 44). The challenge of creating a coherent sense in the complex political and administrative relationships between the bureaucratic body of the EU, the Commission, and political decision-making bodies, such as the Parliament and the Council of Ministers, has been an ongoing concern since before the official confirmation of the EU (Coombes, 1970). One explanation for how the EU generates meaning within itself and its constituent states is provided by Hooghe (2005). According to Hooghe (2005), as a highly autonomous body of the EU, the European Commission has been able to socialize, albeit with some limitations, the norms and principles of shared action required for inter-state coordination and cooperation (Balint et al., 2008).

The debate on the effectiveness of IGOs can be clarified through examples such as the latter, which emphasize the relationship between performance and resilience. Like any organization, IGOs must balance these two necessities. They must create collective conditions, coordinate and manage conflicts, and assess and mitigate risks as to create chances to achieve their goals. As Schemeil (2023: 60) states, "Suboptimal behavior is inevitable in any organization; (a) to learn from the past; (b) to avoid dead ends; (c) to imagine new goals; (d) to create new norms; and (e) to find new sources of value". In other words, organizations create critical conditions for action and goal achievement. Organizing is a process that is more organic than mechanical (Michaud & Theonig, 2003), involving a balance between *exploitation* which involves continuing to do what has worked in the past, and *exploration* which entails investigating and taking risks with new forms or new ends (March, 1991). An organization that neglects this balance may risk losing meaning, relevance, and legitimacy. Exploitation is a logical source of performance, but it is indispensable for organizations to adapt and obtain resilience. The ability of organizations to manage and balance these two contradictory forces is known as ambidexterity (O'Reilly & Tushman, 2013).

One of the conventional approaches that organizations employ is to allocate adequate slack spaces, which provides the flexibility to maneuver in terms of resources and strategies to modify or transform activities that may have been traditionally performed but may no longer be as crucial given alterations in the environment. The availability of these strategic resources and capabilities enables IGOs to adopt various strategies to navigate a complex environment with multiple stakeholders and potential conflicts. The ability to innovate and adapt to turbulent conditions is an essential organizational skill critical to success in a rapidly changing world.

An instance of the most extreme forms of strategic adaptation, where structures, organizational actors, and organizational senses intertwine, resulting in slack and space for ambidexterity, can be observed in the World Trade Organization (WTO). As a highly technical yet deeply heterogeneous political organization, negotiations are often intense and likely to fail because of the diversity of interests of the states. However, the organizational sense has proved crucial: negotiation is essential, stakeholder participation is indispensable, but it is equally important to bring the potential conflict of positions to a successful conclusion.

The World Trade Organization (WTO) has developed a unique combination of formal and informal decision-making processes (Jones, 2009: 85). One such process is the green room, a room painted green where members of the Council Chair may invite delegates to discuss delicate matters in an informal setting. Following these discussions, the General Council may then formalize various decisions. The relationship between formal and informal structures extends beyond the green room, as the General Council has multiple roles in managing organizational slack and responding to diverse challenges and objectives. The Trade Review Board can provide advice on various discussions. At the same time, as the Dispute Settlement Body, it acts as an arbiter, combining the two different logics of reviewing and judging situations. The Heads of Delegations (HODs) also provide a semi-formal platform for states to test and analyze their divergences, debates, and arguments in an open and friendly environment (Schemeil, 2023: 92).

The development of an organizational structure allows for the integration of seemingly irrational issues, as the absence of informal spaces undermines the legitimacy and logic necessary to achieve organizational goals in the face of diversity and contradictions among stakeholders. However, the dual channels of decision-making and participation, both formal and informal, can result in inefficiencies when viewed from a narrow perspective. Nevertheless, these inefficiencies must be considered within the context of the concrete conditions of negotiation and participation required for the existence of the organization. The ability of the World Trade Organization to execute and perform effectively in achieving its objectives requires the creation of conditions through bold schemes that combine formal and informal structures and processes.

However, it is crucial to acknowledge that once specific organizational meanings solidify, altering them can be challenging. Organizations generally tend to resist and maintain the established structure of interpretations, expectations, and commitments that have been effective for them thus far. This process can become dramatic. Weick has provided several examples where contextual change is sudden, and individuals cannot break free from the prevailing network of interpretations. Although this network allows individuals to interact with reality successfully, when the change in context is significant, it can become problematic because it requires the rapid reconstruction of a new meaning. Weick describes the process by which the old meaning quickly ceases to function and collapses, resulting in the collapse of all expectations, commitments, and rationalizations.

The degree of rigidity in sensemaking may not be as pronounced but remains equally significant. The Gender Equity Unit of the International Organization for Migration (IOM) presents a noteworthy case study (Mahon, 2020: 89); as an organization dedicated to *managing migration*, IOM grapples by balancing the welfare of migrants and the role of the countries that fund it. Consequently, some states have impeded the formation of robust administrative structures for IOM at its headquarters. However, the organization has managed to maintain its operations through its field units. In 1997, a gender equity unit was established, embracing the gender equity agenda. The process of integrating this new organizational sense has been long and challenging. The priority has crystallized in the issue of human trafficking; as a result, much of the agenda of the gender unit has been focused on this area. This has left the unit largely dependent on the dominant organizational sense that ensures the support of countries that finance the organization (Mahon, 2020: 92). Sensemaking has practical implications for organizations and their capacity for adaptation and change.

But even organizational change is deeply affected by organizational sensemaking. In the end, all organizations claim, sooner or later, that they reform and change. But what is organizational change? The organizational literature is extensive and clearly shows how organizations also use change to legitimize themselves. Change and reform are always viewed as positive projects, projects that are expected and generally seen in a favorable light due to the positive expectations they generate. However, they are also complex projects that are ultimately difficult to conclude and evaluate objectively. Yet, it is rare for reformers to lose, since these processes take time, once a reform proposal is reaching its end, a new initiative or idea for change emerges (Brunsson, 2009). And the cycle of hope is renewed (Brunsson, 2006). Permanent change seems, rather, to be the constant.

The UN is known for its ongoing and perpetual cycles of reform, characterized by complexity and permanence (Luck, 2003: 2). The issue of UN reform has persisted for many years, and it has been a topic of discussion since 1947 when the United States Congress called for reforms to the financing and administrative systems of the organization (Luck, 2003: 2).

Congress identified several problems at that time, including overlapping responsibilities, weak coordination, the proliferation of mandates and programs, and generous staff compensation (Luck, 2003: 2). However, any proposals for change put forward by a member or group of states are often met with divergent interests or perspectives (Luck, 2003: 2).

Between 1995 and 1997, the UN General Assembly was preoccupied with numerous proposals to enhance the overall efficiency of an organization by altering its structure, decision-making processes, operational methods, financing, and staffing. Despite the various suggestions, stakeholders were not unanimous regarding these reforms. Some actors, for instance, did not consider reducing the scale of contributions as an effective means of improving the efficiency of an organization. Furthermore, it remains uncertain whether the UN's mandate, priorities, and core functions should be altered in addition to modifying administration or funding. These issues were the subject of much debate and discussion during this period (Luck, 2003: 4).

According to Luck, it is necessary to understand the political nature of the multiple and diverse reform efforts of the UN:

> Within the UN context, even seemingly routine matters of administration, personnel, and finance have a way of assuming a political character, should one group of Member States or another come to perceive potential slights to their interest, stature, or priorities. To put crudely, much of the reform debate, at its basest level, is a struggle over political turf, over who is perceived to gain or lose influence within the Organization if the proposed changes are enacted or implemented. Even if the goal of a particular proposal was to enhance efficiency, to some it mattered a good deal in which priority areas these efficiencies were to be carried out, who headed those programs, and whether the balance of attention and resources vis a vis other priorities would be affected. And, at times of relatively low trust between different groups of Member States, in assessing an initiative it mattered considerably to other Member States who was putting forward the proposal and what each group might be expected to gain or lose from it. (Luck, 2003: 5)

During the first three decades of the UN's existence, the question of reform centered on numerical considerations. The central issues were the appropriate size of the Security Council and the Economic and Social Council (ECOSOC), the requisite geographic and ideological balance, and the decision-making process. With the wave of decolonization during the 1950s and the 1960s, the number of UN member states increased from 51 in 1945 to 114 in 1963, with more than half of the members hailing from Asia or Africa, regions previously underrepresented in the structure of the organization. As a result, debates and reforms to increase the number of states in the Security Council and ECOSOC were initiated. The 18th General Assembly session in 1963 proved pivotal, as two resolutions (1990 XVIII and 1991 XVIII) were passed to amend the Charter. The first resolution aimed to ensure greater representation of Asian and African states, while the second resolution expanded the membership of the Security Council from 11 to 15, with 10 non-permanent members distributed according to geographic regions and increased the size of ECOSOC from 18 to 27.

None of the five permanent members of the UN Security Council (UNSC) voted in favor of amendments during the General Assembly, although they refrained from exercising their veto power. Remarkably, two-thirds of the members of the organization approved the amendment, and 76 ratifications were promptly secured. Additionally, the UN grappled with financial constraints due to overdue contributions from permanent members and substantial expenses associated with peacekeeping operations in Congo. The politically costly decision to abstain from vetoing the amendment was further compounded by the ideological struggle to win over newly independent states.

During the 1970s, the ECOSOC expanded from 27 to 54 members based on the proportional principle of growth within the UN. At the time, the UN had 135 members (1973). The primary motivation behind this expansion was to promote justice rather than efficiency (Luck, 2003: 10).

In the 1970s, discussions about reforming ECOSOC extended beyond the number of members to encompass the working methods and coordination capacity of the organization. Due to the lack of development results and 2/3 of the resources of the organization being spent in this area, ECOSOC needed to be revitalized. A group of experts appointed by the Secretary-General and mandated by the General Assembly produced a report with a series of proposals to make the organization more effective. These proposals included small negotiating groups, permanent consultations with member states, further expansion of the number of members, and greater control of specialized agencies. However, the powers of the organization were not expanded; its decisions remained recommendations, it continued to respond politically to the General Assembly, and the specialized agencies and the Bretton Woods institutions (WB and IMF) retained their membership, charters, resources, and governing bodies.

Organizational meaning can produce both rigidity and arguments for change. Weick posits that highly resilient organizations such as high-reliability organizations (HROs) are vital in the face of context-level solid change processes. For example, these organizations construct meaning differently by treating errors as a value in their effects. In HROs, there is great respect for operations, and building organizations that understand the difference between decision-making at the top level and reporting allow for flexibility in the operation, where rules can be bent, and mistakes resolved unexpectedly. This logic is similar to Kleine's (2013: ix) proposal to study the concrete decision-making processes of the EU and the European Commission, both formal and informal, as it is in these informal processes that the meaning of a complex organization like the EU becomes feasible.

Suppose organizations are convinced to embrace values such as the acceptance of error ex ante and recognize that errors are inevitable. In that case, it may be possible to acknowledge that numerous decisions, actions, and interpretations occur at operational levels rather than at the highest decision-making levels. By preparing for surprises, accidents, and errors, organizational change may become manageable if the logic of the context is modified.

Weick's long-standing approach to high-reliability organizing (HROs) has garnered significant interest among numerous organizations. However, implementing this approach is challenging, as many organizational practices prioritize decision-making over operational efficiency and often punish errors. This error-blame culture makes it challenging to consider HROs as a viable option. Nonetheless, overcoming these challenges by fostering commitment and aligning expectations and behaviors among team members is not entirely impossible. A key aspect of sensemaking in HROs is analyzing how interpretations are constructed through the collective behavior of individuals. What may seem like a rational decision, such as a national plan, is a means of making sense of a complex situation. By binding people together through shared expectations and behaviors, HROs can create stability and certainty, even at a high cost.

CONCLUDING REMARKS

Organizations are often viewed as unified entities that function like rational actors and evaluate and make decisions (Allison & Halpering, 1972). Nonetheless, the reality is that they are complex arenas in which coalitions and groups with varying objectives and intentions engage in alliances and conflicts (Cyert & March, 1992). In these settings, diverse groups and individuals make multiple decisions through meaning-making. The complexity of IGOs is heightened by individuals with their own dynamics and a loosely coupled set of organizations, states, and other actors (Weick, 1979).

Why are IGOs perceived as mechanical instruments despite their inherently social nature? This question arises because of their dependence on context, in which inter-organizational relationships are crucial. IGOs are built on the interdependence and interaction of groups and coalitions, requiring communication, stabilization, and sustaining reciprocity in cooperation, as well as, at times, conflictive and competitive dynamics. Since its inception, this paradox has haunted Organization Theory: organizations manifest human behavior (Simon, 1947), which implies complex, uncertain, and dynamic relationships and interactions. A clear example of the uncertainty inherent in organizations is the fact that different parts of the IGO may be unaware of the actions of others, generating unforeseen effects. Thus, the notion of an IGO as a controlled and obedient instrument vanishes in practice, as recognizing interactions and interdependencies among a series of diverse organizations is necessary to speak of an IGO.

Organizations, as social constructs, serve to connect, bind, and relate individuals, thereby influencing and empowering them through the logics of interdependence. Interdependence can be structured and designed to foster constant reciprocity. To achieve this, organizations design behavior through hierarchies, modes of communication, and mechanisms that connect people through rules and norms. These organizational structures are handy for managing uncertainty and facilitating cooperation, thus providing a stable framework for unforeseen changes.

Organizations typically establish routines to maintain stability in relationships and interactions that function effectively in stable environments. However, when stability is jeopardized, these organizations possess the ability to respond and preserve a certain level of stability amid chaos while simultaneously rebuilding their capabilities to return to their perceived state of normalcy. Structuring enables individuals to proactively cope with uncertainty by engaging in sensemaking, which involves making sense of reality and injecting meaning into it to render it comprehensible and manageable, particularly in dynamic and unstable situations.

While there are advantages to establishing a structure through rules, routines, and organizational structures, it can also lead to overstabilization. The meaning built and solidified through daily interactions becomes resistant to change, making it challenging to adjust to new circumstances. Communication, interaction skills, rules, hierarchy, and leadership are essential in routine and non-routine situations. However, it is important to note that introducing order through meaning does not guarantee long-term stability, as it must be continually reproduced and reconstructed. The crucial question in this situation is what happens when the overstabilization of organizational meaning impedes the ability to adapt to new or changing situations. How can this be recognized in an IGO?

It is evident that IGOs, like any other entity, rely not only on the legitimacy conferred by their internal stakeholders but also possess the capacity to establish frameworks and meanings that legitimize their actions within the organization. An IGO bolsters its actions by creating meaning that reinforces its identity and enables it to effectively counter external attacks or criticism.

The apparent incongruity between the more rigid missions or regulations and the often-frenetic speed and operational complexity that IGOs face is intelligently resolved through sensemaking processes that legitimize specific actions and generate the capacity for action. As Von Billerbeck (2020: 215–216) demonstrates, the contradictions that individuals in IGOs experience in their actions do not paralyze action, but sensemaking enables them to interpret, decide, and act. However, this does not occur without grappling with contradictions and criticisms in the face of possible incongruities that other social or political agents may perceive between the normative definitions of the ends and the concrete tactics implemented by IGOs.

Ultimately, the process of sensemaking within organizations is not without consequences. To some extent, it also involves the imposition (or attempt to impose) of specific values and standards on others to guide their actions. The case of international organizations that have positioned themselves as highly technical is particularly relevant. Broome et al. (2018) examine the adverse and limited outcomes that can result when technical and neutral IGOs introduce dynamics such as benchmarks and *best practices*. The authors use the WB's Ease of Doing Business ranking and OECD's Foreign Direct Investment Regulatory Restrictiveness index as examples. According to the authors, these seemingly objective and neutral tools oversimplify the complex realities of the country and regional performance by subtly promoting the idea that there are *ideal* and *pathological* practices and rankings are purely technical matters.

In summary, IGOs establish structure and problem-solving through symbols, agreements, negotiations, and a psychological environment that fosters congruity and order. However, this approach can be inflexible and rigid in the face of new challenges.

REFERENCES

Aart Scholte, J. (2013). Civil Society and NGOs. In T. Weiss & R. Wilkinson (Eds.), *International Organization and Global Governance*. Routledge.

Adler, E. (1997). Seizing the Middle Ground: Constructivism in World Politics. *European Journal in International Relations, 3*, 319–363.

Adler, E., & Bernstein, S. (2005). Knowledge in Power: The Epistemic Construction of Global Governance. In M. Barnett & R. Duvall (Eds.), *Power in Global Governance* (pp. 294–318). Cambridge University Press.

Ahrne, G., & Brunsson, N. (2008). *Meta Organizations*. Edward Elgar Publishing.

Allison, G. (1971). *Essence of Decision*. Little. Brown.

Allison, G. T., & Halpering, M. H. (1972). Bureaucratic Politics: A Paradigm and Some Policy Implications. *World Politics, 24*, 40–79.

Anaya-Muñoz, A. (2017a). Los regímenes internacionales de derechos humanos: la brecha entre compromiso y cumplimiento. *Revista del Instituto de Ciencias Jurídicas de Puebla, 1*(40), 151–181.

Anaya-Muñoz, A. (2017b). International Human Rights Regimes: A Matrix for Analysis and Classification. *Sur. International Journal on Human Rights, 14*(25), 171–188.

Anaya-Muñoz, A., & Saltalamacchia, N. (2019). Factors Blocking the Compliance with International Human Rights Norms in Mexico. In A. Anaya & B. Frey (Eds.), *Mexico's Human Rights Crisis* (pp. 207–226). University of Pennsylvania Press.

Arellano-Gault, D. (2020). *Las trampas de la decisión*. Fontamara.

Arellano-Gault, D., Sánchez, J., & Retana, B. (2014). ¿Uno o varios tipos de gobernanza? Más allá de la gobernanza como moda: la prueba del tránsito organizacional. *Cuadernos de Gobierno y Administración Pública, 1*(2), 9–29.

Balint, T., Bauer, M., & Knill, C. (2008). Bureaucratic Change in the European Administrative Space: The Case of the European Commission. *West European Politics, 4*, 677–700.

Barnett, M., & Coleman, L. (2005). Designing Police: Interpol and the Study of Change in International Organizations. *International Studies Quarterly, 49*(4), 593–619.

Barnett, M., & Duvall, R. (2005). *Power in Global Governance*. In M. Barnett & R. Duvall (Eds.), *Power in Global Governance*. Cambridge University Press.

Barnett, M. N., & Finnemore, M. (1999). The Politics, Power, and Pathologies of International Organizations. *International Organization, 53*(4), 699–732.

Benjamin, C., Brechin, S., & Thoms, C. (2011). Networking Nature: Network Forms of Organizing in Environmental Governance. *Journal of Natural Resources Policy Research, 3*(3).

Boli, J., & Thomas, G. (Eds.). (1999). *Constructing World Culture: International Nongovernmental Organizations Since 1875*. Stanford University Press.

Brechin, S. R., & Ness, G. D. (2013). Looking Back at the Gap: International Organizations as Organizations Twenty-five Years Later. *Journal of International Organizations Studies, 4*(1), 14–39.

Broome, A. A., Homolar, A., & Kranke, M. (2018). Bad Science: International Organizations and the Indirect Power of Global Benchmarking. *European Journal of International Relations, 24*(3), 514–539. https://doi.org/10.1177/135406617719320

Brunsson, N. (2006). *Mechanisms of Hope. Maintaining the Dream of the Rational Organization.* Copenhagen Business School Press.

Brunsson, N. (2009). *Reform as Routine: Organizational Change and Stability in the Modern World.* Oxford University Press.

Checkel, J. (1998). The Constructivist Turn in International Relations Theory. *World Politics, 50*(2), 324–348.

Coombes, D. (1970). *Politics and Bureaucracy in the European Community: A Portrait of the Commission of the E.E.C.* Allen & Unwin.

Cristofaro, M. (2022). Organizational Sensemaking: A Systematic Review and a Co-evolutionary Model. *European Management Journal, 40*(3), 393–405. https://doi.org/10.1016/j.emj.2021.07.003

Cyert, R. J., & March, J. (1992). *A Behavioral Theory of the Firm.* Wiley-Blackwell.

Duffield, J. (2007). What Are International Institutions? *International Studies Review, 9*(1), 1–22.

Finnemore, M. (1996a). *National Interests in International Society.* Cornell Univ. Press.

Finnemore, M. (1996b). Norms, Culture, and World Politics: Insights from Sociology's Institutionalism. *International Organization, 50*, 325–347.

Finnemore, M. (2001). International Organizations as Teachers of Norms: The United Nations Educational, Scientific, and Cultural Organization and Science Policy. *International Organization, 47*(4), 565–597.

Finnemore, M., & Sikkink, K. (2001). Taking Stock: The Constructivist Research Program in International Relations and Comparative Politics. *Annual Review of Political Science, 4*(1), 391–416.

Goodwin-Gill, G. (1999). Refugee Identity and Protection's Fading Prospect. In F. Nicholson & P. Twomey (Eds.), *Refugee Rights and Realities: Evolving International Concepts and Regimes.* Cambridge University Press.

Haas, P. M. (1990). *When Knowledge Is Power: Three Models of Change in International Organizations.* University of California Press.

Haas, P. M. (2002). UN Conferences and Constructivist Governance of the Environment. *Global Governance, 8*(1), 73–92.

Hawkins, D. G. (2004). Explaining Costly International Institutions: Persuasion and Enforceable Human Rights Norms. *International Studies Quarterly, 48*(4), 779–804.

Hooghe, L. (2005). Several Roads Lead to International Norms, But Few via International Socialization: A Case Study of the European Commission. *International Organization, 59*(4), 861–898. https://doi.org/10.1017/S0020818305050307

Hopf, T. (1998). The Promise of Constructivism in International Relations Theory. *International Security, 23*(1), 171–200.

Hyden, G. (1999). Governance and the Reconstitution of Political Order. In R. Joseph (Ed.), *State, Conflict, and Democracy in Africa*. Lynne Rienner.

Janis, I. (1972). *Victims of Groupthink: A Psychological Study of Foreign-policy Decisions and Fiascoes*. Houghton Mifflin.

Jones, K. (2009). *The Doha Blues: Institutional Crisis and Reform in the WTO*. Oxford University Press.

Kaufmann, C., & Pape, R. (1999). Explaining Costly International Moral Action: Britain's Sixtyyear Campaign Against the Atlantic Slave Trade. *International Organization, 53*, 631–668.

Kelley, L. (2008). *The World Health Organization (WHO)*. Routledge.

Kjaer, A. M. (2004). *Governance*. Polity Press.

Kleine, M. (2013). *Informal Governance in the European Union. How Governments Make International Organizations Work*. Cornell University Press.

Koch, M., & Stetter, S. (2013). Sociological Perspectives on International Organizations and the Construction of Global Political Order—An Introduction. *Journal of International Organizations Studies, 4*(1), 4–13.

Krasner, S. (1983). *International Regimes*. Cornell Univ. Press.

Lehmann, I. (2019). From Noah's Ark to Nature. In K. Dingwerth, A. Witt, I. Lehmann, E. Reichel, & T. Weise (Eds.), *International Organizations Under Pressure. Legitimating Global Governance in Changing Times*. Oxford University Press.

Lipschutz, R. (2005). Global Civil Society and Global Governmentality: Or the Search for Politics and the State Amidst the Capillaries of Social Power. In M. Barnett & R. Duvall (Eds.), *Power in Global Governance*. Cambridge University Press.

Luck, E. (2003). Reforming the United Nations: Lessons from a History in Progress. *International Relations Studies and the United Nations Occasional Papers, 1*. ACUNS.

Mahon, R. (2020). Transnational Care Chains as Seen by the OECD, the World Bank, and the IOM. In D. Dolowitz, M. Hadjiisky, & R. Normand (Eds.), *Shaping Policy Agendas: The Micro-Politics of Economic International Organizations*. Edward Elgar Publishing.

Maitlis, S. (2014). Sensemaking in Organizations: Taking Stock and Moving Forward. *Academy of Management Annals, 8*(1). https://doi.org/10.546 5/19416520.2014.873177

Malmborg, F. (2022). Narrative Dynamics in European Commission AI Policy. Sensemaking, Agency Construction, and Anchoring. *Review of Policy Research, 40*, 757–780. https://doi.org/10.1111/ropr.12529

March, J. (1991). Exploration and Exploitation in Organizational Learning. *Organization Science, 2*, 71–87.

McFarlane, N. (2013). Regional Organizations and Global Security Governance. In T. Weiss & R. Wilkinson (Eds.), *International Organization and Global Governance*. Routledge.

Merton, R. (1942). *Social Theory and Social Structure*. Free Press.

Michaud, D., & Thoenig, J. (2003). *Making Strategy and Organization Compatible*. Palgrave Macmillan.

Muppidi, H. (2005). Colonial and Postcolonial Global Governance. In M. Barnett & R. Duvall (Eds.), *Power in Global Governance*. Cambridge University Press.

O'Reilly, C., & Tushman, M. (2013). Organizational Ambidexterity: Past, Present and Future. *Academy of Management Perspectives, 27*, 324–338.

Oestreich, J. (2012). *International Organizations as Self-Directed Actors: A Framework for Analysis*. Routledge.

Pellicer, O. (2022). La OEA a los 50 años ¿hacia su fortalecimiento? *Política Exterior 54*, 19–36.

Polzer, T. (2001) Corruption: Deconstructing the World Bank Discourse. *Working Paper* No. 01-18, Development Studies Institute, LSE.

Price, R., & Reus-Smit, C. (1998). Dangerous Liaisons? Critical International Relations Theory and Constructivism. *European Journal in International Relations, 4*, 259–294.

Reichel, E. (2019). Navigating Between Refugee Protection and State Sovereignty. In K. Dingwerth, A. Witt, I. Lehmann, E. Reichel, & T. Weise (Eds.), *International Organizations Under Pressure. Legitimating Global Governance in Changing Times*. Oxford University Press.

Rheinhardt, A., & Giola, D. (2021). Upside-down Organizational Change: Sensemaking, Sensegiving and the New Generation. In M. S. Poole & A. H. Van de Ven (Eds.), *The Oxford Handbook of Organizational Change and Innovation*. Oxford University Press. https://doi.org/10.1093/oxfordhb/9780198845973.013.4

Risse, T., Topp, S., & Sikkink, K. (1999). *The Power of Human Rights. International Norms and Domestic Change*. Cambridge University Press.

Rosenau, J. (1995). Governance in the 21st Century. *Global Governance, 1*, 13–44.

Roy, A. (1998). The End of Imagination. *Frontline (India), XV*(16).

Ruano, L. (2023). *La Unión Europea como potencia normativa: visiones desde Latinoamérica*. Documentos de Trabajo, 86. Madrid: Fundación Carolina. https://doi.org/10.33960/issn-e.1885-9119

Ruggie, J. (1998). What Makes the World Hang Together? Neo-utilitarianism and the Social Constructivist Challenge. *International Organization, 52*, 855–887.

Schemeil, Y. (2004). Expertise and Political Competence. Consensus Making Within the World Trade Organization and the World Meteorological Organization. In B. Reinalda & B. Verbeek (Eds.), *Decision Making Within International Organizations*. Routledge.

Schemeil, Y. (2023). *The Making of the World. How International Organizations Shape Our Future*. Verlag Barbara Budrich.

Scott, J. (1998). *Seeing Like a State: How Certain Schemes to Improve the Human Condition Have Failed*. Yale University Press.

Scott, R. (2008). *Institutions and Organizations* (3rd ed.). Sage.

Shaffer, G. (2005). Power, Governance, and the WTO: A Comparative Institutional Approach. In M. Barnett & R. Duvall (Eds.), *Power in Global Governance*. Cambridge University Press.

Simon, H. (1947). *Administrative Behavior*. Macmillan.

Simon, H. (1957). *Models of Man: Social and Rational*. John Wiley & Sons.

Stiles, K. (2012). Disaggregating Delegation. Multiple Agents in the International Maritime Safety Regime. In J. Oestreich (Ed.), *International Organizations as Self-Directed Actors: A Framework for Analysis* (pp. 168–194). Routledge.

Urquhart, C., Cheuk, B., Lam, L., & Snowden, D. (2024). Sense-making, Sensemaking and Sense Making—A Systematic Review and Meta-synthesis of Literature in Information Science and Education: An Annual Review of Information Science and Technology (ARIST) Paper. *Journal of the Association for Information Science and Technology*. https://doi.org/10.1002/asi.24866

Von Billerbeck, S. (2020). "Mirror, mirror on the wall:" Self-legitimation by International Organizations. *International Studies Quarterly, 64*(1), 207–219.

Weaver, C., & Nelson, S. (2016). Organizational Culture. In J. Cogan, I. Hurd, & I. Johnstone (Eds.), *The Oxford Handbook of International Organizations*. Oxford University Press.

Weick, K. (1979). *The Social Psychology of Organizing*. McGraw Hill.

Weick, K. (2001). *Making Sense of the Organization*. Blackwell.

Weiss, T., & Wilkinson, R. (2013). International Organization and Global Governance. What Matters Why. In T. Weiss & R. Wilkinson (Eds.), *International Organization and Global Governance*. Routledge.

Wendt, A. (1992). Anarchy is What States Make of it. The Social Construction of Power Politics. *International Organization, 46*(2), 391–425.

Wendt, A. (1998). Constitution and Causation in International Relations. *Review of International Studies, 24*(4), 101–117.

Wendt, A. (1999). *Social Theory of International Relations*. Cambridge Univ. Press.

Woods, N. (2004). Groupthink. The IMF, the World Bank and Decision-making Regarding the 1994 Mexican Crisis. In B. Reinalda & B. Verbeek (Eds.), *Decision Making Within International Organizations* (pp. 109–122). Routledge.

Zamudio-González, L. (2020). *International Intervention Instruments Against Corruption in Central America. Governance, Development, and Social Inclusion in Latin America*. Palgrave Pivot. https://doi.org/10.1007/978-3-030-40878-7_6

CHAPTER 6

Organizations and Institutions: IGOs Decisions, Adjustments, and Transformation Within the Context of the Technical-Political Discourse in the International Arena

INTRODUCTION

Institutions play a crucial role in comprehending the operations of IGOs. The International Commission against Impunity in Guatemala (CICIG) was established in 2006 as a pioneering and daring endeavor, an international organization endowed with legal and moral authority to investigate and prosecute individuals, groups or criminal factions embedded in the Guatemalan state. In essence, an IGO has the potential to intervene in the institutional and legal framework of a sovereign country that had been subverted by political actors and criminal groups, rendering actual law enforcement practically unattainable. It was believed by many actors inside and outside Guatemala that only an international entity could act autonomously, depoliticized, and assist Guatemala in bolstering the rule of law and democracy within the country. However, the initial proposal put forth by the United Nations (UN), which allowed for independent investigation and prosecution, was not sanctioned by national authorities. The scheme ultimately adopted protracted political negotiations with various stakeholders in Guatemala—political and civil society groups—and implemented a hybrid or mixed approach that included prosecutors, lawyers, forensic investigators, criminalistic experts, legal instruments, and both international and local personnel.

© The Author(s), under exclusive license to Springer Nature   189
Switzerland AG 2025
L. Zamudio-González, D. Arellano-Gault, *International Organizational Anarchy*,
https://doi.org/10.1007/978-3-031-82392-3_6

Endorsed by the Guatemalan administration, international benefactors fully funded the CICIG, and although it was not a permanent UN entity, it was granted unrestricted access to gather intelligence and operate within the nation. The UN Secretary-General handpicked the Commissioner, while the staff members were not part of the UN system and did not possess diplomatic immunity. The mandate of the organization was to investigate corruption and impunity, but it was not authorized to make arrests or press charges against the individuals involved. However, the advanced investigative capabilities of the CICIG provided invaluable assistance to the Guatemalan government agencies responsible for criminal prosecution.

The institutional framework established for CICIG required the Guatemalan government to request UN support every two years, placing the existence of the organization at the mercy of the political elite, who paradoxically could be under investigation by CICIG. This political environment necessitated CICIG to adapt to its surroundings and to focus on anti-corruption investigations rather than the original objective of eliminating impunity. This shift in focus allowed the organization to develop successful investigations and contribute to create strong, autonomous judicial institutions with technical capabilities (Zamudio González, 2020). The organization gained legitimacy and support from civil society despite facing political and economic interests within the state. The original contradiction of corruption was a clear challenge for CICIG, as it had to support the government while investigating corruption (Arellano-Gault & Rojas-Salazar, 2021).

The institutional design of the initial arrangement proved to be a substantial obstacle for CICIG, as various political figures in Guatemala subsequently accused it of breaching its impartiality mandate. These accusations claimed that the CICIG pursued its interests and agenda rather than maintaining neutrality. In 2019, after a prolonged period of tension and conflict, coinciding with an investigation into the misuse of resources by the ruling party for political campaigns, CICIG was forced to shut down because of its inability to secure the renewal of its mandate.

The case of the CICIG illustrates the significance of institutions. Organizations, including CICIG, function within complex and uncertain environments, which necessitates using strategies characterized by limited rationality to address inherent complexity and unpredictability. Initially developed to address particular challenges, these strategies often become entrenched and generalized, ultimately legitimizing the organization's existence.

In this section, we want to address the widespread assumption that IGOs (International Governmental Organizations) exist under the idea (or hope) that they *know what they are doing*, make decisions, and act based on specialized and technical knowledge to solve complex problems. The widely shared idea in modern societies that organizations *know what they are doing* can be seen as a very strong institution, as a belief shared by many people and groups, which is recreated and reproduced daily. Of course, the decision-making processes of an IGO are as limited as those of any organization, as they also face constraints of time, information, capabilities, and resources. The idea that legitimizes them as highly intelligent and extremely rational collective agents faces clear limitations in practice, where the capacities and knowledge of the people who compose them, the technologies they possess, and the resources at their disposal are finite. And often, they tend to be scarce.

This, however, contrasts with the expectations placed upon them. To the extent that they present themselves as an ordered, technical whole, capable of acting rationally and depoliticized, they gain legitimacy—the shared belief that, indeed, they have the tools and knowledge to address complex problems. The uncertainty of the real world remains, but it is assumed that an organization is one of the best ways to face it and thus achieve intricate ends. In many ways, this belief is an illusion, as has been widely shown in this book; organizations are people facing highly uncertain situations with limited resources and rationality. But without the illusion that knowledge, technique, coordination, and intelligence can solve the most complex problems, no organization would exist.

The complexity of UN Peacekeepers' role in carrying out Peacekeeping Operations provides a prime example of the challenges intergovernmental organizations (IGOs) face. These operations aim to secure peace in scenarios fraught with violence and conflict among ethnic, religious, and political groups, each embedded within unique local, cultural, and historical contexts. Achieving such a goal is notably difficult without a well-equipped, trained army at the UN's disposal, ready to intervene immediately and without limitations.

Furthermore, it is not merely presumed that an organization can navigate these complexities and coordinate diplomatic, resource, humanitarian, military, and political efforts through organizational techniques. Significantly, the context has led to the introduction of ambitious new agendas beyond the traditional roles of peacemaking (negotiating peace) and peacekeeping (establishing ceasefires to cool down or de-escalate conflicts). These include 'peacebuilding' (implementing peace agreements) and *State-building* (creating post-conflict institutions and strengthening the rule of law) as outlined by Zamudio-González and Culebro (2013).

The aspirations of what an IGO can achieve have reached the highest levels. The UN, for instance, has undertaken highly ambitious operations aimed at rebuilding governments in failed states while also addressing their international legal status. A notable example is the Transitional Administration in East Timor (UNAMET), which was mandated to rebuild the government and subsequently transfer authority to national officials (Martin & Mayer-Rieckh, 2005).

The reality of IGOs often conflicts with the perceptions of rationality and neutrality, which are typically associated with them. The need to negotiate and bargain with diverse stakeholders makes it difficult to maintain this illusion of rationality. For example, the UN must balance its role as a neutral and technical entity with the necessity to impose certain norms or conditions to defend human or social rights. This can sometimes lead to conflicts with certain powerful actors and their interests. The ability of IGOs to operate effectively in the international arena requires a constant balance between their stated neutrality and the complex geopolitical realities they must navigate.

IGOs face numerous ethical and political dilemmas and must make strategic decisions while adapting to the ever-changing global landscape. However, decision-making and action are not always straightforward. To function effectively, IGOs must manage the interdependencies they create with other actors, groups, and organizations, negotiate and bargain, and build solutions while recognizing that time and resources are limited. Furthermore, they must be adaptable to create viable conditions. While formal plans, mandates, and objectives may outline what is desired, the reality is that numerous factors, including accidents and unforeseen events, often influence the results. The disparity between the perceived instrumental rationality of IGOs and the political and operational realities they face has been well-documented in previous chapters.

A central issue in IGOs is the tension between technical rationality and the complex social and political realities they encounter. While the literature often portrays IGOs as functional entities—tools or obedient machines primarily focused on achieving their formally assigned objectives—the reality is more nuanced. Like any other organization, IGOs are sustained by a network of social relationships that create multiple interdependencies.

6 ORGANIZATIONS AND INSTITUTIONS: IGOS DECISIONS, ADJUSTMENTS…   193

As a result, managing or operating an IGO as if it were a simple machine, is a significant challenge.

For instance, in peacekeeping operations, achieving the objective involves the interaction of diverse agents, such as local governments, donors, the Security Council, legal and illegal armed groups, local and global business groups, populations, NGOs, and many others. It is necessary to recognize the varying degrees of interdependence among these actors. This means that from the perspective of an IGO, achieving an outcome can be much more complicated than simply following rules and procedures and applying instruments as if they were following a guide or issuing a prescription. Instead, it requires navigating the complex social and political dynamics inherent in the web of relationships that sustain IGOs.

Furthermore, it is essential to acknowledge that, in the discourse on the conflicts between technical and political rationality, IGOs operate in a systemic environment (Chap. 3), and subsequently, what they rationally strive for is not limited to accomplish formal objectives. What is rational at the systemic level is ensuring survival. This depends on their capacity to navigate through a complex geopolitical and organizational environment, for which legitimacy is required in the eyes of member states and other relevant stakeholders. Unfortunately, the CICIG failed to achieve this. The skills of individuals within an IGO cannot be limited to technical, managerial, or bureaucratic capabilities. They must also possess political, negotiating, bargaining, and consensus-building abilities. The interplay between the illusion of instrumental rationality and political reality is a fundamental characteristic of any modern governmental, corporate, or international organization.

IGOs embody the paradox between the necessity for technical and neutral expertise and the reality of navigating complex political landscapes. The intersection of rationality and political legitimacy is crucial in comprehending contemporary organizations, as they are legitimized for their accomplishments. However, the nonlinear and often irrational nature of human action within organizations poses a challenge. Recognizing the role of surrounding institutions and understanding their interplay with IGOs is essential. It is worth noting that modern organizations are considered institutions.

This chapter provides a comprehensive overview of the concept of institutions from an organizational perspective. This will facilitate a deeper understanding of organizational decisions as institutions. Indeed, institutions enable us to reconcile the paradox of being perceived as a rational, technical entity while simultaneously being capable of addressing a wide range of uncertain situations (some of them political) as a group of individuals. This chapter begins by re-examining the seminal ideas on institutions that have significantly informed the study of IGOs since the inception of International Relations (IR). Subsequently, this chapter delves into the organizational perspective of institutions, aiming to comprehend the dynamic interplay and intersection between IGOs and institutions.

Drawing upon Brunsson's (2007) insights, organizational decisions have emerged as a potent institutional variable. In practical applications, organizational decisions are far more intricate than mere reflections before action. In many cases, actions do not necessarily arise from decisions, and some decisions may not lead to any discernible actions. Nevertheless, the multiplicity and diversity of decision action chains are well-documented. However, the institution of decisions has played a pivotal role in enabling organizational decisions to serve a broader purpose beyond mere selection or choice. Instead, organizational decisions facilitate negotiation, justification, mobilization, and coordination or involve other actors in decision-making.

Prior to exploring into the intricacies of organizational decision-making, it is necessary to examine some of the fundamental concepts that have shaped the perspective of institutions from an IR standpoint. These concepts serve as a comprehensive framework for understanding the existence and actions of IGOs and how they make decisions.

Institutions and Regimes in IR: the Search for Order in Anarchy

In the field of IR, institutions hold a significant position that surpasses that of organizations. However, the dynamics between institutions and IGOs have received limited attention, and the process by which organizations transform into institutions has not been thoroughly examined. Even though organizations develop strategies that eventually solidify into institutions, there has been no in-depth study on how organizations create institutions and how institutions, in turn, establish parameters, procedures, logics, and mechanisms that organizations must adhere to (DiMaggio & Powell, 1983; Meyer & Rowan, 1977). Consequently, organizations are expected to operate *rationally* by employing techniques that align with institutional logic.

Persuading others that an organization is a rational, technical, neutral, and apolitical entity is a key and highly effective strategy for these entities, as this perception disperses suspicions of self-government, discretion, and autonomy, which are always at the core of IR. In this field, states are the most important actors and constantly grapple while maintaining their sovereignty and ability to control the organizations they have created. However, as discussed in Chap. 2, political actions are essential for their survival and existence (Barnett & Coleman, 2005; Cox, 1996; Cox & Jacobson, 1973; Gruber, 2000). It is important to note that organizations operate, make decisions, and act in uncertain environments; therefore, they constantly define, delimit, and create their own realities based on political criteria. This political logic within institutions is a significant gap in the literature on IR as the concept of institution is well-established but is often analyzed without any consideration of IGOs.

Institutions: The Long and Confusing Path of a Concept

Institution is a concept that has multiple meanings in the social sciences. It is employed across disciplines such as Sociology, Political Science, Economics, and Anthropology. Research Institutions (RI) are no exception. Generally, institutions are considered mechanisms that facilitate coordination, communication, exchange, and agreement. Given this, it is unsurprising that, at different times, this discipline has viewed IGOs as institutions or components of larger institutions, such as international order or international regimes (Brechin & Ness, 2013). In this sense, IGOs are components or elements of a broader whole, whether they are the relationships between nations or institutional mechanisms aimed at fostering order in the international sphere (Finnemore & Sikkink, 1998; Haggard & Simmons, 1987; Keohane, 1982).

Institutions create certainty and stability in interactions between states, which is especially relevant in the international arena, characterized as an anarchic environment, that is, without a hierarchical order or a central integrating authority (Keohane & Nye, 1973, 1987; Keohane, 1982, 1986). From this perspective, institutions play a fundamental role in building global governance, as they lay the foundations for cooperation within anarchy. Indeed, it can be thought that in many ways, global governance is interpreted as an institution of institutions: the way regimes, organizations, state actors, NGOs, companies, and other actors are able to construct frameworks or schemes for participation or interaction to make decisions. In this sense, while global governance itself is an institution, this same institution designs, configures, and shares other institutions, which are indeed extremely powerful. Following this, Haas (2002) points to institutions like international conferences, and Reinalda and Verbeek (2004) highlight the influence of IGOs on various national public policies, not to mention the influence of various instruments that specialized organizations promote in areas such as economic development, environmental care, anti-corruption, among others.

Institutions in the field of IR are vital because they can be observed as deliberately created tools that aim to coordinate actions and policies to tackle transnational and global issues. However, there has been much debate as to whether institutions can be consciously designed. Furthermore, from this perspective, there is a significant challenge. States typically create, manage, and oversee institutions as tools that encourage cooperation or strengthen the implementation of rules and processes. Nevertheless, institutions can also influence their creators. This raises the challenging question of how institutions come into existence, at what point they transition from being controlled instruments to mechanisms that shape the behavior of their creators, how institutional change occurs on the international stage, and what factors contribute to such changes. The answers to these questions are not straightforward.

By exploring various perspectives, such as economic and sociological institutionalism, the field of IR has provided answers and explanations to comprehend better and even guide the development of international institutions. For economic institutionalism, institutions are the *rules of the game*, encompassing both formal and informal norms, which establish the specific incentives that will influence the behaviors of diverse actors with varying interests (North, 1990; Olson, 1992; Williamson, 1996, 2010; Williamson & Winter, 1993). This, in turn, reduces uncertainty as institutions generate stability and order by following the rules of the game. Moreover, institutions are a product of history, where path dependence is created, causing them to endure over time, even if it is not entirely rational or practical from different perspectives. Furthermore, according to economic institutionalism, formal and informal institutions are equally important (North, 1990). Formal institutions include norms, regulations, laws, and organizations legally established and legitimized by an authority such as the state. In contrast, informal institutions comprise traditions, customs, and unwritten rules that shape the behavior of agents (North, 1990).

Sociological institutionalism posits that institutions are social constructs represented by systems of rules, norms, and practices that define the interpretation and behavior of actors in diverse social contexts. These institutions are powerful enough to shape the beliefs, values, dynamics, and interaction logic of individuals. They are established, accepted, and legitimate patterns deeply rooted in culture and social structures. March and Olsen (1995, 2011) argue that there are two logics: consequences and appropriateness. The former is based on instrumental rationality, where means and ends are linked, and people act based on the consequences of their actions. Conversely, the latter is based on various elements, such as history, culture, and moral considerations (March, 2010), and establishes signals for action. This logic of appropriateness facilitates the construction of meaning, which is socially legitimate, as well as the social dynamics and interactions within organizations. Institutions are crucial in consolidating the logics of appropriateness, which, although contextual, can also become universal.

Institutions are central to IR theory, with neoliberalism and constructivism employing them in their respective frameworks. In neoliberalism and constructivism, institutions are viewed as mechanisms for cooperation, control, transaction cost reduction, influence, meaning creation, and social conventions. These perspectives have been influential in IR literature, leading to discussions on global governance, bureaucratization, and regimes, as detailed in Chap. 5 of this book.

Neorealism and Neoliberalism

Institutional logic is highly relevant in the field of IR. However, since the 1980s, the debate has been dominated by two main currents: neorealism and neoliberalism. These perspectives have placed international institutions at the center of the discussion as instruments of cooperation between states and devices used by states to achieve their ends, primarily maintaining their status quo. In both views, institutions are viewed as configurations, mechanisms, rules, and logics that generate stability and certainty from the outset, fostering cooperation and coordination.

Neorealism posits that more powerful states establish institutions as additional tools to exert control and secure resources without violence or coercion. In this sense, institutions, including IGOs, serve the interests of their creators and they are mandated to follow directives. They possess no autonomy as the primary focus is on state sovereignty. However, these institutions are limited in their capabilities, as cooperation among states is uncommon. Rational agents seek to maximize utility in a competitive environment, challenging coordination and collaboration. In the neorealist view, cooperation is temporary and unstable, and states often employ dominant mechanisms. This skepticism towards institutions is reflected in the limited recognition of IGOs as actors in their rights, restricting our understanding of their roles.

Neoliberalism and constructivism differ in their views of the role and nature of cooperation in IR. Although both views acknowledge the anarchic nature of the international system, they differ in the rationality of states, with neoliberals focusing on states pursuing their ends. In this sense, the institutional environment shapes the behavior and rationality of states, creating institutional logic. Both perspectives view institutions as crucial in determining the behavior of actors. In an anarchic context, states are seen as selfish and utility-maximizing actors competing in a constantly unstable environment, a function of their environment characterized by high uncertainty, scarce resources, and survival pressures.

It is essential to consider the interactions among states to examine the development of international order, each with its unique goals and resources. In this institutional framework, there are no dominant actors or actors capable of imposing authority. Considering this, states seek ways to simplify the complex situations they encounter, which aligns with the ideas put forth by Pfeffer and Salancik (1978), Oliver (1991), and Barnett and Coleman (2005). Acquiring more power or greater discretion and fostering cooperation are strategies that may be effective or legitimate. However, cooperation presents a challenge in ensuring compliance with agreements, as institutional logic dictates that these agreements cannot be enforced through coercion beyond social and economic sanctions, which may not necessarily alter the behavior of states.

The paradox of institutions in these two currents lies in the fact that, although they are often viewed through a narrow and limited state lens, the very structure of organizational order is based on institutional logic. In this sense, institutions are vital as they directly impact state interests and identities. The behavior of states is shaped by this powerful institution, which is so ingrained that it often goes unnoticed.

IGOs are typically viewed as institutional modalities rather than organizations capable of endorsing endogenous logics. This means they are not considered autonomous and do not define their interests. Instead, they are seen as instruments or actors that pursue, defend, and promote the interests of the states. According to neorealism, the most powerful states impose their interests on IGOs, whereas neoliberalism suggests that IGOs address the collective problems faced by states. However, this often-dominant view of IGOs and institutions has been contested. Constructivism, for example, rejects the conceptualization of institutions in both Neo-realism and neoliberalism. Instead, it adopts a different perspective on the role of institutions in IR.

Constructivism

Following the constructivist view, institutions are understood to be a collection of norms attended to by states as a matter of rationality and the significant impact of these norms on forming identities, meanings, and appropriate behaviors (Duffield, 2007). These norms manifest in processes, discourses, symbols, beliefs, and customs, which shape the international governance structure (Checkel, 1998; Finnemore & Sikkink, 2001; Haas, 2002; Hopf, 1998; Villanueva, 2018; Wendt, 1992).

According to constructivists, international reality is created by institutions that include material and ideological elements (Haas, 2002; Keohane, 1999). In constructivism, institutions shape reality by defining and delimiting mechanisms and frameworks of interpretation that determine what is considered legitimate and acceptable in the international arena. As a result, states share a common understanding of complex situations, including their meanings, beliefs, and visions (Duffield, 2007). The socialization, education, persuasion, discourse, and inculcation of norms are critical in this regard, as they help establish, reproduce, and solidify institutions, ultimately serving as the foundation of international governance.

The formation of institutions, however, is a process that takes place within a highly intricate global context, which means that they do not develop straightforwardly but rather emerge from the interactions between various actors with different and often conflicting objectives. Therefore, institutions are not static entities but continuously evolving and adapting to changes. They play a crucial role in shaping the behavior of states, fostering a sense of identity and cooperation. However, institutions are also vulnerable to the influence of actors who have agendas and pursue their interests (Haas, 2002).

Constructivism is different from neorealism and neoliberalism, which assume instrumental rationality. Instead, constructivism focuses on the roles of ideas, norms, knowledge, culture, and politics (Finnemore & Sikkink, 1998, 2001; Ruggie, 1998). It employs a social analysis approach that posits that human interaction is primarily driven by ideological factors, which are more than just shared beliefs and play a significant role in shaping the interests of agents, particularly states (Adler, 1997; Duffield, 2007; Finnemore & Sikkink, 1998, 2001; Price & Reus-Smit, 1998; Wendt, 1999).

Unlike neorealism and neoliberalism, constructivism views IGOs as more than mere mechanical tools. Constructivism posits IGOs as a distinct set of complex actors with resources, capabilities, powers, and autonomy in the international arena (Brechin & Ness, 2013). The *new institutionalism* and *world society theory* offer a more nuanced perspective on the functioning of IGOs by accounting for the unique environment of the international system. Consequently, constructivism acknowledges the emergence of diverse agents with increased legitimacy and social control beyond the state, leading to significant environmental changes and institutional logics.

IGOs are inherently significant because they impact the behavior of states and their identities beyond mere rational-instrumental considerations and coordination around jointly identified and agreed objectives (Duffield, 2007). IGOs affect states that establish themselves independently. This perspective acknowledges the political nature of IGOs in terms of their power. However, this approach is moderate because constructivism fails to address how power is a crucial factor in understanding the performance of IGOs. IGOs possess a substantial degree of discretion and autonomy to such an extent that they determine their interests, adjust their mandates, and make decisions that affect other actors in the international arena.

The strength of constructivist institutional theory is closely linked to its application in global governance and international regimes. However, this approach creates paradoxes, contradictions, and gaps. When an institution becomes sufficiently robust to influence its creators, it remains a point of analysis and discussion. Additionally, the conceptual confusion of equating an organization with an institution persists under this theory. The emergence and evolution of institutions that define the behavior and interests of states are also areas of inquiry. Despite these challenges, constructivist currents remain a significant area of study and debate.

International Regimes

From an institutional logic perspective, another stream that has gained significant relevance is that of international regimes, whose definition is closely aligned with that of institutions, as they are described as principles, norms, rules, and decision-making procedures (Keohane, 1982; Axelrod & Keohane, 1985; Haggard & Simmons, 1987; Young, 1986; Barnett & Finnemore, 1999; Brechin & Ness, 2013). In this context, regimes function not as actors but as mechanisms comprising systems of rules, conventions, and other institutional logics. The institutional paradox emerges because regimes are processes that are designed, executed, and maintained by various actors and organizations, yet they also establish patterns of behavior, guidelines for beliefs, logics of appropriateness, and definitions that shape the actions of these actors. Consequently, regimes are institutions created by actors, which in turn formulate norms and principles that these actors are expected to follow. Additionally, regimes are influenced and supported by other previously established regimes, creating a network that mutually reinforces these structures (Barnett & Finnemore, 1999; Brechin & Ness, 2013).

Per Scott (2008), argues that IR regimes are systems that combine actors and activities, along with discourses and norms, all collaboratively created to address a collective action problem. These regimes are closely related to constructive arguments and global governance and allow multiple actors to co-create logics of action and appropriateness. This, in turn, influences and shapes reality while also constraining actions, strategies, and decisions. As discussed in the previous chapter, international regimes can be seen as a new approach to dealing with external pressures in the international environment.

The relationship between global governance and regimes is discernible, as the constructivist perspective posits that decision-making depends on agreements that incorporate symbolic, value-based, and material aspects. Consequently, regimes are adaptable and pursue various objectives, primarily by focusing on resolving collective challenges. These regimes have formulated policies responding to context-specific requirements, state interests, and international concerns.

The concept of an international regime remains undefined; various perspectives exist on its meaning, as there are multiple definitions of international regimes ranging from patterns of behavior that reflect convergent norms and expectations to mechanisms that provide explicit prescriptions

(Young, 1986). Additionally, regimes may vary in different dimensions, such as strength, organizational form, scope, and mode of allocation, and can be analyzed using at least four theoretical approaches: structural, game-theoretic, functional, and cognitive (Haggard & Simmons, 1987; Hasenclever et al., 1999). Each theoretical approach has its strengths and limitations in explaining the formation, maintenance, and transformation of international regimes.

In international regimes, one of the most significant offerings is incorporating political logic as a crucial element in comprehending the formation and application of regimes. This perspective acknowledges the intricate political interactions and recognizes the power imbalances between states, IGOs, and transnational corporations. International regimes, which encompass principles, norms, rules, and decision-making procedures in a specific area of IR, are established based on the interests, power struggles, and influence of certain actors over others (Axelrod & Keohane, 1985). Within these regimes, defined roles, rules, and conventions govern the relationships among members and grant them specific attributions and powers, albeit limited by the constraints of the international system.

The regimes theory generally studies IGOs briefly. The main preoccupation is to study the relationship between regimes and powerful or hegemonic actors (Keohane & Nye, 1987). Other approaches investigate cooperation from a game-theoretic perspective, focusing on how cooperation can develop under anarchic conditions lacking supranational authority to ensure compliance (Keohane & Nye, 1987). Additionally, functionalist approaches assume that regimes have a particular purpose within a broader framework that explains their purpose and necessity (Keohane & Martin, 1995).

The final remarks of Keohane and Nye (1987) highlight the shortcomings of this theoretical approach in that it fails to fully comprehend the intricate nature of IR, as subnational and systemic factors are not considered for a complete understanding of global politics. Furthermore, the concept of regime remains vague as it encompasses a variety of terms, practices, and mechanisms. Although IGOs are essential, they are not analyzed as organizations but as components or actors of the regime. According to the authors, it could be assumed that IGOs are understood beyond an instrumental perspective but still from a unidimensional standpoint as unitary actors, without any consideration of their internal complexity, values, dynamics, and meanings. At the very least, this perspective sparked reflection on the autonomy, power, discretion, and influence of IGOs and their impact on the international arena.

Organizations and Institutions: The Internal Organizational Logic of Institutions

As previously mentioned, the notion of institutions is prevalent in various disciplines, including Sociology, Political Science, International Relations, and Economics. However, it is challenging to establish a singular definition or agreement on the concept as it remains a contested concept to some extent, with substantial variations among disciplines. Nevertheless, this chapter introduces an alternative perspective on institutions, specifically the organizational view. According to this view, there is skepticism regarding the potential for *institutional design* (Goodin, 2012), as institutions are seen as intricate social constructions with complex relationships between diverse actors and where organizations influence and are influenced by institutions. While rules and principles can be designed and are crucial in the international order (Sommer et al., 2022), from an organizational standpoint, such a design is just one aspect among several others, both in terms of organizational outcomes and performance. An institution can be studied highly abstractly as formal and informal norms that become widely accepted or recognized by a wide range of social actors as legitimate, necessary, rational, or correct. This general view of the concept of institutions has been employed and adapted to examine more specific societal issues, such as organizations. From the perspective of organizational theory, the study of institutions is not solely focused on analyzing external or social institutions. Most importantly, it involves understanding how organizations utilize, adapt, adopt, reproduce, and introduce various institutional logics within themselves.

Institutions are constructions established through actions and time and continuously enacted. These actions result in the development of recurring behaviors, which can sometimes become customs, traditions, or the basis for certain beliefs. Consequently, creating and designing institutions is not straightforward, and it is difficult to create them instrumentally or rationally. However, they can become strong ideas and solid practices considered inevitable or even *natural* (Lawrence & Suddaby, 2006).

Institutions are fundamental to the functioning of organizations as they establish expected guidelines and rules for behavior and interaction. Over time, institutions have become deeply ingrained beliefs and produce behavioral frameworks that shape the behavior of individuals within the organization. Institutions can be formal and informal, with formal institutions established by authority and encompassing rules, norms, and hierarchical relationships, as seen in codes, regulations, organization charts, and process maps. On the other hand, informal institutions are social interactions that occur outside of formal structures and include power relations, reciprocity, disputes, conflicts, negotiation, and cooperation. In this informal sphere, the discussion of the previously analyzed pathologies is situated.

The potency of institutions is derived from their capacity to diminish uncertainty. This effectiveness is such that they can maintain stability over time. Nevertheless, this stability also renders them inflexible, restricting their transformation even when they are no longer operational or consistent with their original context. Consequently, institutions typically undergo incremental modifications rather than abrupt shifts and exhibit resistance to change.

The World Trade Organization (WTO) reform is a good and useful case to understand the internal dynamics of institutions within an IGO. Although perceived as a member-driven organization, the WTO continues to deliberate enhancing its autonomy—an institutional autonomy (Footer, 2011, p. 380) that aligns with its framework. Like numerous IGOs, the WTO operates on two decision-making levels: serving as a forum for states and establishing a general course of action. In this context, autonomy signifies independent decision-making and separate action mechanisms from states. By 2025, an Executive Steering Committee is expected to establish institutionalized autonomy. What accounts for the longer process of defining such a structure within the WTO when compared to other IGOs? According to Footer (2011, p. 386), comprehending institutions within the logic of action of the WTO necessitates acknowledging its history, such as the progression from the General Agreement on Tariffs and Trade (GATT) to the WTO. The history and rules of an organization are significant, and constructing institutionalized autonomy involves adjusting entrenched norms and customs. Organizations develop and endorse a set of practices that are crucial for helping their members make sense of their actions and decisions. These practices contribute to creating organizational memories and provide reasons that lend legitimacy to the organization itself. Overall, institutions exert a profound influence on organizations.

The influence of institutions on an organization, such as sensemaking, is not only because the construction of meaning becomes *sedimented* over time, but it also transforms into an element that appears almost natural or inevitable. A sedimented institution embodies a normalized logic to the extent that it may be considered inevitable, closing off other possible alternatives for action. It is important to remember that institutions are ideas, discourses, and interpretations of reality, and thus are socially and culturally constructed. This clarification is crucial because, in contemporary thought, institutions are often transformed into a substantive artifice, to the point where they are seen as powerful tools for directing and instrumentally constructing reality. However, institutions become enacted, and organizations play key roles in this enactment.

Despite their ability to offer explanations and create meaning, institutions may also perpetuate biases by denying or neglecting the elements of complexity. Moreover, although institutions can reduce uncertainty, they may also increase uncertainty when they do not align with the context or become so powerful that they restrict the margin for action and decision-making or limit strategies for acquiring information. This creates a paradox: institutions necessitate to stabilize to address the context until they solidify, but their rigidity subsequently generates uncertainty as they become less flexible and less adaptable to changes in the context. Thus, institutions can limit their organizations.

Similarly, organizations create symbols, images, and narratives that sustain and validate them. Consequently, institutions develop through social and organizational interactions, which are influenced by institutions. Thus, institutions advocate interpretations that substantially shape how organizations operate and their structural features and characteristics. Therefore, the most persistent institution views the organization as an entirely rational tool. From this point, a series of other assumptions have emerged that reinforce the notion of organizations as rational instruments, such as the necessity of having clear objectives to pursue, the alignment of the goals and values of the members with those of the organization, the organization as an administrative apparatus that prioritizes generating solutions to achieve objectives through expected and concrete outputs, and so on.

The institution of the organization, which establishes it as a rational entity, is also linked to the notion that it is a powerful mechanism open to change, as change is planned and executed rationally. Although every organization is prone to making mistakes, this can be avoided if the organization is open to learning. Reforming organizations is a continuous process, and there is always hope that, with a group of intelligent reformers, change will alleviate the problems and conflicts currently hindering the progress of the organization.

Although the highly structured perspective of change has been scrutinized (Brunsson, 2009; Tsoukas & Chia, 2014), it remains a commonly held paradigm for studying and comprehending organizations. However, the question remains: How realistic is this approach? According to Graham Allison, a prominent figure in IR, the answer depends on the analytical lens an individual chooses.

POLITICS AND RATIONAL ORGANIZATIONAL TECHNIC: NECESSARY BUT UNCOMFORTABLE BEDFELLOWS

Allison (1971) conducted a seminal study to examine how the analytical lenses through which a social phenomenon is analyzed (in this instance, the Cuban missile crisis in the 1960s) can significantly influence the observations and conclusions drawn. In his work, which concentrated on US policy and decision-making, Allison proposed three distinct analytical lenses to comprehend the choices made by President John F. Kennedy and his team in a situation of extreme uncertainty, with limited information, and amidst conflicting interests of diverse groups: (1) the rational approach (Model I), (2) the organizational approach (Model II), and (3) the bureaucratic policy approach (Model III).

Interpretation and decision-making processes vary greatly depending on the analytical perspective employed. Through the rational approach from Model I, it can be asserted that the institution in question is genuine and regularly utilized. For instance, many media outlets frequently employ phrases such as *the US determined, the UN decided, the Security Council concluded,* and so on, without giving it much thought. It is presumed that people possess the will to pursue general objectives and are knowledgeable about employing various means to achieve them. Consequently, it is assumed that organizations, governments, and even nations operate similarly to individuals, functioning as unified actors who make decisions, possess preferences, and adjust their means to attain their objectives. This notion is referred to as the unified rational actor, which posits that individuals, organizations, governments, and even nations make decisions. Therefore, the focus shifts to determine the preferences of entities such as the OECD or Mexico as a nation, identifying available alternatives, and evaluating the outcomes obtained. When employing rational thinking, one would opt for the option that offers the best potential outcome given the prevailing circumstances and probabilities.

The second analytical perspective is the organizational approach of Model II, which contrasts with the rational model, positing that decision-makers are various organizations with their own objectives, priorities, and logic. These organizations and their bureaucracies confront high levels of uncertainty and respond with standardized procedures to the ongoing risk of making decisions with incomplete information. In essence, they may not tackle general problems, which can be difficult for a single actor or organization to solve. Consequently, organizations respond to this uncertainty through standardized and routine processes. When examining the missile crisis through the lens of different organizations attempting to safeguard their decision-making domains, a narrative emerges distinct from the parsimonious and straightforward view of the rational model. The organizational perspective challenges the assumption of a unified rational actor and allows for examining other factors influencing decision-making, such as routines, procedures, and procedural knowledge within the organizations.

Finally, the bureaucratic policy approach of Model III posits that decision-makers are not rational actors but individuals who are constantly engaged in battles and conflicts. They exist within the arenas of interaction where numerous players are involved. Instead of making rational decisions for a general problem, they make several decisions to tackle problems, aiming to secure positions to influence decisions at the highest political or organizational level.

Each model has its own paradigmatic logic and approach for incorporating actors and their decisions based on assumptions. In the case of the rational approach, the fundamental assumption is the existence of a unified rational actor, which is a collective entity made up of various individuals and groups but acts as a single unit. This collective actor possesses the objectives, values, and preferences from which it selects and acts congruently with the preferences of the collective. When a country, government, or organization confronts a problem, it will select action alternatives that will enable it to address the issue, establishing goals, objectives, means, and ends. Because the unified rational actor is rational and congruent, to select the most effective means to solve the problem is possible. However, what happens to individuals when a unified rational actor is assumed?

Generally, it is implied that they can subordinate their interests to those of the collective actors.

The simplifying view of the unified rational actor is just that: highly simplistic and easily empirically questionable. However, it is a very popular and useful perspective that is often used without much thought. Empirically, it is possible to trace the workings of an organization or government. When this is done, a different conclusion is reached, where decisions and actions are taken and performed by specific, identifiable individuals. The "black box" is not so opaque and can be studied. What happens, rather, is that this black box allows for the identification of the obvious, namely, individuals with different interests, in specific contexts, facing time and resource constraints that present an image of a complex, even disordered context where multiple rationalities, sometimes in outright competition, come into play. The clean and simple metaphor of the unified rational actor unfolds to reveal a world that is practically chaotic, disordered, filled with conflicts, battles, doubts, and errors. In the analysis and study of IGOs, this rational model has been key, but it is becoming less useful as IGOs are not unified entities, nor are they monoliths that can be assumed to act as individual decision-makers.

Organizational analysis reveals that IGOs are characterized by non-unified collective entities. These entities comprise various groups and coalitions, as outlined in Chap. 4. These groups and coalitions often encounter problems characterized by a high degree of uncertainty. Throughout this book, several of these wicked problems (Rittel & Webber, 1973) have been referenced, such as how to address a pandemic, rebuild a collapsed state, and how to tackle and address global crime. In Model II, it is assumed that there is not just one decision problem but several: addressing a wicked problem involves creating the conditions for defining it, measuring it, and framing it within the realm of the possible while also satisfying specific criteria (as discussed in Chap. 4 regarding satisficing criteria). This is achieved through rules and processes that establish standardized forms that enable organizations to intervene in a viable and legitimate manner. For instance, an IGO such as the WHO cannot act against a pandemic without convincing various national actors to support its strategies; the International Police Organization (INTERPOL) cannot connect national police forces without the endorsement of their respective governments, and the UN cannot intervene in a nation such as East Timor to rebuild the state and its administration without reaching agreements with the political groups within the population of that country. Organizations create processes, legitimize paths, and agree on rules allowing for decision-making and action, but they may not know how to solve their problems initially. They must establish conditions for processes and rules that enable different actors and groups to communicate, analyze, decide, and act.

Therefore, when considering a country or an IGO where multiple governments and organizations are involved, Model II highlights the significance of the relationships between organizations in loosely coupled systems (Weick, 1976) as crucial components of the outcome of the interaction and interdependence among various decision-makers and stakeholders.

The lenses of Model II offer powerful analytical capabilities, revealing the limitations of Model I. For instance, Model II highlights the illusion of control. In this model, control over decision-making and action processes is always in question. It is impossible to control a network of agents and organizations, each functioning according to their routines, processes, and standards. Organizations establish rules and routines to protect themselves from uncertainty. Consequently, decision-making is not linear but is characterized by constant negotiation, interaction, correction, and improvement using various toolboxes. This dynamic decision-making approach often leads to unforeseen and uncontrollable effects, as discussed in Chap. 4.

Model II presents a simplified perspective on organizations, as evidenced by several organizational approaches examined in this book. While standardized routines and processes are among the organizational tools used, they are not the only ones. Individuals, groups, and coalitions recognize that they operate in the context of relationships, interactions, and interdependencies. Allison's Model III, known as bureaucratic politics, incorporates this dynamic arena where positions are contested among various groups and individuals. This model posits that decisions arise from political processes. In the governmental arena, individuals and groups make decisions that require interaction with others, confronting each other based on organizational logics. Model III builds upon Model II by asserting that commitments are established among the actors due to the existence of routines, rules, norms, and procedures. This is because cooperation may be necessary in certain circumstances despite the different objectives being pursued.

Similarly, in the game of interdependence, there is competition in which coalitions strive to attain better positions. Therefore, the organization can be considered an arena where the actions of organizations manifest as a multitude of actors negotiating, interacting, and competing within certain limits, although with margins of freedom that are sought to be exploited and utilized. Through this process, groups acquire decision-making positions, gaining organizational power and influence. Consequently, a significant problem, as posited in Model I, can be broken down into numerous minor problems that arise from the actors occupying positions.

The control was significantly reduced in Model II, while it was even more limited in Model III. Despite this reduction, Model III maintains certain structural elements, such as rules, procedures, and organizational culture, which stabilize interactions. Moreover, positional games of political actors require the logic of interaction and, therefore, interdependence. Additionally, Model III must consider the influential role of certain individuals or leaders in the technical-political-bureaucratic games (Biermann & Siebenhuner, 2009).

Consider the example of Marinus van der Goes van Naters, a skilled bureaucrat in a political game within the Council of Europe in 1954 (Brouwer, 1998). Considering the historical tensions between France and Germany regarding the status of the Saar region, particularly its rich coal mines, and the desire to avoid a new regional conflict, France proposed the creation of an independent state that would be economically tied to France. To this end, France established a customs barrier in 1946, and in an electoral process coincidentally resulted in a pro-French party gaining a majority in 1947. However, the German government of Konrad Adenauer rejected these unilateral measures and the election, effectively paralyzing the accession of both countries to the European Defense Community (EDC).

The Council of Europe, established in 1949 under the leadership of Dutch politician Marinus van der Goes van Naters, entered the political-bureaucratic game. A fervent advocate of European integration and supporter of granting the Saar a European status, van Naters recognized that a bilateral solution was not feasible. Instead, he sought to give Saar the European status within a supranational structure, specifically the European Political Community (CPU) of economic and military cooperation associated with the EDC. Van Naters negotiated with officials in Paris and Bonn, meeting tirelessly with Adenauer, Bidault, and Schuman to seek economic concessions from the French and grant political freedom in the Saar demanded by Bonn. However, the proposal failed to gain traction because of the French defeat in Dien Bien Phu in 1954, which left the French government in a situation of instability. The impossibility of forming the

EDC ultimately closed the door to a supranational solution, and Saar returned to Germany in 1957.

In the event of limited capacity on both sides, the Council attained considerable independence and devised a fresh approach to resolving this matter. Discussions were conducted at multiple levels, and amendments were proposed. As Haas (1968, p. 139) elucidates, it did not pursue the most basic common ground; it did not encourage division but intentionally reframed the disagreement to develop a comprehensive resolution.

Individuals and their leadership roles are significant in both institutional and organizational settings (Sanz-Carranza, 2015). Despite the constant influx of people into various positions and playing games in different arenas, the prevailing notion is that organizations are coherent and rational entities that operate through decision-making schemes and purposeful action. However, relying solely on rational models is not sufficient. In practical applications, it is necessary to incorporate the elements offered by organizational and political models, as suggested by Allison. The dynamic relationship between institutions and organizations is complex and intertwined.

On the one hand, institutions, observed in a highly rational manner, shape organizations. On the other hand, organizations also influence the formation of institutions by operating in the real world. This reciprocal relationship suggests that institutions are not static entities but are constantly evolving in response to the actions of organizations.

The INTERPOL is a subject of ongoing debate regarding its classification as a genuine intergovernmental organization or an international non-governmental organization (NGO) (Deflem, 2010). Unlike other intergovernmental organizations established through treaties, INTERPOL operates without a formal treaty, whose primary objective is to foster cooperation among diverse national police forces (Calcara, 2020). However, the institutional framework and decision-making mechanisms involving multiple states pose challenges, necessitating the strategic prioritization of issues (Martha, 2010).

INTERPOL members comprise national police forces, which are structural components of various states (Savino, 2010). In addition to the General Assembly, Executive Committee, and General Secretariat, the organization includes National Central Bureaus established by each member state, forming an integral part of the INTERPOL's structure (Savino, 2010). The overall mission of INTERPOL is to promote police cooperation; however, this endeavor involves addressing diverse countries, legal systems, and administrative regimes, some of which present challenges regarding legality and human rights (Calcara, 2020).

Institutional logic underpins the significance of international police cooperation in addressing organized crime, globalized crime, and safeguarding vulnerable nations from major criminals (Deflem, 2010). However, practical implementation requires INTERPOL to resolve concrete issues and make decisions, which may present difficulties, given the diverse contexts and challenges involved.

For example, during the 1970s, protecting INTERPOL's institution of neutrality meant that terrorism was considered a political matter in which the organization should not intervene. The real conditions of the 1980s and 1990s required a gradual modification of this definition for practical organizational reasons. By 2017, terrorism was officially legitimized as a factor for the organization's intervention. Another example of the dynamic interaction between institutions and organizations can be observed in the operational difficulty INTERPOL faces in maximizing cooperation between police bodies and avoiding being ensnared by the questionable policies of various states that use INTERPOL in cases of political persecution. Indeed, the red notices that serve to detain individuals whom countries identify as criminals require a complex organizational process. These can be issued by the National Central Bureaus, following instructions from the countries. INTERPOL, via the General Secretariat and its staff, must analyze in record time whether such requests are legally substantiated and are not instruments for persecuting political adversaries, for example. The time it takes for this review, which in practice allows INTERPOL to erase an unsubstantiated red notice, is considerable. This duration already allows for the intimidation and threatening of the individuals subject to the alert.

Furthermore, the deletion of such an alert is announced in the bulletin of the state in question. However, an individual may still face prosecution in another country if an additional or related red alert is raised. The operational limits and challenges of IGOs are critical to understand how institutions function in practice. Institutional effects are often severely affected by the capacities and situations that organizations generate, learn, cope with, and reproduce.

INTERPOL has cultivated an organizational culture that distinctly separates political from apolitical cooperation between national police forces. Maintaining an apolitical stance is crucial for the organization, as the professional execution of its activities could adversely affect state considerations and their short-term agendas. However, INTERPOL recognizes that isolating itself from the institutional influences of states could be counterproductive. States may fear that such isolation could lead INTERPOL to act in ways that violate their sovereignty and pursue its own interests (Barnett & Coleman, 2005, p. 604). This delicate balance between maintaining autonomy from states and gaining recognition, support, and legitimacy has been critical throughout the history of INTERPOL. We are discussing an organization that was born without a treaty between states and gradually advanced in its formalization without becoming a structure too closely tied to the interests of the states. Thus, the relationship between IGOs and their institutional environment involves the existence and use of various strategies, ranging from following established norms, negotiating with other organizations and even ignoring or confronting them (Oliver, 1991; Pache & Santos, 2010; Pfeffer & Salancik, 1978). To this end, they generate mechanisms such as professionalization and the creation of epistemic communities, as supported by constructivist theory, as well as rules, norms, and agreements that foster certainty for organizations and stakeholders alike.

The relationship between management and policy in IGOs can be effectively illustrated through the case of the International Criminal Court (ICC), which was established in 2002 to end impunity and punish perpetrators of war crimes, genocide, and crimes against humanity. Despite its significance, the ICC has faced criticism for its high cost, low effectiveness, and inappropriate political bias, as it has mainly focused on cases from African countries. Although the Court has successfully investigated a few cases, the number of cases that have resulted in effective sentences is even lower (Goodman, 2020).

In its 20 years of operation, with a budget of nearly €1.5 billion, the institution has made only ten convictions and four acquittals. This is primarily due to the institutional mechanisms. It lacks the means to enforce arrests and bring suspects before the Court and has no prisons to enforce sentences. The investigation, trial, and sentencing processes were handled entirely by its 124 member states. Generally, the state brings cases before the Court, whether they provide evidence and contribute to the confirmation of charges at hearings. Without evidence, cases do not proceed, as was the case in 2011 with the Kenyan president, Uhuru Muigai Kenyatta, whose case was dismissed due to a lack of evidence.

The effectiveness of the Court in conducting investigations and prosecutions is closely tied to the collaboration of member states. States typically cooperate when their political interests are aligned, but predicting their cooperation can be challenging for the Prosecutor. Consequently, it has become essential for the Prosecutor to assess the situation to initiate informal suits. Nevertheless, the level of uncertainty remains high even with these efforts.

The judicial system, particularly the Court, mediates the relationship between politics and administrative management. The involvement of the United Nations Security Council (UNSC), including referring cases to the International Criminal Court or suspending them, also reflects regional and international political dynamics. In 2009, the UNSC, under Chapter VII of the Charter, referred the case of Omar al Bashir, President of Sudan, to the ICC. Sudan had not ratified the Rome Statute, which granted ICC jurisdiction, but the UNSC argued that the situation threatened international peace and security. Despite this, 19 countries disregarded the arrest warrant, nine of which ratified the Rome Statute. It was not until 2021 that the government of Sudan surrendered Omar al Bashir to the ICC.

Hence, it is essential to consider the institutional logic that defines the relationship between policy and technique and the relationship between policy and management when discussing the efficiency of IGOs.

The Institution of the Decision: Rationality and Irrationality

The institution that has propelled organizations to be rational and technical entities is indeed very potent. Nevertheless, IGOs are also political and social entities consisting of individuals with diverse interests, motives, and capabilities and are constantly in conflict and disagreement. The political actions and decisions of stakeholders in an IGO are not insignificant. However, they are commonly regarded as *irrational elements*, which can positively impact the performance and rationality of the organizations themselves. Consequently, IGOs assert their unity as rational actors, even if they are not.

A prominent institution plays a crucial role in addressing the paradoxes or contradictions that organizations encounter. Organizational theory has widely discussed how organizations resolve such issues. Specifically, the category of decision has become an institution that is essential in helping individuals and organizations to navigate a world in which they must legitimize themselves as rational, even though they operate in a complex and conflict-ridden environment. According to Brunsson's (2001, 2003, 2006, 2007; Brunsson & Olsen, 2008) research, the decision-making process is not just about selecting options or alternatives but also legitimizes actions in a complex reality. The key lies in understanding how human beings with limited rationality in organizational settings conceptualize decisions as instrumental and a basis for legitimacy, enabling action in a complex world.

Brunsson's primary contention was that decision and decision-making constitute institutions in the contemporary world. Making a decision is a powerful metaphor for how humans regularly make choices. Decision-making is a fundamental expectation of individuals throughout their lives, aimed at directing and governing their actions. The exercise of human agency is generally guided by the notion that decisions are being made. Thus, decision-making is generally perceived as an internal, reflective, and endogenous act individuals perform. This being the case, decision-making being reflective, conceived prior to action, it allows for the existence of rationality. Essentially, one decides before taking an action. This metaphorical institution has been legitimized and solidified as a substantive truth for rational conduct.

Brunsson posits that the institution of decision-making extends beyond the notion that decisions are merely the product of selection; instead, it encompasses the myriad of causes and consequences that arise from these choices. While selection is undoubtedly a critical factor in decision-making, it is merely one component of a more complex process that involves psychological and social factors. Individuals do not make decisions in isolation; they are constantly influenced by their surroundings and the cultural practices and heuristics prevalent in their locality. They are also cognizant that their choices will impact others and that these impacts may vary. Thus, decision-making involves considering how to implement a decision and how others perceive and react to it. The possibility of error and risk also play a significant role in the decision-making process.

The issue is not merely to contend that decision-making cannot be rational. Rather, it is to comprehend how, in a world where rational decision-making is presumed to be the norm and internalized as a fundamental institution that promotes order and stability, individuals encounter a reality characterized by insurmountable contradictions and perpetual uncertainties. Which political, organizational, or group leaders would willingly admit to their peers, stakeholders, superiors, or subordinates that they cannot act rationally by setting goals, charting courses, and establishing well-defined technical pathways? Hardly anyone. However, this situation implies that these individuals and groups will have to confront a reality that is practical, contingent, and constantly changing (as discussed in Chap. 3). This reality is not one of complete control but rather one in which rationality is multiple and constantly clashes (as explored in Chap. 4). Furthermore, in this reality, resources are always limited and in flux. Brunsson is unequivocal on this point, and he argues that to exist within an organizational world grounded in rationality, one must learn to navigate the irrational.

Decision-making in the real world involves more than simply choosing among alternatives, which is the first element of decision-making according to Brunsson. It is crucial to understand decision-making beyond just selecting options to ensure it is rational. This process also involves mobilization—the second element of decision-making—engaging individuals who must not only make choices but also implement these decisions in real-world scenarios and secure the necessary resources to turn the chosen idea into reality. In this way, decisions foster cooperation and coordination among groups, aiming to achieve equilibrium and consensus that prevent organizational collapse or paralysis. Thus, decision-making serves to legitimize the notion of taking concrete actions to address problems.

The third element is that, in addition to choosing and mobilizing, the institution of decision-making assigns responsibilities, thereby driving action and establishing differentiated patterns of action among actors. Consequently, when decisions are made, specific effects are produced, and in cases in which these effects do not occur, it is possible to justify, learn, and assign responsibilities. However, this decision does not inevitably result in success.

The fourth element is the creation of legitimacy: organizations communicate. Decision-making allows for discussion, the creation of metaphors, the definition of reasons, and the sharing of arguments; it strengthens bonds, re-legitimizes values, and generates hope. Thus, the belief that rational decision-making involves controlling one's destiny enables organizations to deploy their cognitive and motivational capacities. These elements are necessary for individuals to act and coordinate with each other. Mobilizing, assigning responsibilities, and legitimizing are not classic rational processes but are, in their *irrationality*, key for organizations to function.

The International Labor Organization (ILO) is an IGO that has established a robust normative framework for actors to make decisions by representing strategic issues. According to Louis (2019), states, trade unions and employers' organizations are the primary actors that can have substantive representation. NGOs have been gaining influence over the past few decades. The ILO, which places non-state actors on an equal footing with state actors in decision-making processes, implies a complex governance process. The Secretariat is primarily responsible for managing relationships with these actors to optimize the tripartite negotiations in which the ILO continuously engages. The entry of diverse NGOs has been viewed as both an opportunity and challenge and *tripartism* has been developed to express this potential. Despite the reluctance of various actors within the organization, NGOs have been seen as valuable allies by employers and unions to mobilize opinions and raise concerns in important audiences (Louis, 2019, p. 54). The ILO serves as a prime example of the different roles that decisions play within an institution and the various dynamics that organizations deploy to make decisions.

In this context, it can be posited that the irrational aspect is essential for establishing a rational decision-making institution. For organizations to effectively execute decisions, they must confront challenges beyond simply making choices. They necessitate compromises, coordination, conflict resolution, and the development of communication logics that enable individuals to accept decisions, their associated responsibilities, directives, and beliefs in particular normative patterns. Organizations imbue values, and in an uncertain world, specific values may legitimize behaviors, bias, and disregard alternatives, creating a finite list of options. Indeed, this is not a rational endeavor, as it does not originate from exhaustive analysis. However, as Simon elucidates, pre-decision spaces are fashioned within organizations, where decision foundations are established to facilitate faster, more logical choices with more significant resource consideration and, to embrace the ambiguity that consensuses and agreements may not necessarily guarantee a favorable outcome. At the very least, they ensure that actions are taken and then they can be deemed legitimate and acceptable. This is the mechanism through which Brunsson resolves the paradox that the institution of a decision requires substantive non-rational elements for its legitimacy and existence.

When discussing the assignment of responsibility, it is essential to recognize the dynamics of an uncertain and multicausal world. This perspective suggests that individuals and organizations have some control over outcomes, but numerous other factors beyond their control influence the effects of their decisions. Making decisions with some awareness of the potential consequences within their control is deemed necessary, even if not wholly. According to Brunsson, decisions involve choosing or mobilizing resources and establishing certain responsibilities. By acknowledging the existence of controllable and non-controllable effects, he established limits and justifications for the assignment of responsibilities. It is one thing to make a mistake due to an incorrect calculation and another to do so due to insufficient information.

Furthermore, given the uncertain nature of the context, the conditions can change, making it crucial to define what is controllable. Promising complete control may be counterproductive and acknowledging that the best decision was made with the available information allows learning and strengthening of future alternatives. Additionally, establishing punishments and rewards based on decision outcomes helps to maintain the illusion of control.

One of the most exciting effects of assigning responsibility as part of the decision-making process is the ability to justify an ex-post. For successes, it is possible to trace back the chains of actions and responsibility. This can also be performed for failures. Once an organizational disaster is generated, it is relatively easy to return in time and put individuals in rational situations where they made certain decisions to identify their miscalculations, motivational failures, lack of information, or lack of intelligence. The saga of the decision as an institution is strengthened because, ex-post, it is relatively easy to make this reconstruction and maintain the idea that the decisions generate the results in organizations.

An example of this learning process regarding the not-so-rational steps of decision-making in organizations is given by the description of Romero Dallaire (Dallaire, 2003), a Canadian officer in charge of directing the United Nations Blue Helmets operation in Rwanda as the Force Commander of the Assistance Mission to Rwanda (1993–1994). Dallaire describes with great candor the decision-making and action processes he had to develop before starting this mission. Upon arriving at the UN building in New York, he came into contact with staff from the Department of Peace Keeping Operations (DPKO) on the 36th floor, 'full of people at small desks, working in a sweatshop'. He also found that the Department of Political Affairs (DPA) was in competition and disagreement with the DPKO, and even with the undersecretary general regarding the operation. All of them, characters with different qualities, responsibilities, and attention spans. The conceptualization of the mission was also not clear. Although there was some agreement around a small and simple mission,

6 ORGANIZATIONS AND INSTITUTIONS: IGOS DECISIONS, ADJUSTMENTS... 219

understanding that after the failure in Somalia (1993), it would not be easy to find funders

Establishing an operation in Rwanda necessitated agreements with internal and external parties within the UN. Gaining entrance required the assent of local actors in Rwanda, the endorsement of the government of Uganda, and the backing of countries with financial means to fund the mission. Additionally, it called for the support of offices responsible for peacekeeping operations and logistical entities, such as the Field Operation Division. Negotiating with all these parties was essential to the success of the endeavor.

What classification of operations does Rwanda represent? As a peacekeeping mission under Chapter VII, which allows for the use of force, or an operation under Chapter VI.5, which restricts intervention to maintain principles of neutrality, acceptance, and limited use of force? Which design is more likely to gain approval from the Security Council, that implies continuous support with resources and political backing? Dallaire emphasizes his isolation and lack of organizational support during this process, as he had to independently raise funds and finance the operation through alternative means, such as the World Bank (WB) and International Monetary Fund (IMF).

Determining the size of a mission staff extends beyond a mere selection process, encompassing the mobilization and assignment of responsibilities and legitimizing the mission. For example, the staff size was reduced from an ideal 5500 to a reasonable 2500, despite the US and Russian governments insisting that 325 people were sufficient (Dallaire, 2003, p. 83). Organizations operating in complex situations and under multi-actor governance mechanisms, such as many IGOs, face lengthy and arduous processes of mobilization and legitimization. Dallaire reported that he received no feedback or formal approval of his proposals to enhance the operation and that the United Nations Assistance Mission for Rwanda (UNAMIR) was deployed before substantive rules of operation had been agreed upon or the political representative of the mission, the Special Representative of the Secretary-General (SRSG), had been appointed (Dallaire, 2003, pp. 98–99).

Furthermore, to better comprehend the organizational structure of the UN in this situation, an extended quotation from the conversation between Dallaire and Per O. Hallqvist, who was appointed as the Chief Administration Officer:

"Hallqvist made it abundantly clear to me that he was a stickler for process and that he expected it to take upwards of six months before UNAMIR as administrative and logistical support system was fully functional. He told me that the UN was a "pull system", not a "push system" like I was used to with NATO, because the UN had absolutely no pool of resources to draw on. You had to make a request for everything you needed and then you had to wait while that request was analyzed. If you did not ask, you did not get.... In a push system, food and water for the number of soldiers deployed is automatically supplied. In a pull system, you have to ask for those rations...The civilian UN logistician, and not the operational commander, has the power of supply. If he judges that the item is required, the UN will supply it; if not, it won't." (Dallaire, 2003, pp. 99–100)

It is not within the purview of this book to delve into the rationale behind the pull system organization of the UN. However, the quest for a rational ideal necessitates the creation of structuring, innovation, and the invention of methods to effectively handle the numerous demands and constraints stemming from diverse interests, resource scarcities, and organizational cultures that prioritize state sovereignty and prevent the UN from morphing into a supranational government.

Concluding Remarks

Legitimacy is an essential aspect of institutional decision-making. According to Brunsson, the central tenet of legitimacy is the belief that rational decision-making can yield outcomes. Legitimacy is rooted in the idea that organizations operate on two separate planes, decision, and action; however, these planes are interconnected in practice. Decision-making requires justification, communication, and convincing individuals to coordinate their efforts toward a common goal. In society, the decision-making process is a visible act expressing commitment. Thus, it is a process of negotiation, communication, interaction, and strategic use of information. It is limited by rationality in the strictest sense of the word because it involves controlling ambiguity.

Often, decisions that must be put into action must be made. In doing so, it is expected to find a disconnection between the values of the organization and the outcomes that the decision supposedly achieves. Furthermore, there is a lack of clarity regarding the results. This ambiguity serves as a space for justification, allowing decisions to persist despite the inability to control everything. Ultimately, ambiguity enables damage control and can be used to justify inevitable failures. It is essential to recognize that organizations make decisions and communicate messages that determine what is considered acceptable and legitimate.

Decision-making is not opposed to action. Instead, numerous fundamental organizational, social, cognitive, motivational, and commitment-related factors lie between decision-making and action. Consequently, in the complex and uncertain realm of multiple causes and effects, organizations do not adopt an illusory stance that everything is under control nor a desperate stance that nothing can be controlled. Instead, they adopt a proactive approach to ensure viability in technical and discursive terms.

Dingwerth et al. (2019) investigated the altered dynamics of legitimizing IGOs. Specifically, they examined five organizations: the World Trade Organization, the African Union, the International Atomic Energy Agency, the International Union for Conservation of Nature, and the Office of the UN High Commissioner of Refugees. Through these case studies, the authors observed that the legitimacy game has become crucial for IGOs to make decisions as the world becomes increasingly complex. Consequently, IGOs have adapted to their complex environment by creating new arguments and compromises, which paradoxically increase complexity, as noted by Luhmann in Chap. 3. This adaptation has led to IGOs serving states and incorporating their individuals. In doing so, these organizations are forced to explain and justify their goals and the processes, structures, and the mechanisms they use. The legitimization waves of IGOs are changing, and this is essential for their decisions and actions to make sense and allow the individuals, and groups that compose them to justify themselves and understand what to do and how to do it while maintaining a minimum hope of achieving something, which is seen as positive by an increasing number of stakeholders.

Brunsson argued that a helpful approach for comprehending the organizational logic of establishing sufficient legitimacy to function is to relate the abstract rationality of decision-making to the practical rationality of action. Analytically separating decision-making and action is likely a significant obstacle to comprehensively examining the procedures through which individuals within an organizational framework undertake their work and attempt to grapple with intricate challenges. Individuals often recognize the necessity to carry out other processes to initiate any action, which constitute prerequisites for making decisions and acting. However, these processes are neither linear nor ambiguous. They involve mobilization, consensus building, responsibility allocation, and legitimizing potential actions. Interestingly, all these steps are crucial, but individuals within organizations may not always know how to undertake them effectively.

The study of IGOs is intricate because of their profound interrelationships and interdependencies which are internationally engendered and fostered. The effective management of such organizations requires the ability to coordinate these interrelationships. Orchestration, a governance mechanism that emerged as a means of operationalizing the dynamics of complex interdependence (Keohane & Nye, 1973), is crucial for introducing and ordering diverse intermediary actors between the IGO and its target public (Abbott et al., 2015, p. 4). Considering the intricate political and decision-making challenges IGOs face, governance has shifted towards more distributed and decentralized schemes, necessitating new coordination logics among international actors. Understanding how IGOs influence, mobilize, define, and structure international order is essential, and this process is less linear and orderly than acknowledged by many theoretical perspectives. IGOs are critical in defining, operationalizing, and implementing various governance mechanisms, each with its challenges. Noteworthy studies include how the EU incorporates orchestration mechanisms into regulatory and policy implementation (Blauberger & Rittberger, 2015) and how the ILO manages its complex structure by including more agents, such as trade unions and employer associations (Baccaro, 2015).

Nowadays, decisions and solutions are less determined by individual entities, such as governments, corporations, or international organizations. Instead, they are increasingly influenced by complex interrelationships and interdependencies established among these entities. Each actor and organization are influenced by their unique dynamics, including political and technical factors and strategic considerations. Despite this interconnected world, rational decision theory remains a widely accepted and legitimizing framework, providing a sense of control and order in the face of uncertainty. This final chapter, along with others, reveals a more nuanced and dynamic picture of organizational and inter-organizational behavior characterized by ambiguity and complexity. Understanding this logic is essential for navigating the paradoxes, constraints, and opportunities associated with the management of international organizations. This goes beyond simply identifying *pathologies* or *dysfunctions* and requires a more comprehensive and sophisticated approach to decision-making.

Institutions have a significant influence as they possess a weighty presence and lasting impact. They facilitate action and streamline processes yet simultaneously introduce biases, restrict options, and render specific issues, practices, values, and norms natural. Conversely, they render others as unnatural. How institutions interact with one another, specifically concerning IGOs, is particularly important. Although the rational design of institutions is challenging, many hope to improve international organizations and IGOs through this approach. Just as organizations are comprised of individuals engaging in formalized spaces, games, interactions, and interdependencies, institutions are also influenced by, and often created and perpetuated by, such organizations. Moreover, institutions are shaped by more than just incentives; the logics of appropriateness also play a crucial role in their development.

References

Abbott, K., Genschel, P., Snidal, P., & Zangl, B. (2015). Orchestation: Global governance through intermediaries. In K. Abbott, P. Genschel, P. Snidal, & B. Zangl (Eds.), *International organizations as orchestrators*. Cambridge University Press.

Adler, E. (1997). Seizing the middle ground: Constructivism in world politics. *European Journal of International Relations, 3*, 319–363.

Allison, G. T. (1971). *The essence of decision: Explaining the Cuban missile crisis.* Harper Collins.

Arellano-Gault, D., & Rojas-Salazar, G. (2021). Dealing with the "original contradiction" in fighting corruption in countries with systemic corruption: A critique of the cases of Brazil and Mexico and their multi-organizational strategies. In J. Pozsgai-Alvarez (Ed.), *The politics of anti-corruption agencies in Latin America*. Routledge.

Axelrod, R., & Keohane, R. O. (1985). Achieving cooperation under anarchy: Strategies and institutions. *World Politics, 38*(1), 226–254.

Baccaro, L. (2015). Orchestation for the "social partners" only: Internal constrains on the ILO. In K. Abbott, P. Genschel, P. Snidal, & B. Zangl (Eds.), *International organizations as orchestrators*. Cambridge University Press.

Barnett, M., & Coleman, L. (2005). Designing police: Interpol and the study of change in international organizations. *International Studies Quarterly, 49*(4), 593–619.

Barnett, M., & Finnemore, M. (1999). The politics, power and pathologies of international organizations. *International Organization, 54*(4), 699–732.

Biermann, F., & Siebenhuner, B. (2009). The role and relevance of International Bureaucracies: Setting the stage. In F. Biermann & B. Siebenhuner (Eds.),

Managers of global change. The influence of international environmental bureaucracies. MIT Press.

Blauberger, M., & Rittberger, B. (2015). Orchestrating policy implementation: EU governance through regulatory networks. In K. Abbott, P. Genschel, P. Snidal, & B. Zangl (Eds.), *International organizations as orchestrators.* Cambridge University Press.

Brechin, S. R., & Ness, G. D. (2013). Looking back at the gap: International organizations as organizations twenty-five years later. *Journal of International Organizations Studies, 4*(1), 14–39.

Brouwer, J. W. (1998). An early window of opportunity. The intervention by the Council of Europe in the Saar problem 1952-1954. In B. Reinalda & B. Verbeek (Eds.), *Autonomous policy-making by international organizations.* Routledge.

Brunsson, N. (2001). The irrationality of action and action rationality: Decisions, ideologies and organizational actions. *Organizational Studies: Critical Perspectives on Business and Management, 1*, 245–261.

Brunsson, N. (2003). Organized hypocrisy. In B. Czarniawska & G. Sevon (Eds.), *Northern lights.* Liber.

Brunsson, N. (2006). *Mechanisms of hope. Maintaining the dream of the rational organization.* Copenhagen Business School Press.

Brunsson, N. (2007). *Consequences of decision-making.* Oxford University Press.

Brunsson, N. (2009). *Reform as routine.* Oxford University Press.

Brunsson, N., & Olsen, J. (2008). *La reforma de las organizaciones.* CIDE.

Calcara, G. (2020). Balancing international police cooperation: INTERPOL and the undesirable trade-off between righs of individuals and global security. *Liverpool Law Review., 42*, 111–142. https://doi.org/10.1007/s10991-020-09266-9

Checkel, J. (1998). The constructivist turn in international relations theory. *World Politics, 50*(2), 324–348.

Cox, R. (1996). The executive head: An essay on leadership in international organization. In R. Cox (Ed.), *Approaches to world order.* Cambridge.

Cox, R., & Jacobson, H. (Eds.). (1973). *The anatomy of the influence. Decision making in international organization.* Yale University Press.

Dallaire, R. (2003). *Shake hands with the devil. The failure of humanity in Rwanda.* Carroll & Graf P.

Deflem, M. (2010). *The policing of terrorism: Organizational and global perspectives.* Routledge.

DiMaggio, P. I., & Powell, W. W. (1983). The iron cage revisited: Institutional isomorphism and collective rationality m organizational fields. *American Sociological Review, 48*, 147–160.

Dingwerth, K., Witt, A., Lehmann, I., Reichel, E., & Weise, T. (2019). *International organizations under pressure. Legitimating global governance in challenging times.* Oxford University Press.

Duffield, J. (2007). What are international institutions? *International Studies Review, 9*(1), 1–22.

Finnemore, M., & Sikkink, C. (1998). International norms dynamic and political change. *International Organization, 52*(4), 887–917.

Finnemore, M., & Sikkink, C. (2001). Taking stock: The constructivist research program in international relations and comparative politics. *Annual Review of Political Science, 4*(1), 391–416.

Footer, M. (2011). Future imperfect: Institutional autonomy and the WTO. In R. Collins & N. White (Eds.), *International organizations and the idea of autonomy. Institutional independence in the international legal order.* Routledge.

Goodin, R. (2012). *The theory of institutional design.* Cambridge University Press.

Goodman, S. (2020). The effectiveness of the international criminal court: Challenges and pathways for prosecuting human rights violations. *Inquiries Journal, 12*(9). https://doi.org/10.2139/ssrn.4228603

Gruber, L. (2000). *Ruling the world: Power politics and the rise of supranational institutions.* Princeton University Press.

Haas, E. (1968). *The uniting of Europe.* Stanford University Press.

Haas, P. M. (2002). UN conferences and constructivist governance of the environment. *Global Governance, 8*(1), 73–92.

Haggard, S., & Simmons, B. (1987). Theories of international regimes. *International Organization, 41,* 491–517. https://doi.org/10.1017/S0020818300027569

Hasenclever, A., Mayer, P., Rittberger, V., Murillo, S. L., & Castro y Ortiz, F. J. (1999). Las teorías de los regímenes internacionales: situación actual y propuestas para una síntesis. *Foro Internacional, 39*(4), 499–526.

Hopf, T. (1998). The promise of constructivism in international relations theory. *International Security, 23*(1), 171–200.

Keohane, R. (1982). The demand for international regimes. *International Organization, 36*(2), 325–355.

Keohane, R. (1986). Reciprocity in international relations. *International Organization, 40*(1), 1–27.

Keohane, R. (1999). Ideology and professionalism in international institutions: Insights from the work of Douglass C. North. In E. James, M. Alt, & E. Ostrom (Eds.), *Competition and cooperation: Conversations with Nobelists about economics and political science.* Russell Sage Foundation.

Keohane, R., & Martin, L. L. (1995). The promise of institutionalist theory. *International Security, 20*(1), 39–51.

Keohane, R., & Nye, J. (1973). Power and interdependence. *Survival, 15*(4), 158–165.

Keohane, R., & Nye, J. (1987). Power and interdependence revisited. *International Organization, 41*(4), 725–753.

Lawrence, T., & Suddaby, R. (2006). Institutions and institutional work. In S. Clegg, C. Hardy, T. Lawrance, & W. Nord (Eds.), *The Sage handbook of organization studies*. Sage.

Louis, M. (2019). Who decides? Representation and decision-making at the International Labor Organization. In C. Gironde & G. Carbonnier (Eds.), *The ILO @ 100*. Brill/Nijhoff.

March, J. G. (2010). *The ambiguities of experience*. Cornell University Press.

March, J. G., & Olsen, J. P. (1995). *Democratic governance*. Free Press.

March, J. G., & Olsen, J. P. (2011). The logic of appropriateness. *Oxford Handbooks Online*. https://doi.org/10.1093/oxfordhb/978019960445

Martha, J. (2010). *The legal foundations of Interpol*. Hart Publishing.

Martin, I., & Mayer-Rieckh, A. (2005). The United Nations and East Timor: From self-determination to state building. *International Peacekeeping, 12*(1), 124–145. https://doi.org/10.1080/1353331042000286595

Meyer, I. W., & Rowan, B. (1977). Institutional organizations: Formal structure as myth and ceremony. *American Journal of Sociology., 80*, 340–363.

North, D. (1990). *Institutions, institutional change and economic performance*. Cambridge University Press.

Oliver, C. (1991). Strategic responses to institutional pressures. *Academy of Management Review, 16*(1), 145–179.

Olson, M. (1992). *La lógica de la acción colectiva*. Limusa.

Pache, A. C., & Santos, F. (2010). When worlds collide: The internal dynamics of organizational responses to conflicting institutional demands. *Academy of Management Review, 35*(3), 455–476.

Pfeffer, J., & Salancik, G. (1978). *The external control of organizations: A resource dependence perspective*. Harper and Row.

Price, R., & Reus-Smit, C. (1998). Dangerous liaisons? Critical international theory and constructivism. *European Journal of International Relations, 4*(3), 259–294.

Reinalda, B., & Verbeek, B. (2004). *Decision making within international organizations*. Routledge.

Rittel, H., & Webber, M. (1973). Dilemmas in a general theory of planning. *Policy Sciences, 4*(2), 155–169.

Ruggie, J. (1998). What makes the world hang together? Neo-utilitarianism and the social constructivist challenge. *International Organization, 52*, 855–887.

Sanz-Carranza, A. (2015). Agents as brokers: Leadership in multilateral organizations. *Global Policy, 6*(3), 277–289.

Savino, M. (2010). Global administrative law meets soft powers: The uncomfortable case of Interpol red notices. *New York University Journal of International Law and Politics, 43*, 263–336.

Scott, R. (2008). *Institutions and organizations* (3rd ed.). Sage.

Sommer, T., Squatrito, T., Tallberg, J., & Lundgren, M. (2022). Decision-making in international organizations: Institutional design and performance. *The Review of International Organizations, 17*, 815–845.

Tsoukas, H., & Chia, R. (2014). On organizational becoming: Rethinking organizational change. *Organization Science, 13*(5), 567–582. https://doi.org/10.1287/orsc.13.5.567.7810

Villanueva, C. (2018). Theorizing cultural diplomacy all the way down: A cosmopolitan constructivist discourse from an Ibero-American perspective. *International Journal of Cultural Policy, 24*(5), 681–694. https://doi.org/1 0.1080/10286632.2018.1514033

Weick, K. (1976). Educational organizations as loosely coupled systems. *Administrative Science Quarterly, 21*(1), 1–19.

Wendt, A. (1992). Anarchy is what states make of it. The social construction of power politics. *International Organization, 46*(2), 391–425.

Wendt, A. (1999). *Social theory of international relations.* Cambridge University Press.

Williamson, O. E. (1996). *The mechanisms of governance.* Oxford University Press.

Williamson, O. E. (2010). Transaction cost economics: The natural progression. *American Economic Review, 100*(3), 673–690.

Williamson, O. E., & Winter, S. G. (1993). *The nature of the firm: Origins, evolution, and development.* Oxford University Press.

Young, O. R. (1986). International regimes: Toward a new theory of institutions. *World Politics, 39*(1), 104–122.

Zamudio González, L. (2020). *International intervention instruments against corruption in Central America.* Palgrave Macmillan.

Zamudio González, L., & Culebro Moreno, J. E. (2013). Los procesos de implementación de los acuerdos de paz. Aportes desde el nuevo institucionalismo. *Análisis Político, 26*(77), 175–194.

CHAPTER 7

Conclusions: The Power of Interdisciplinary Cross-Fertilization Between International Relations and Organization Studies

International Governmental Organizations (IGOs) play crucial roles in the international system, but their influence largely depends on their organizational nature. As distinct entities, IGOs exhibit unique characteristics that both explain their increasing importance and shed light on the criticisms and concerns they generate from governments, corporations, and individuals worldwide.

The idea that they are organizational actors that have an influence and play a role in shaping international reality has significant implications. First, organizations possess capabilities that enable them to create rules, establish regimes, implement policies, orchestrate actions, convince others, form alliances, and enforce regulations on states and their citizens. Second, and less obviously, these actors comprise individuals who operate within their organizational dynamics, making decisions based on internal management, policy, and political schemes. As a result, the dynamics within these international organizations directly impact the decisions and actions they undertake, ultimately shaping the international environment.

A third implication could be drawn from the existence of organizations in the international system: the increasing significance of the inter-organizational variable. IGOs have been weaving a complex tapestry of

© The Author(s), under exclusive license to Springer Nature Switzerland AG 2025
L. Zamudio-González, D. Arellano-Gault, *International Organizational Anarchy*,
https://doi.org/10.1007/978-3-031-82392-3_7

229

networks and interrelationships with other organizations, as well as a mixture of norms, agreements, conventions, conferences, and a myriad of instruments for engagement, dialogue, and conflict resolution. All these instruments and actions have become increasingly intertwined, forming deep interconnections that can stabilize and consolidate, acquiring a near-permanent or inevitable existence. Inter-organizational relationships—where not only various IGOs but also other types of international organizations participate—have gradually turned into a web, a grid from which it is increasingly difficult for states, and all other actors in the international arena, to escape. As Schemeil (2023) points out, states may at some point decide to withdraw or stop funding an IGO, but it is highly unlikely that they can escape the existing inter-organizational framework that connects virtually all states and their citizens.

The role of IGOs as organizational actors is now an undeniable reality for understanding the dynamics of the international order. The question that remains an enigma for many disciplines is: how can these actors, known as organizations *motu proprio*, be understood within the logic of the international system? Especially when it is recognized that, as *motu proprio* actors, their specificity is deeply organizational, and thus political-administrative both internally and in their behavior toward the environment. This is an international environment where states remain powerful and decisive agents, but no longer the only ones.

The answer explored in this book is one: IGOs are actors in the international arena bound by their own specificity—being organizations. If we use the metaphor of power as a game in a specific arena, it can be said that states have certain *tokens* that they use to play in the political arena. Companies and NGOs have their own tokens, derived from their specificity: size, capacity to influence, available resources, and the particular disposition of their environment, among others. IGOs are no exception: they also have certain tokens to play their role, negotiate, and act strategically.

IGOs possess tokens that are inherently tied to their organizational specificity. With their specificity, states are powerful, diverse, and intricate territories, populations, and political spaces. For a long time, they have been key actors and unique determinants. However, the international arena is becoming increasingly inter-global rather than just inter-national. In other words, while nation-states remain key players and determinants, they are no longer the only players in the game. IGOs have entered the arena with their own dynamics, instruments, and positions, thus making them distinct players with their attributes.

Along the chapters of this book, the three fundamental aspects of IGOs have been thoroughly examined, which encapsulate and elucidate their distinctiveness: (a) they are organizations inhabited by concreate real persons, (b) their members are typically states, and (c) they are increasingly engaging in a web of intricate interdependencies and interconnections, not only between states and IGOs but also with a multitude of other stakeholders. These three essential aspects are intimately intertwined, as detailed below.

In this book, we have argued that IGOs are best understood as organized anarchies (see Chap. 2; Cohen et al., 1972). Organized anarchies are organizations that function in environments where preferences and goals are multiple and often ill-defined. The members of such organizations, including the states that support the IGO, may lack a clear, unified understanding of its objectives. Additionally, the methods for solving problems or achieving goals—referred to here as *technologies*—are often unclear or nonexistent. In this context, *technology* refers to the operational methods or procedures of the organization, which are frequently complex or poorly understood by its members. As a result, decision-making often relies on trial and error, intuition, or experience, rather than a rational, systematic approach. In several cases examined in this book, the efforts of IGOs to address intricate and even *wicked* problems vividly illustrate this key characteristic of organizational anarchy.

Furthermore, in organized anarchies, participation in decision-making is variable and inconsistent. Members, including decision-makers, may come and go, with their level of involvement fluctuating due to personal interests or external demands. Consequently, decisions are made by different groups of people at different times, leading to inconsistency and unpredictability in the decision-making process. Often, there is no clear hierarchy of authority, and the roles of participants may be poorly defined or constantly shifting. As explored in the last two chapters, IGOs depend on the involvement and interaction of multiple individuals and groups, both inside and outside the organization, to legitimize and give meaning to their actions and decisions.

A key feature of organized anarchies is the *garbage can* model of decision-making. In this model, decisions do not follow a linear or rational process but result from the convergence of four streams: problems, solutions, participants, and choice opportunities. These streams are independent and often disconnected, meaning that decisions emerge from random combinations of problems, available solutions, and the participants involved at a given time, rather than from deliberate strategic planning. Chapter 4 discusses how IGOs must experiment with and defend various decision-making approaches, even while they work to legitimize these processes and negotiate with diverse stakeholders, often with conflicting interests.

IGOs as organized anarchies are quite capable of influence and affect the international reality. And they, as organizations, play a substantive game, both internally and externally. In this game, as organizations, the tokens that IGOs can use and play, are determined by their anarchic organizational logic. In other words, as organizations, they are seen as instruments: they serve a purpose, they have a function. That function is defined by their ability to act, pursue goals, and achieve them. This book has shown that this functionalist view is powerful but limited. It is powerful because it provides a strong ideology that legitimizes them—they exist because (it is assumed, expected, or idealized) they have the knowledge and technology to accomplish things and achieve goals. However, existing as an organization to achieve objectives implies being a sophisticated instrument with almost unique knowledge and capabilities. This is because, as organizations, their great strength lies in confronting reality directly, in specific and unique situations. Organizations understand reality by acting upon it directly.

IGOs are social constructs comprising individuals who must relate and connect to understand and collaborate. Therefore, the most effective method to mobilize and coordinate people is not always straightforward. First, organizations must establish political and managerial conditions that make addressing their specific situations through actions and tasks feasible. These actions are always carried out under uncertainty and risk. Hence, individuals within IGOs strive to be perceived as rational and logical by both internal and external stakeholders in order to legitimize their actions. With a basic legitimacy agreement in place, IGOs, like any other organization, develop the capabilities, knowledge, and technologies they consider the most rational and viable options for achieving their goals. Their organizational specificity serves as both a limitation and an opportunity. This is a limitation because IGOs cannot replace states, at least not under the current conditions of political legitimacy that recognize states as the primary agents for amalgamating the world. However, this organizational specificity enables IGOs to legitimize themselves as agents that can achieve objectives through a complex network of relationships that extend beyond territorial and political boundaries and involve a variety of civil associations, companies, groups, and individuals in a global arena that is increasingly interconnected.

IGOs possess a high level of specificity, which is closely linked to their ability to manage and organize themselves effectively. To the extent that they can administer and organize efficiently, they can influence the external relationships in which they are involved. While understanding the strategic games that occur within organizations can be challenging for those who are not part of them, it is essential to comprehend the unique characteristics and specificities of an organization. Only those who delve deeply into the specific work of an organization can gain insights into its inner workings and learn how to navigate it to make the actions of the organization effective. The organizational game is unique and specific; it requires being part of the organization to comprehend and play it fully. This specificity is crucial because the positioning of IGOs in international political games is closely connected to their technical, political, and management capabilities. Outsiders may be able to observe and intuit how to understand an organizational anarchy, but, generally, they will have a limited capacity to do so.

Clearly, the tokens that IGOs possess would not exist without states. Here, the interaction is multifaceted: states, as members of IGOs, finance them and often participate in their decision-making processes, yet they also frequently become subjects of action by the IGOs. States, in their plurality, differ in power and in their correlation of forces. Thus, for the organizational game to be effective, IGOs are compelled to play their tokens under these conditions of dependence on states. However, this dependence occurs in an arena of diverse, often conflicting states with varying degrees of influence and power. It is a fluid and changing dependence that typically leaves gaps and spaces for maneuver and learning on the part of IGOs. These spaces for maneuver are highly flexible. The clearest example of this process of increasing complexity in the relationship between states and IGOs is the ongoing tendency of the latter to differentiate and specialize through multiple instruments, agencies, conventions, and regulations. The fact that IGOs are creations of states is a key source of their constraints, but also of opportunities—allowing the tokens that IGOs play to be used and reimagined in innovative and bold ways. Of course, as with any innovation process, this cannot be free of risks.

The growing intricacy of the network of connections between states, corporations, and other national and international organizations has opened up new opportunities for IGOs as organized anarchies. This web of interdependence is becoming increasingly robust and resilient. The unwritten rules, agreements, negotiations, and collaborations in which numerous IGOs have engaged, deliberately and inadvertently, have resulted in acquiring new resources and capabilities to participate in this complex and differentiated game. As explained in Chap. 3, this game has become hyperdifferentiated using the parlance of various systems theories.

In sum, IGOs are primarily organizations, anarchic ones, that possess their internal logic, which plays a significant role in determining their actions and impact within the international arena. IGOs operate within a complex network of relationships and instruments involving a wide range of actors in this arena. The internal organizational structure of IGOs, characterized by agency, presents significant challenges in comprehending how these organizations can effectively address the issues they are tasked with resolving. IGOs must bridge the gap between their internal micro-logic and external meso-logic to overcome these challenges, which involves managing relationships with stakeholders, including states, at various levels of management and politics. Both logics require distinct management and political strategies, and mastering both is crucial for the success of IGOs.

IGOs often face challenges and exhibit paradoxical behavior due to their organizational nature. Situational context plays a crucial role in understanding these behaviors, which can be attributed to micro-, meso-, or macro-levels. The micro-level refers to the internal logics and dynamics of the organization. In contrast, the meso-level encompasses the interactions between IGOs and other actors, such as states, international organizations, and companies. The macro-level involves the political and management game that emerges from the interplay between these actors and their respective regulations and regimes. To effectively navigate this network of agents and regulations, it is essential to consider these three levels and their respective organizational logics and dynamics.

The international order has always been decentralized, lacking a single hierarchy or a central authority to impose coherence and uniformity. Instead, it is shaped by a multitude of social and collective actors, including diverse entities like International Governmental Organizations (IGOs). Despite this complexity, there remains a normative hope that these varied actions and interactions can still forge a livable and civil order. Such an order would need to be self-organized, characterized as non-hierarchical, imperfect, mutable, ambiguous, and flexible, reflecting the dynamic and ever-changing nature of global relations. These actors introduce their own logic: one that is substantively organizational, playing within an anarchic yet self-organized game. Understanding this reality is one of the most spectacular and exciting challenges in continuing to build the hope that an international order (more just, equitable, peaceful, and sustainable) can exist. *International anarchy meets organized anarchies.*

References

Cohen, M., March, J., & Olsen, J. (1972). A garbage can model of organizational choice. *Administrative Science Quarterly, 17*(1), 1–25.

Schemeil, Y. (2023). *The making of the world. How International Organizations shape our future.* Verlag Barbara Budrich.

INDEX

A
Advisory Committee on Administrative and Budgetary Questions, 122
African Union (AU), 12, 13, 80, 155, 221
Allison, G. T., 15, 19, 33, 147, 148, 206, 209, 211
Amnesty International, 67
Anarchy/anarchies, 2, 4–8, 16, 20, 29, 35, 53, 55, 57, 85, 86, 103, 194–203, 231, 233, 235
Asian Infrastructure Investment Bank, 15
Association of Southeast Asian Nations (ASEAN), 124, 125

B
Boutros-Ghali, Boutros, 119, 120
Brunsson, N., 22, 31, 64, 194, 206, 215–218, 220, 221

Bureaucracy
Bureaucracy/bureaucracies, 24, 33–35, 37, 96, 100–104, 106–108, 112, 116–128, 147, 150, 151, 169, 207
Bureaucratic logic, 36, 118
Bureaucratic theory, 31, 33, 36
Bureaucratization, 103, 128, 146, 150–152, 197
Business non-governmental organizations (BINGOs), 2

C
Complex adaptive systems (CAS), 73, 74
Central American Integration System (SICA), 18
Central Commission for the Navigation of the Rhine (CCNR), 17
Chaos theory, 71
Chernobyl, 96

© The Author(s), under exclusive license to Springer Nature Switzerland AG 2025
L. Zamudio-González, D. Arellano-Gault, *International Organizational Anarchy*,
https://doi.org/10.1007/978-3-031-82392-3

237

238 INDEX

China/chinese, 15, 19
Civil service, 35, 105
Cognitive frameworks, 148, 150
Cold War, 55, 119
Collective action, 109, 115, 132, 152, 162
problem, 201
Common Foreign and Security Policy (CFSP), 67
Complex adaptive systems, 55, 58, 73
Complexity theory, 5, 6, 31, 37, 46, 47, 54, 55, 59, 60, 62, 64, 66, 67, 70, 72, 73, 75, 81, 82, 85, 86, 114, 128, 148, 164, 166, 167, 182, 183, 190, 191, 203, 205, 221, 222, 233, 234
Congress of Vienna, 16–18
Constructivism, 22, 29, 30, 135, 145, 148, 149, 197–200
Constructivist, 102, 104, 148, 154, 157, 158, 199–201, 213
Contingency, 75
Council of Europe, 210
COVID-19, 1, 49, 98, 113, 155
Crimean War, 17
Crozier, M., 100, 116–120, 127, 130, 132
Cuban Missile Crisis, 206

D
Danube River Commission, 18
Decision-making, 3, 5, 7, 13, 14, 17, 19, 21, 24, 25, 27–29, 34, 38, 57, 59, 66, 76, 81, 85, 87, 96, 98–102, 104, 107, 113, 114, 118, 119, 123, 125, 130, 145, 148, 149, 152, 153, 156, 158, 161, 163, 164, 166, 167, 169, 191, 192, 194, 201, 202, 204–207, 209–211, 215–218, 220–222, 231, 233

Department of Political Affairs (DPA), 218
Durkheim, E., 53, 65, 97

E
Economic and Social Council (ECOSOC), 46, 83
Economic institutionalism, 28, 196
Economics, 195, 203
Episteme, 158
European Commission, 15, 67, 170
European Commission for Agriculture, 15
European Political Community, 210
European Union (EU), 12, 13, 18, 48, 67, 99, 104, 112, 114, 156, 170, 222
Extraordinary Chambers in the Courts of Cambodia, 80

F
Food and Agriculture Organization (FAO), 45, 66
Foreign Affairs Council, 67
Fukuyama, F., 25
Functionalist, 30, 48, 50, 56, 64, 76, 97, 99, 100, 116, 129–131, 133, 146, 202, 232

G
Gavi Alliance, 37
General Agreement on Tariffs and Trade (GATT), 204
General Assembly, 46, 47, 82, 83, 119, 125, 211
General systems theory/general theory of systems, 50, 53, 58, 60, 64, 65, 167

INDEX **239**

Genocide, 12, 49, 79, 117, 158, 159, 163, 213
Global Alliance for Vaccines and Immunization (GAVI), 11
Global Financial Crisis of 2008, 158
Global Fund, 63, 64
Global Fund to Fight AIDS, Tuberculosis, and Malaria (GFATM), 63
Global governance, 36, 49, 56, 103, 107, 154–158, 195–197, 200, 201
Globalization, 16, 49, 53, 155, 157
Global Outbreak Alert and Response Network (GOARN), 11
Governance, 2, 6, 7, 12, 13, 31, 32, 36, 45, 57, 63, 72, 74, 95, 104, 118, 130, 132, 153–158, 217, 219, 222
Governmental NGOs (GONGOs), 2

H
Homeostasis, 63, 70
Human Rights Watch, 67
Hybrid international organizations (HIGOs), 2

I
IGOs, 1–8, 11–26, 28, 30–38, 46–49, 51, 57, 58, 62–69, 71, 72, 74, 77–80, 84–88, 95–130, 132–135, 143–171, 182, 183, 189, 191–200, 202–204, 208, 209, 212–214, 216, 219, 221–223, 229–234
Impersonalization, 128, 150
India/Indian, 15
Institution, 7, 8, 16, 20, 25–29, 49, 65, 79, 81, 85, 86, 104, 134,

145, 147, 155, 157, 158, 190, 192–201, 203–206, 211, 212, 215, 223
Inter-American Development Bank (IDB), 109, 110
Interdependence equilibria, 133
International Atomic Energy Agency (IAEA), 18, 60, 61, 87, 95, 96, 221
International Civil Aviation Organization, 18, 86
International Commission against Impunity in Guatemala (CICIG), 1, 12, 14, 162, 189, 190, 193
International Committee of the Red Cross (ICRC), 17
International Conferences, 196
International Criminal Court, 13, 18, 49, 114, 213, 214
International Criminal Police Organization (INTERPOL), 13, 18, 86, 208, 211–213
International Criminal Tribunal for Rwanda, 79
International Criminal Tribunal for the Former Yugoslavia, 79, 80
International governance, 16, 24, 149, 154, 199
International Governmental Organizations (IGOs), 1, 2, 11, 37, 47, 95, 148, 191, 229, 234
International institutions, 27
International Labor Organization (ILO), 13, 216
International Maritime Organization (IMO), 164, 165
International Meteorological Organization, 18
International Monetary Fund (IMF), 2, 18, 30, 32, 45, 151, 159, 161, 219

240 INDEX

International order, 8, 16, 18, 27, 31, 54, 62, 128, 134, 135, 195, 198, 203, 222, 230, 234, 235
International organization, 2, 12, 18, 20, 29, 45, 98, 106, 107, 111, 189, 193
International politics, 17, 50, 51, 53, 55–57, 103, 149
International Public Administration (IPA), 100, 104–106, 108, 135
International regimes, 28, 29, 134, 150, 152, 195, 200–203
International Relations (IR), 2–4, 6, 8, 19–24, 26, 27, 29–31, 35–37, 47–54, 56, 58, 85–88, 100–104, 108, 114, 128–130, 134, 135, 147–149, 152, 154, 194–203, 206
International system, 2, 4, 5, 16, 20–21, 26–28, 48, 50–55, 68, 80, 86–88, 198, 200, 202, 229, 230
International Telecommunication Union (ITU), 45, 118
International Telegraph Union (ITU), 18, 118
International Union for Conservation of Nature (IUCN), 168, 221
Irrationality, 78, 162, 214–220
Isomorphism, 50–52
Israel, 15

J

Joint United Nations Programme on HIV/AIDS (UNAIDS), 64, 68, 72, 74
Journal of International Organizations Studies (JIOS), 20

K

Kant, I., 4, 20, 52
Kenya, 2
Keohane, R. O., 26–28, 195, 199, 201, 202, 222

L

League of Nations, 14, 18
Limited rationality
   bounded rationality, 7, 8, 162, 165–167, 190, 215
Logics of appropriateness, 197, 201, 223
Luhmann, N., 50, 58, 74, 75, 77, 84–86
   Luhmannian, 50, 56, 58, 59, 74–78, 80–86, 166, 221

M

Macro-dynamics, 134
Meso-dynamics, 134, 135, 234
Meta-organization, 31, 32
Micro-dynamics, 53, 55, 134, 135, 234
Multi-stakeholder governance model, 63

N

Neo-institutionalism, 26, 30
Neoliberal, 4, 198
Neoliberal governmentality, 156
Neoliberalism, 26, 27, 29, 33, 197–200
Neo-realism, 4, 27, 199
Non-governmental international organizations, 19
Non-governmental organizations (NGOs), 2, 5, 24, 34, 37, 57, 63, 67, 69, 72, 85, 86, 153–156, 168, 193, 196, 217, 230
North Atlantic Treaty Organization (NATO), 2, 11–13, 15, 18, 37, 155, 170, 220

O

Office of the United Nations High Commissioner for Refugees (UNHCR), 12, 18

Organisation for Economic
Co-operation and Development
(OECD), 18, 207
Organizations, 2–8, 11–26, 29–38,
45–50, 52, 57–59, 62–67, 69, 71,
72, 77–87, 95–106, 108–119,
121, 123, 124, 127–135,
143–148, 151–155, 158–171,
181–183, 190–198, 201–209,
211–214, 216–223, 229–234
change, 7, 74, 131
pathology, 33
stability, 8
studies, 23
theory, 3, 4, 8, 21, 23, 31, 35, 37,
49, 64, 73, 86, 100, 104, 114,
132, 134, 135, 147, 148, 203
Organization of American States
(OAS), 12, 18, 155
Organized anarchy, 4, 5, 7, 8, 34, 35,
231–233, 235

P
Palestine, 15
Paradox of rationality, 34
Parsons, T., 65, 97
Peacekeeping, 12, 37, 69, 84, 86, 114,
120, 122, 159, 191, 193, 219
Permanent Court of
Arbitration, 13, 17
Political and Security Committee, 67
Political Science, 195, 203
Power, 2, 3, 5–7, 14, 16, 17, 20, 21,
24–28, 33, 34, 36–38, 52, 53,
56, 57, 69, 96, 99–101, 105,
108, 112–114, 118–121, 127,
128, 131–133, 147, 149–151,
153–158, 165, 198, 200,
202–204, 210, 220, 230, 233
dynamics, 21, 119, 120, 133,
149, 157
institutional power, 157–158

productive power, 158
structural power, 158
Principal agent theory, 8, 23, 28, 30,
36, 102, 135, 147
Public administration, 4, 105,
108, 150
Punctuated equilibrium, 73, 74

Q
Quasi-non-governmental organizations
(QUANGOs), 2

R
Rational Choice, 30
Realism, 4, 26, 29, 30, 33, 53, 55
Russia/Russian, 15
Russian invasion of Ukraine, 11

S
Secretariat of the Department for
Development Support and
Management Services, 121
Secretary-General, 46, 83, 120–122,
125, 190, 219
Security Council, 47, 67, 125, 193,
206, 219
Sedimented institution, 205
Sensegiving, 168
Sensemaking, 115, 167–171, 182,
183, 205
Shanghai Cooperation
Organization, 15
Simon, H., 21, 55, 126, 134, 160,
164, 167, 217
Sociological institutionalism, 197
Sociology, 195, 203
Somali Civil War, 158
Special Court for Sierra Leone, 13, 80
Specialist Chambers for Kosovo, 80
State-building, 192

242 INDEX

Structural-functionalism, 58, 64, 65
Systems theory, 48, 49, 51, 56, 58, 59, 61, 64, 65, 70, 74–76, 85, 86

T
Three Mile Island, 96
Transaction cost reduction, 197
Transaction cost theory, 27
Trans-governmental organizations, 2
Transnational relations, 57

U
Underorganization, 69
UN High Commissioner for Refugees (UNHCR), 66
UN Interim Administration Mission for Kosovo (UNMIK), 13
Union of International Organizations (UIO), 18–19
United Nations (UN), 12–18, 37, 45–47, 62, 63, 66, 67, 79, 80, 82–84, 87, 99, 107, 114, 119–121, 125, 126, 153, 155, 157, 159, 162, 163, 170, 189–192, 206, 208, 214, 218–221
United Nations Development Program (UNDP), 45
United Nations Educational, Scientific and Cultural Organization (UNESCO), 15, 63
United Nations General Assembly, 13, 83
United Nations High Comissioner for Refugees (UNHCR), 12, 18, 66, 76–78, 81, 83, 151

United Nations Population Fund (UNFPA), 62, 67
United Nations Security Council, 15, 17, 214
United Nations Transitional Administration in East Timor (UNTAET), 12, 13, 80
Universal Postal Union (UPU), 18
UNOPS, 121, 122

W
Wallerstein, I., 47
Waltz, K., 4, 50, 52, 53
Warsaw Pact, 14
Weber, M.
Weberian, 31, 98, 102, 103, 110, 118, 127, 150
Weick, K., 168, 171, 209
Westphalian model, 49
Wicked problems, 34, 208, 231
World Bank (WB), 18, 49, 63, 85, 113, 130, 131, 151, 170, 183, 219
World Economic Forum, 157
World Health Organization (WHO), 1, 2, 11, 12, 14, 15, 18, 63, 64, 72, 74, 87, 113, 143, 144, 155, 208
World Meteorological Organization (WMO), 166
World policy model, 33
World system, 47
World Trade Organization (WTO), 15, 18, 156, 166, 204, 221
World War II, 18, 52

Printed in the United States
by Baker & Taylor Publisher Services